SO-ALB-072

9/21/10
$45.00

Bloom's Literary Themes

Alienation
Death and Dying
Human Sexuality
Rebirth and Renewal
The American Dream
The Grotesque
The Hero's Journey
The Labyrinth

Bloom's Literary Themes

THE GROTESQUE

Bloom's Literary Themes

THE GROTESQUE

Edited and with an introduction by
Harold Bloom
Sterling Professor of the Humanities
Yale University

Volume Editor
Blake Hobby

 BLOOM'S
LITERARY CRITICISM
An imprint of Infobase Publishing

CHABOT COLLEGE LIBRARY

PN
56
.G7
G76
2009

Bloom's Literary Themes: The Grotesque

Copyright © 2009 by Infobase Publishing
Introduction © 2009 by Harold Bloom

All rights reserved. No part of this book may be reproduced or utilized in any form or by any means, electronic or mechanical, including photocopying, recording, or by any information storage or retrieval systems, without permission in writing from the publisher. For information contact:

Bloom's Literary Criticism
An imprint of Infobase Publishing
132 West 31st Street
New York NY 10001

Library of Congress Cataloging-in-Publication Data
The grotesque / edited and with an introduction by Harold Bloom ; volume editor, Blake Hobby.
     p. cm. — (Bloom's literary themes)
  Includes bibliographical references and index.
  ISBN 978-0-7910-9802-8 (acid-free paper) 1. Grotesque in literature. I. Bloom, Harold. II. Hobby, Blake.
  PN56.G7G76 2009
  809'.915—dc22   2008042984

Bloom's Literary Criticism books are available at special discounts when purchased in bulk quantities for businesses, associations, institutions, or sales promotions. Please call our Special Sales Department in New York at (212) 967-8800 or (800) 322-8755.

You can find Bloom's Literary Criticism on the World Wide Web at
http://www.chelseahouse.com

Cover design by Takeshi Takahashi
Text design by Kerry Casey

Printed in the United States of America

IBT EJB 10 9 8 7 6 5 4 3 2 1

This book is printed on acid-free paper.

CHABOT COLLEGE LIBRARY

Contents

Series Introduction by Harold Bloom: Themes and Metaphors

1. Topos and Trope

What we now call a theme or topic or subject initially was named a *topos*, ancient Greek for "place." Literary *topoi* are commonplaces, but also arguments or assertions. A topos can be regarded as literal when opposed to a trope or turning which is figurative and which can be a metaphor or some related departure from the literal: ironies, synecdoches (part for whole), metonymies (representations by contiguity) or hyperboles (overstatements). Themes and metaphors engender one another in all significant literary compositions.

As a theoretician of the relation between the matter and the rhetoric of high literature, I tend to define metaphor as a figure of desire rather than a figure of knowledge. We welcome literary metaphor because it enables fictions to persuade us of beautiful, untrue things, as Oscar Wilde phrased it. Literary *topoi* can be regarded as places where we store information in order to amplify the themes that interest us.

This series of volumes, *Bloom's Literary Themes*, offers students and general readers helpful essays on such perpetually crucial topics as the Hero's Journey, the Labyrinth, the Sublime, Death and Dying, the Taboo, the Trickster and many more. These subjects are chosen for their prevalence yet also for their centrality. They express the whole concern of human existence now in the twenty-first century of the Common Era. Some of the topics would have seemed odd at another time, another land: the American Dream, Enslavement and Emancipation, Civil Disobedience.

I suspect though that our current preoccupations would have existed always and everywhere, under other names. Tropes change across the centuries: the irony of one age is rarely the irony of another. But the themes of great literature, though immensely varied, undergo transmemberment and show up barely disguised in different contexts. The power of imaginative literature relies upon three constants: aesthetic splendor, cognitive power, wisdom. These are not bound by societal constraints or resentments, and ultimately are universals, and so are not culture-bound. Shakespeare, except for the world's scriptures, is the one universal author, whether he is read and played in Bulgaria or Indonesia or wherever. His supremacy at creating human beings breaks through even the barrier of language and puts everyone on his stage. This means that the matter of his work has migrated everywhere, reinforcing the common places we all inhabit in his themes.

2. CONTEST AS BOTH THEME AND TROPE

Great writing or the Sublime rarely emanates directly from themes since all authors are mediated by forerunners and by contemporary rivals. Nietzsche enhanced our awareness of the agonistic foundations of ancient Greek literature and culture, from Hesiod's contest with Homer on to the Hellenistic critic Longinus in his treatise *On the Sublime*. Even Shakespeare had to begin by overcoming Christopher Marlowe, only a few months his senior. William Faulkner stemmed from the Polish-English novelist Joseph Conrad and our best living author of prose fiction, Philip Roth, is inconceivable without his descent from the major Jewish literary phenomenon of the twentieth century, Franz Kafka of Prague, who wrote the most lucid German since Goethe.

The contest with past achievement is the hidden theme of all major canonical literature in Western tradition. Literary influence is both an overwhelming metaphor for literature itself, and a common topic for all criticism, whether or not the critic knows her immersion in the incessant flood.

Every theme in this series touches upon a contest with anteriority, whether with the presence of death, the hero's quest, the overcoming of taboos, or all of the other concerns, volume by volume. From Monteverdi through Bach to Stravinsky, or from the Italian Renaissance through the agon of Matisse and Picasso, the history of all the arts demonstrates the same patterns as literature's thematic struggle with itself. Our country's great original art, jazz, is illuminated by what the great creators called "cutting contests," from Louis Armstrong and Duke Ellington on to the emergence of Charlie Parker's Bop or revisionist jazz.

A literary theme, however authentic, would come to nothing without rhetorical eloquence or mastery of metaphor. But to experience the study of the common places of invention is an apt training in the apprehension of aesthetic value in poetry and in prose.

1

Astonishment is the mode of the Grotesque, though this is tinged with distaste, unlike the transcendent astonishment induced by the Sublime.

Oddly, "grotesque" as a word as based upon *grotto*, a cave, underground and phantom-infested. The Shakespearean Fool fused the Grotesque and the Uncanny or Sublime, most notably the Fool in *King Lear*.

For me, the great modern master of the Grotesque was the now rather neglected Victorian poet Robert Browning (1812-1889). Our era dumbs down with shocking ferocity, and the neglect of Browning largely reflects his intellectual energy and the authentic, achieved difficulty of his best poems. His particular masterpiece in the Grotesque mode is the superb *Childe Roland to the Dark Tower Came*, a dramatic monologue that is also an internalized quest-romance.

Of all literary forms, quest-romance has undergone the most astonishing transfigurations from the *Odyssey* through Spenser's *The Faerie Queene* on to Joyce's *Ulysses*, Proust's *In Search of Lost Time*, and Mann's *The Magic Mountain*. Such metamorphic propensities now render quest-romance into an all but indefinable genre: it has expanded by progressive internalization until further inwardness scarcely seems possible. What, from *Don Quixote* and *Hamlet* onwards, is not to some degree an internalized search to re-beget the individual self? Freud, who increasingly takes his proper place as a great literary artist, and *not* a scientist, is the theoretician of modern quest-romance.

To understand this, commence by casting out the odd notion that Freud's prime concern was human sexuality. Instead it was the

individuation and augmentation of the ego, where sexuality necessarily played a key developmental role. If we can speak of Freud's
own quest-romance it would be his drive to free cognition from its
sexual past. In a brilliant perception Freud surmised that all cognition
began with a child's curiosity as to gender differences, a curiosity that
remains an endlessly moody brooding in most of us but that an elite
group could transcend, by way of an intellectual discipline and of a
profound immersion in culture. And yet our discomfort with culture
grows incessantly. In Freudian quest-romance, we always are marching
on to defeat because each of us is her or his own worst enemy. We have
a will-to-fail, an unconscious sense of guilt, a sado-masochistic drive
beyond the Pleasure Principle.

2

Freud was the last and greatest of the Victorian prophets: Samuel
Butler, Thomas Carlyle, Ralph Waldo Emerson, John Ruskin, Walter
Pater, Matthew Arnold and, in Germany, Schopenhauer and Nietzsche.
Browning, a fiercely Protestant sensibility but scarcely a pious Chris-
tian, was the lifelong disciple of Percy Bysshe Shelley, archetypal High
Romantic rebel against the established order, Christianity included.
From his early poetry—*Pauline* and *Paracelsus*—which were essentially
Shelleyan voyages to the impossible ideal—on to his mature dramatic
monologues, Browning was faithful to the spirit of Shelley. But the Shel-
leyan Sublime is transformed into Browning's Romantic Grotesque, as
it had been by Shelley himself in his verse-drama, *The Cenci*.

Browning's darkly splendid *Childe Roland to the Dark Tower Came*
is a controlled phantasmagoria in thirty-four six-line stanzas, spoken
by a nameless "childe" or candidate for knighthood. The poem's title
is taken from a snatch of anonymous song uttered by Shakespeare's
Edgar (impersonating madness) in *King Lear* (III, IV, 173):

> Child Rowland to the dark Tower Came,
> His word was still, "Fie, foh, and fum,
> I smell the blood of a British man."

That brief bit of weird lyric was enlarged by Browning into a grand
nightmare of a poem, dependent for many of its grotesque singulari-
ties upon a chapter, "Of Things Deformed and Broken," in *The Art of*

Painting in All Its Branches, by Gerard de Lairesse, a book in his father's library that Browning had memorized in his childhood.

By tradition, the poem's obsessed monologist is known as Childe Roland, which is true to the poem's imaginative pattern though not to its letter. Childe Roland is an unique quester, because he *wants to fail*. His heart springs up at "finding failure in its scope." All his companions in the quest have been disgraced as cowards and traitors, and though he himself is both heroic and loyal his love for his forerunners augments his manic intensity to fail as they did.

The reader increasingly is made aware that he can give no credence to what the Childe thinks he sees. If we rode by his side we would see a wretched landscape no doubt, but not nearly as apocalyptic as the one Roland fiercely describes. The culminating negative vision represents an apotheosis of the grotesque:

> If there pushed any ragged thistle-stalk
>   Above its mates, the head was chopped; the bents
>   Were jealous else. What made those holes and rents
> In the dock's harsh swarth leaves, bruised as to baulk
> All hope of greenness? 'tis a brute must walk
>   Pashing their life out, with a brute's intents.
>
> As for the grass, it grew as scant as hair
>   In leprosy; thin dry blades pricked the mud
>   Which underneath looked kneaded up with blood.
> One stiff blind horse, his every bone a-stare,
> Stood stupefied, however he came there:
>   Thrust out past service from the devil's stud!

We hear a little child's voice here, desperate at being left alone with a suffering beast. And then suddenly the crisis of his life and quest burningly assaults Roland:

> What in the midst lay but the Tower itself?
>   The round squat turret, blind as the fool's heart,
>   Built of brown stone, without a counterpart
> In the whole world. The tempest's mocking elf
> Points to the shipman thus the unseen shelf
>   He strikes on, only when the timbers start.

That "round squat turret," both unique and commonplace, is a kind of grotto peculiarly raised up. Even as "all the lost adventurers my peers" ring his ordeal, Roland sounds his slug-horn in defiance of his fate, and concludes dauntlessly if ambiguously: '*Childe Roland to the Dark Tower Came*'. Through him, Browning recalls Shelley's "trumpet of a prophecy" (from the conclusion to the "Ode to the West Wind") and thus establishes again his relationship to his prime precursor.

THE AMERICAN AND EUROPEAN GROTESQUE

"Notes on the Grotesque: Anderson, Brecht, and Williams"
by James Schevill,
in *Twentieth Century Literature*, (1977)

INTRODUCTION

For James Schevill, the American Grotesque stems from both the American evangelical tradition, which he refers to as a "grotesque version of Christianity," and from the goal of "individual, materialistic success." Analyzing three exemplar authors, each a radically different stylist working in a different form (the novel, drama, and poetry), Schevill first defines the characteristics of the grotesque and then observes the ways it has appeared as a trans-continental art form.

Popular concepts of *grotesque* still prevent our understanding the importance of this idea in American society. While traveling across the United States this past Bicentennial summer of 1976, I asked many people of widely differing backgrounds and occupations their

---

Schevill, James. "Notes on the Grotesque: Anderson, Brecht, and Williams." *Twentieth Century Literature*, Vol. 23, No. 2 (May 1977): 229–38.

immediate reactions to grotesque. The great majority of answers emphasized three elements—*distorted, fantastic, ugly*.

The problem remains that *grotesque* is essentially something we distrust, the hidden demonic fantasy that still torments and attracts us, the shadow we repress because we don't want to confront this central problem in our society. In recent years we have learned much about the grotesque tradition in art and literature. Important books on the subject have been written by such scholars as Wolfgang Kayser, Frances K. Barasch, Peter L. Hays, Philip Thomson, and Willard Farnham. We recognize the French and Italian background of the word, particularly the Italian *grottesca* with its vision of a special style of opera or art. The *Oxford Universal Dictionary* with its impeccable British-European tradition defines *grotesque* as "A kind of decorative painting or sculpture in which portions of human and animal forms are fantastically interwoven with foliage and flowers." Today, linguistically and emotionally, we associate the word with the terrifying and beautiful gargoyles of the great Gothic cathedrals. As Otto von Simson writes in *The Gothic Cathedral*, "Two aspects of Gothic architecture are without precedent and parallel: the use of light and the unique relationship between structure and appearance." Hidden, functioning as rain-spouts to release dark weather, the gargoyles represent the bestial counter-forces of light. That these dark, bestial forms can be beautiful too if released into the open air by modern photographic techniques is the psychological lesson we have learned again and again in the twentieth century.

Today in the age of concentration camps it is relatively easy for anyone interested in the arts to associate beauty and terror (strange, that this relationship seems so modern when the Greeks knew it intimately). Especially the comic tone in contemporary literature and drama, as in Joyce's *Ulysses* and Beckett's *Waiting for Godot*, reflects a unique combination of terror, fear, beauty, and laughter. As long ago as our Civil War, in the early 1860s, *grotesque* was applied to clowns and buffoons. After the First and Second World Wars, Korea, Vietnam, the Russian invasions of Hungary and Czechoslovakia, the Middle-Eastern disasters, and the constant threat of nuclear warfare, artists and writers have used increasingly stylistic variations on the world as *grotesque* to emphasize their themes. In Germany Günter Grass, in Italy Cesare Pavese, in France Beckett, Genet, and Ionesco, in

England a poet like Ted Hughes in *Crow*, all exemplify visions of the grotesque. Throughout Europe the side of grotesque that is defined as "fantastically absurd" has led to the major theatrical style called "Theatre of the Absurd."

In America Heller's *Catch 22*, Pynchon's *Gravity's Rainbow*, Hawkes's trilogy of novels from *Blood Oranges* to *Travesty* are recent examples of grotesque styles in fiction. We are beginning to recognize[1] the depth of the grotesque tradition in American literature from, say, Hawthorne, Melville, and Poe's *Tales of the Grotesque and Arabesque*, with its emphasis on the supernatural and fantastic, to Anderson's *Winesburg, Ohio*, Nathanael West's 1930s grotesques, and certain of Faulkner's obsessed stories and novels such as *Light in August*. Yet we still have difficulty in defining the sources of the unique American sense of *grotesque*.

What I shall call *American Grotesque* comes, I believe, from two major sources. First, the evangelical splintering of our country into hundreds of separatist movements with all the puzzles, repressions, and violence that the splintering has produced. The American evangelical tradition is often so fanatic in its religious intensities and obsessions that it would put Christ to shame if he could see his hardshell to say nothing of hardsell imitators. In our frenetic attempt to conquer the west, tame the land, subdue and eliminate the Indians, we put the stern-zealot Christ to work. Thus we achieved often a grotesque version of Christianity. It is this grotesque Christianity that Sherwood Anderson shows so well in *Winesburg, Ohio* in such characters as Reverend Curtis Hartman, Jesse Bentley, Louise Bentley, and David Hardy.

The second major source of *American Grotesque* is the goal of individual, materialistic success. Wright Morris writes in his photographic novel, *The Home Place*, speaking of a Nebraska farm family: "Independence, not abundance, is the heart of their America." As the nineteenth century changed into the twentieth century, an increasingly grotesque relationship grew between independence and abundance. Abundance, the goal of technological, urban society, was put ahead of independence. However, official lip service continued to be paid to the ideal of individual independence. Throughout the country the connection between the individual and the community became distorted. Today we struggle with the contradiction of a democracy founded on agrarian frontier ideals that persist doggedly amidst the realities of a secret technology that runs our country.

As a pioneer into the mythology of *American Grotesque*, Sherwood Anderson has never received just recognition for his discoveries. In my first biography of Anderson, published in 1951, I suggested the need for an anthology of Anderson's work that would show the full range of his concept of *grotesque*. Alas, this has never happened. Even so astute a poet and critic as Horace Gregory in his editions of *The Portable Sherwood Anderson* has failed to show the significance of the *grotesque* in Anderson's fiction.

In *Winesburg, Ohio*, which Anderson called originally *The Book of the Grotesque*, he defines *grotesque* with the Emersonian insight that "the moment one of the people took one of the truths to himself, called it his truth, and tried to live his life by it, he became a grotesque and the truth he embraced became a falsehood." If we apply this to American politics as a test, we find several recent presidents stressing proudly that they work fourteen hours a day at the job. Evidently on the surface we are reassured by the idea of an immensely hard-working president, although the minute we begin to consider this seriously we realize how grotesque it is that anyone can claim to work fourteen hours a day with any real quality. Anderson's real insight, then, is to show how *American Grotesque* masquerades as a rigid defense of truth. The style of *grotesque* in Anderson's terms is an idiomatic American irony developed out of Mark Twain and other frontier writers. In this connection it is important to note that the writer in the opening "Book of the Grotesque" section in *Winesburg* is a symbolic, Mark Twain-like figure with his white mustache, cigars, and Joan of Arc fantasies hovering in his memories. Anderson felt deeply how Mark Twain's life and work embodied a clear sense of *American Grotesque*. If Anderson were alive today he would view with amazement how his vision of the grotesque has emerged from the Vietnam disaster in the far more bitter style of a playwright like David Rabe, a novelist like Robert Stone in *Dog Soldiers*, and other young writers who are emerging.

Criticism of Anderson has been limited too much to American sources and relationships. This has prevented us from seeing how the ironic American aspects of *grotesque* are connected with European Epic and Absurdist styles. No mention has been made of the singular link between Anderson and Bertolt Brecht, whose epic theater has transformed the modern stage. In Brecht's work there is a short poem called "Coals for Mike":

I have heard, that in Ohio
At the beginning of this century,
A woman lived in Bidwell in poverty,
Mary McCoy, widow of a brakeman
By the name of Mike McCoy.
Every night from the thundering trains of the
Wheeling Railroad
The brakemen threw some lumps of coal
Over her picket fence into her potato patch,
Shouting quickly with harsh voices:
For Mike!
And every night,
When the lumps of coal for Mike
Crashed against the rear wall of her cabin,
The old woman got up, drunk with sleep,
Stumbled into her coat,
And heaped the lumps of coal aside,
Gift of the brakemen to Mike, dead
But not forgotten.
She got up long before the grey light of dawn
And cleared her gifts away from the world's eyes,
So that the men would not get into trouble
With the Wheeling Railroad.
This poem is dedicated to the comrades
Of the brakeman, Mike McCoy
(Died because of weak lungs
On a coal train in Ohio)
For comradeship.

Mike McCoy? Bidwell, Ohio? These names sound familiar. In the Brecht memorial edition of *Sinn und Form*, printed in Berlin after his death in 1953, Elizabeth Hauptmann, Brecht's longtime colleague and secretary, published some old diary notes which reveal the source of the poem. The note dated August 6, 1926, reads: "Around Easter

Brecht discovered a new rental library. *Poor White* by Sherwood Anderson made a great impression on him." After reading it, he wrote the poem, "Coals for Mike." The episode about the widow, Mary McCoy, is in Chapter 12, Book Four, of Anderson's novel.

It is easy to see how Anderson's short, direct, colloquial style, his populist concerns, and his focus on the social problem of the transition from an agricultural to an industrial society would fascinate Brecht. Yet today we see even more central connections in style between Brecht and Anderson. There is a curious relationship between *grotesque* and epic in both writers. The epic form, as Brecht developed it out of Shakespeare and other sources such as contemporary film techniques, is marked by short, fragmented rhythms and quick scenes portraying an entire community or society. In epic drama the characters are not fully rounded in depth, but grotesque in the distortions that society has imposed on them. It is especially interesting in this regard that Brecht's work is so often set in America. Unconsciously, Brecht felt a deep connection between the distortions in American society and the distortions in German society after the First World War. As I wrote in my theater book, *Breakout*:

> The image of America in Brecht's work is puzzling—fantastic, brutal, chaotic, materialistic, romantic, daring, primitive and sophisticated at the same time—a strange mixture of attraction and repulsion, the same attitudes that Brecht revealed in conversation about the United States. Reading Brecht's work and talking to him was a lesson in what the United States meant to Europeans in the 1920s, and a warning why the United States is still regarded by Europeans as a grotesque mixture of raw materialism and free openheartedness.

Consider Brecht's play, *In the Jungle of Cities*, written shortly before he read *Poor White*, but revised afterwards, a revision that may well have been influenced particularly in the relationship between agricultural and industrial environments by his reading of *Poor White*. *In the Jungle of Cities* is about a mysterious battle to the death in Chicago between a Chinese lumber dealer, Schlink, and a clerk in a rental library called George Garga. As Brecht describes it, "It is the year 1912 in Chicago. You are witnessing an inexplicable wrestling match and the destruction of a family that has come from the prairie lands to the great city jungle." Although the conflict between Schlink and Garga is based on the love-hate relationship between Verlaine and Rimbaud, it is no accident that the grotesque environment and characters and the episodic form relate not only to German Expressionism but also to Brecht's reading of Sherwood Anderson as well as his encounter with American films and gangster stories.

Unfortunately Anderson did not live long enough to perceive the incredible influence that epic forms would assume after the Second World War. Yet he could relate instinctively to the Cubist distortions of perspective that reached America in the Armory Show of 1913, to the pointillistic techniques of Gertrude Stein, to the collage techniques of presenting fragmented images and rhythms that dominated the European arts after the First World War. He sensed how this new twentieth-century feeling of fragmentation, of clashing "objects-in-space" from many different cultures as Hugh Kenner calls them, contributes to a portrayal of the *grotesque*. His intuitive understanding, his native American sense of how *grotesque* related to European movements in the arts enabled him to create two pioneer works in modern literature, *Winesburg, Ohio* and *Poor White*. Anderson's moving definition of writing as "cutting and nailing on steps by which one attempts to reach some unattainable height" indicates the kind of formal craftsmanship for which he has received insufficient credit. At the end of his life in 1938 and 1939, when he was writing his *Memoirs*, Anderson began to perceive consciously what he had done with his concept of the *grotesque* by using serial, epic techniques. On December 16, 1939, he wrote to his friend, Roger Sergel: "I am trying to do a series. The idea is really, Roger, to do an autobiography in a new way, not in the life of the teller but in lives that touch his life . . . much as I used the figure of George Willard in *Winesburg*." Cut short by his untimely death, the *Memoirs* remains one of Anderson's most successful books, a rare combination of form and subject matter that penetrates deeply into his views of *American Grotesque*.

At the center of Anderson's sympathy for the grotesque is a compassion for the relationship between beauty and ugliness. Anderson's compassion is like the spirit with which Theodore Roethke defines *grotesque* in his poem, "Long Live the Weeds":

> All things unholy, marred by curse,
> The ugly of the universe

The rough, the wicked and the wild
That keep the spirit undefiled.
With these I match my little wits
And earn the right to stand or sit
Hope, love, create, or drink and die:
These shape the creature that is I.

An extraordinary recent relationship, barely noticed in American literature because it involves the concept of *grotesque*, is that between Sherwood Anderson and William Carlos Williams. To Williams, as to Anderson, the grotesque is often beautiful because it is openly human and exposed. As a doctor Williams exposed himself deliberately to the ways in which poverty distorts life. As Williams writes in "A Beginning on the Short Story," "I lived among these people. I knew them and saw the essential qualities (not stereotype), the courage, the humor (an accident), the deformity, the basic tragedy of their lives—and the importance of it. You can't write about something unimportant to yourself. I was involved."

In such fine stories of Williams as "The Knife of the Times," "The Use of Force," and "Jean Beicke," we see the true development of Anderson's insights into *American Grotesque*. Even the styles, the terse, colloquial tone, are similar. It is a shame that the too easy compartmentalization of Williams as poet and Anderson as short story writer prevents our understanding their deep connections in both style and theme. Perhaps the reason we fail to understand this relationship is because we Americans still reject the link between beauty and ugliness that is essential to understand *grotesque*. Despite recent trends in the arts we cling to our specialized, sentimental idea that ugly is ugly. Only after the disasters of the Second World War, Korea, and Vietnam have we begun to perceive a little how *grotesque* can produce beauty if viewed in a compassionate way. The photographer Diane Arbus, with her unique insights into *American Grotesque*, has helped greatly to focus attention on this problem. As we see clearly in her best photographs and in the work of Anderson and Williams, only an unusual compassion can relate ugliness to beauty in the world of *American Grotesque*.

I would like to attempt a final definition of *American Grotesque* as distinguished from European versions of *grotesque*. In his influential essay on *King Lear or Endgame*, Jan Kott writes:

> In the final instance tragedy is an appraisal of human fate, a measure of the absolute. The grotesque is a criticism of the absolute in the name of frail human experience. That is why tragedy brings catharsis, while grotesque offers no consolation whatsoever . . . In the world of the grotesque, downfall cannot be justified by, or blamed on, the absolute. The absolute is not endowed with any ultimate reasons; it is stronger, and that is all. The absolute is absurd. Maybe that is why the grotesque often makes use of the concept of a mechanism which has been put in motion and cannot be stopped.

When Kott says that "grotesque offers no consolation whatsoever," he seems to me wrong. Treated with artistry and compassion the grotesque can console. Many artists, European and American, testify to this. The difference lies in tone. The confrontation of existential questions has led to savage comedy, black humor, the pursuit of style and techniques into abstract areas where human elements are increasingly missing. All of these pervasive problems of meaning and faith lead to dominant trends in the arts that lift technique above content. Art becomes the masks of art rather than the direct confrontation of experience.

After the Second World War, caught in the age of concentration camps, the European artist began to struggle with Camus' sense of the absurd:

> A world that can be explained by reasoning, however faulty, is a familiar world. But in a universe that is suddenly deprived of illusions and of light, man feels a stranger. He is an irremediable exile, because he is deprived of memories of a lost homeland as much as he lacks the hope of a promised land to come. This divorce between man and his life, the actor and his setting, truly constitutes the feeling of Absurdity.
>
> [From *The Myth of Sisyphus*, as quoted
> by Martin Esslin in *The Theatre of the Absurd*.]

Naturally European artists after the Second World War tended to reflect a grotesque world in which man had become an absurdist cipher. Yet in the great works of European Grotesque, such as Beckett's

Waiting for Godot and *Endgame*, there is undeniable compassion in the urge to struggle and continue, to seek the necessity of companionship absurd though it may be in the face of vacancy.

American Grotesque still flows from a basic American optimism about the possibilities of democracy, religion, money, goods, power, conflicting with an increasing pessimism about the corporate and military forces that dominate our country. *American Grotesque*, then, creates an energetic style of vision that still searches for belief in a way that European visions of *grotesque* have given up. It is impossible for *American Grotesque* to be absurdist in the European sense of Camus' definition, or in the way that Martin Esslin elaborates that definition in his *The Theatre of the Absurd*.

A final vision of how *American Grotesque* continues to exert its particular tone and force . . . Traveling across the United States this past Bicentennial summer of 1976, my wife and I drove into Lake Havasu, an extraordinary new real estate boondoggle built out of the hot Arizona desert to celebrate the transplanting stone by stone of London Bridge to arch over an artificial lake. In 110 degree heat I walked with my dog over the bridge and she yelped as her paws encountered the burning pavement. British flags fluttered stoically side by side with American flags in the hot breeze creating an ironic opposition. I wrote these lines to celebrate the endurance of American Grotesque and to explore its meaning:

> Through the refrigeration of calculated transplants, personal hearts, kidneys, tissues, why not transplant an impersonal bridge? Number each huge stone-block forming the Victorian arch, dismantle the green Art Nouveau lamps, eliminate the Thames River, transfer every floating detail to hot dry Arizona desert. Scrub off the history of dirty time, the Wasteland images ("London Bridge is falling down"), erect the bridge again in shining, grotesque flight across a man-made lake . . .
>
> Spectres applaud shrewd real estate surgery, P. T. Barnum, Melville's Confidence Man, the venerable nineteenth century tycoons burst clapping out of their spectacular graves to celebrate this satirical Mark Twain promotion, culture for the cactus.

What fails is the invisible, furious American resistance. Landscape resists, language resists, Sherwood Anderson's grotesques resist searching for their lonely, individual salvation. William Carlos Williams resists crying, "T. S. Eliot, you cannot come home again!" The new frontier desert community resists, struggles for its identity. The American concept of *grotesque* resists, crying through tangled webs of ambition, evangelical fervor writhing with the desire for material possessions:

"*Grotesque* is the vulnerable, pathetic fantasy we distort in our simultaneous search for love and property. *Grotesque* is the mystery we eliminate to create the revolt of simple things, goods, that desire mystery. *Grotesque* is what we become when we seclude ourselves in the suburban community closed to wonder, the mechanical mirage of technological comfort. *American Grotesque*, the sad, searching patron of beauty, struggles to balance the intolerable weight of fantasies that shatter the sky with the glow of their singular distortions."

NOTES

1. I say "beginning to recognize" deliberately because even such a seminal work of American literary history as F. O. Matthiessen's *American Renaissance* does not consider the concept of grotesque as something central to American society.

As I Lay Dying
(William Faulkner)

" 'Great God, What They Got in That Wagon?':
Grotesque Intrusions in *As I Lay Dying*"
by Michael Gillum,
The University of North Carolina at Asheville

Outrageous, absurd, or outlandish situations are common in William
Faulkner's narratives. For example, Ike Snopes in *The Hamlet* is deeply
in love with a cow. The Indians in "Red Leaves" imitate their Euro-
American neighbors by acquiring black slaves, but only use them to
haul a derelict steamboat twelve miles overland to serve as the head-
man's palace. At the end of *The Sound and the Fury*, Benjy Compson, a
mentally defective member of a distinguished family, bawls his lungs
out in downtown Jefferson because the family carriage is circling
the Confederate Memorial in the direction opposite to what he is
used to. Tonally diverse as they are, all these situations are grotesque.
Grotesque art is art with bad manners. It challenges our ideals and
our notions of proper order with dissonant elements—disgusting,
embarrassing, incongruous, or frightening intrusions. To date, the
most systematic analysis of the literary grotesque is Philip Thomson's.
He writes that, structurally, the grotesque consists of "a mixture of
both the comic and the terrifying (or the disgusting, repulsive etc.)
in a problematical (i. e. not readily resolvable) way. . ." (21), adding
that the content of the grotesque must include "abnormality" (25). In
keeping with Thomson's point about contrasts being problematic or
irresolvable, a fundamental quality of the grotesque is its complexity

and uncertainty of tone. The grotesque is incongruous, and incongruity is funny. However, the grotesque incongruity may be so jarring and disturbing that revulsion or sympathy overpowers the sense of comedy. *As I Lay Dying* is the Faulkner novel that operates most consistently in the mode of the grotesque. Its travesty of funerary ritual, and mockery of the ideal of family solidarity, tests readers' assumptions and values.

The tone of *As I Lay Dying* is extremely complex and uncertain, as witnessed by the astonishing range of contradictory interpretations the book has inspired. For Patricia R. Shroeder, it is formally a comedy with Anse Bundren as its comic hero; whereas for Robert Merrill it is a tragedy with Darl as its tragic hero. While Shroeder's Anse is purely comic, Cleanth Brooks saw the Bundren patriarch as "one of Faulkner's most accomplished villains" (154). The novel's openness of meaning stems in part from the radical narrative technique, in which fifteen different first-person narrators relay fragments of the story and comment on the action. For example, in a sequence near the end, the smart-aleck drugstore clerk MacGowan tricks and sexually exploits Dewey Dell Bundren, pregnant outside of wedlock and desperately trying to negotiate an abortion. From MacGowan's perspective as narrator of the incident, it is a funny story about getting the better of a stupid country girl with loose morals. But readers are aware that Dewey Dell, as a "ruined maid," faces a grave situation. She is probably unmarriageable, unlikely to be able to support herself and a child, certain to be a pariah if she stays within the rural community. Although the text does not present Dewey Dell with a great deal of sympathy, it does give readers access to her interior panic and denial. The tension between comedy and pathos is irresolvable except in the minds of individual readers.

Of the dissonant elements that characterize the grotesque, one of the most prominent is the grossness of the human body, emphasized by Joyce Carol Oates, who says in the "Afterword" to *Haunted* that the grotesque "always possesses a blunt physicality" (304). The grotesque in art often reminds us that the body, with its smells, wastes, unruly appetites, and deformities, calls into question human idealisms and human pretensions. In his influential study of Rabelais, Mikhail Bakhtin showed that literary treatments of the grotesque body can serve variously to celebrate animal vitality, to humiliate satiric targets, or, in a darker vein pertinent to Faulkner's novel, to remind us of our inevitable decay and death (308–17). When Yeats wrote in "Sailing to

Byzantium" that his soul was "fastened to a dying animal," he captured exactly this darker aspect of the grotesque body. In Yeat's figure we see the contrasting ideal or normative element, in this case the "soul," that must be engaged in some way if the effect of the grotesque is to be felt.

In *As I Lay Dying*, Anse Bundren is a grotesque character partly because of his moral deformity: his lack of self-understanding, his parasitic and manipulative relations with others, his pious posturing. But he is also physically deformed and ugly, with his toothless mouth, humped back, and splayed feet with no nails on the little toes. At the end, on learning that Anse has married a popeyed "duck-shaped" woman (260), the reader may feel a bit queasy at the prospect that these two grotesque bodies will join in a sexual union. However, the grotesque body that commands our primary attention in *As I Lay Dying* is not Anse's, but rather the corpse of Addie Bundren.

The action of *As I Lay Dying* consists of Addie's death and the family's week-long effort to move her body from rural southern Yoknapatawpha County to Jefferson, over forty miles distant, for burial in her father's family plot. Essentially, the action is an absurdly extended funeral procession, complicated by a river in violent flood, as well as a series of misjudgments and bizarre acts by the Bundrens. Since, as we have seen, the effect of the grotesque depends on a contrast with the ideal or normative, we should think first about what a funeral and funeral cortege ought to be.

Among rural Americans circa 1929, most people died at home. It was normal for neighbors to visit during a deathwatch, or to gather the day after a death to pay their respects. It was normal for the women-folk to wash and dress the corpse. Burial usually occurred on the second or third day, a plain coffin having been hastily constructed or purchased. A married woman normally was buried with her husband's family in a nearby family plot. There was a cortege or ritual procession from the home or church to the gravesite. Finally, there would be a graveside ceremony with a clergyman usually officiating.

The funerary process for Addie Bundren is abnormal in every way. At the beginning of the narrative, the deathwatch is underway. The neighborly Tulls are visiting as they should be, with Cora nattering incongruously about her egg business and pretending Addie will get well. But then there is a shocking eruption of violence in Jewel's interior monologue as he approaches the house. He hates the Tulls for "sitting there, like buzzards" and staring at Addie (15). He hates Dewey Dell's fanning. He fantasizes about being alone on a high hill with his mother, "and me rolling rocks down the hill at their faces, picking them up and throwing them faces and teeth and all by God. . ." (15)—these are his family members and his helpful neighbors! Later, Jewel will openly insult Vernon Tull by suggesting that his friendly visit is an intrusion on Addie's privacy (17). Above all, Jewel hates the sound of Cash's tools at work on Addie's coffin right under her window "where she can see him" (14). Since everyone but Jewel acknowledges that Addie is dying, it is proper for Cash to have begun work on the coffin. Surely, though, among normal families the project would be hidden away in the barn rather than set up ten feet from the sickbed, intruding on the ceremony of death. So the noise of coffin-building provides a soundtrack for the days of the deathwatch. This macabre arrangement culminates in the moments before death, when Addie shouts, "You, Cash!" and looks out the window. The proud carpenter holds up two boards and mimes the shape of the finished box; she looks without reacting, and then she dies (48).

Incongruous events continually upset the decorum of death. Earlier that day, the boy Vardaman caught and butchered a huge fish, which he reported was "full of blood and guts as a hog" (38). In a scene of low comedy, the fat and elderly Doc Peabody has to be hauled up the steep path to the house by a rope. Anse grumbles about having to pay him, while Peabody and the Tulls realize that Anse is too cheap to have summoned a doctor unless it was already too late to do any good. Then, at the climactic moment of death, the family circle is incomplete or (as we shall see later) deliberately broken. Addie and the third son, Jewel, have loved each other with a furious but unexpressed intensity. As Addie is dying, Dewey Dell says, "It's Jewel she wants" (47), but Jewel is not there because Darl and Jewel have gone off on a trip to sell a load of wood for a measly three dollars. Then shortly after the death, and with the trip to Jefferson in prospect, Anse is thinking, "Now I can get them teeth" (52), Vardaman thinks at least briefly about bananas and the toy train, and Dewey Dell broods about an abortion. No doubt they are all grieving as well, but each has a private, selfish interest that contradicts social ideals about how people respond to the death of a loved one.

Young Vardaman, the only son to witness Addie's death directly, goes wild with grief and traduces the funerary atmosphere with a series of comical, gruesome, and violent acts. He lashes Peabody's horses until they run away, attacks Cora while she is cooking the fish that Vardaman has confused with his mother, and keeps opening the window so the corpse gets rained on. Then, in the novel's first truly horrifying moment, the family discovers that Vardaman, using Cash's auger to drill holes in the sealed coffin lid, has drilled three holes in the corpse's face.

Here we encounter one of the plot's central motifs: Addie's corpse is the grotesque body in its dark sense, a reminder of mortality. Funerary ritual is a system for affirming the life that is now finished, for consoling the bereaved, and for asserting the bonds of community that survive the loss of an individual member. But above all, funerary ritual serves to cover the naked indignity of death. While already a series of ugly or comic intrusions have compromised that covering-up, Vardaman's thoughts and interventions radically expose the indignity. We may wonder why he thinks, "My mother is a fish" (84). From an early age, farm children are inured to the death of animals and the spilling of blood and entrails. Thus, when the boy commented earlier on the fish's huge mass of guts, he was not only bragging about his manly prowess in catching such a "hog," but also making clear that he could handle the messiness of death. But when Addie dies later that day, perhaps his first close contact with human death, he makes the appalling connection: his mother is dead meat, like the fish. Then he converts that similitude, too terrible to be faced, into a disguised form: my mother is a fish. This thought is the reason he attacks Cora when she takes the bloody fish fillets out of the pantry and starts to cook them. He thinks at a later point that Addie may be some other fish and still alive, so it is not she in the coffin. But, in his confusion, he also thinks the corpse needs to breathe, so he must open the window above the deathbed and drill holes in the box once she is nailed up inside it.

The Bundrens continue to call what is in the box "Addie" or "Ma" in the days leading up to the burial, but the text does not let readers forget that what the box contains is dead meat. The dead meat is grotesquely clothed in Addie's wedding dress, although Addie despised Anse and has denied her Bundren-hood by demanding to be buried with her father's family. The corpse is placed backwards in the coffin, frustrating Cash's meticulous custom engineering. And finally the corpse is mutilated by three holes drilled in its face. Although

Cash plugs the holes in the lid with perfectly fitted dowels, and the women veil the mangled face (enacting the idea of funeral as cover-up), the holes in the flesh are still there.

After the neighbors gather for a memorial service at the house, the funeral's course is suspended for two more days because Jewel and Darl broke a wagon wheel on the wood-delivery mission. By the time they finally load the coffin in the wagon, the corpse has already begun to stink; the brothers are "breathing through [their] teeth to keep [their] nostrils closed" (98), and the buzzards have already appeared (94). The Bundrens will travel for six days under a miasma of death-stench with an aerial escort of vultures filling out the meager one-wagon funeral cortege. For the reader, the spectacle is horrifying and disgusting, but it is also darkly comic. The Bundrens made this impression during their stop in the town of Mottson:

> It was Albert told me about the rest of it. He said the wagon was stopped in front of Grummet's hardware store, with the ladies all scattering up and down the street with handkerchiefs to their noses, and a crowd of hard-nosed men and boys standing around the wagon, listening to the marshal arguing with the man. He was a kind of tall, gaunted man sitting up on the wagon, saying it was a public street and he reckoned he had as much right there as anybody. . . . It had been dead eight days, Albert said. . . . It must have been like a piece of rotten cheese coming into an ant-hill, in that ramshackle wagon that Albert said folks were scared would fall all to pieces before they could get out of town. (203)

This is one of several points in the novel where outsiders catch the smell and react with horror and indignation, reminding readers again and again of how disgusting and shameful it is to be hauling a rotting corpse around the countryside. However, the perspective offered by the narrator Moseley, Albert's boss, is undeniably comic. He sees the Bundrens as crazy and ridiculous hayseeds. Here is the stolid Anse, stubbornly defending his right to use a public street and "spend his money where he wants" (204)—hardly the issue, of course—while the town ladies scatter like chickens to escape the smell, and the swaggering males show they are manly enough to take it. The scene that Moseley describes is comic-grotesque in the way the disgusting and incongruous intrude upon a settled order. But, on reflection, if the fictional world were projected into the future, someday Moseley and Albert will be what Addie is now. The Bundrens' wagon is a *memento mori* for the town folk, and their panicky reaction to it is, in its way, as ridiculous as the Bundrens' behavior.

One of the most unique things about *As I Lay Dying* is the way it treats the final stage of the Bundrens' funeral rite. The text does not present Addie's burial at all. The long, painful, and humiliating journey, the crazed attempt to ford the swollen river, Jewel's heroic rescue of the coffin from the burning barn, Cash's terrible suffering with the broken leg in the jolting wagon—all these were endured for the purpose of burying Addie according to her wishes. Although some readers have thought Anse led the family to Jefferson for the sake of the false teeth, Anse could have buried Addie at New Hope and then gone to town for the teeth under much easier circumstances. Their suffering shows that they were really doing it out of a sense of obligation to Addie. So it is a surprising anticlimax when we are denied a scene of grave-digging and burial along with the characters' observations and reactions. Instead, we get Cash's brief, offhand statement that the burial occurred: "But when we got it filled and covered and drove out the gate . . ." (237). With this deliberate minimizing, Faulkner denies readers access to the expected climax and fulfillment. The sudden vacuum in the story has the effect of devaluing the Bundrens' odyssey—often compared to that other *Odyssey*—and devaluing in particular the heroic elements of the story, rendering them grotesque by dissolving the purpose behind them. When the driving force of Addie's will and her role in the family structure are suddenly obliterated, that absence seems to drain significance away from whatever the Bundrens have done.

So we see how the text deforms the ideal pattern of funerary ritual into the grotesque at every turn. The sounds of Cash's saw and adze make a harsh background music for Addie's dying. The narration interweaves comic incidents with the preparation for death, while social and familial tensions disturb the ceremonial atmosphere of the deathwatch. Then all hell breaks loose as Vardaman strikes violently at Peabody and Cora and desecrates the corpse. While the improvised memorial service seems to be one part of the process that goes properly, readers are darkly aware that the presiding preacher Whitfield was Addie's secret lover and the father of her son Jewel.

Most importantly, the funerary process not only fails to conceal the indignity of death, but actually parades that indignity across two counties as the stinking corpse with attendant buzzards makes its halting progress. And finally, the climactic burial is apparently wiped away from the consciousness of the narrators and hidden from the reader.

On arriving at Jefferson, the Bundrens are understandably anxious to "get her underground" (235), but in the seven narrative segments that are set in Jefferson, the only reference made to Addie after her burial comes with Anse's obviously insincere bullying of Dewey Dell when he takes her money: "[M]y own daughter, the daughter of my dead wife, calls me a thief over her mother's grave" (256). Obviously, he makes a travesty of Addie's memory by invoking it only to further his own shabby purpose. Otherwise, everyone seems to forget about Addie after the burial. Even Vardaman's anguish is displaced by thoughts of bananas, the toy train, and observations of a stray cow, perhaps a ghostly echo of the lost mother (251). We can suppose that Jewel has not forgotten, but the text does not allow him a voice. So when the novel's last sentence names the duck-shaped woman as "Mrs. Bundren," Addie has disappeared altogether, and along with her, any high motivation for the journey, which turns out to be more a disposing-of than a tribute.

This erasure of Addie connects with the text's subversion of another idealism, the idea of the family united in love. The terrible tensions among the Bundrens emerge in Jewel's furious monologue, where he apparently wishes that Cash and Anse had died after suffering their accidents and imagines himself smashing everyone with stones in order to protect Addie and keep her to himself alone (15). Later, Jewel was absent at the moment of his mother's death. Reading closely, we come to realize that Darl, probably motivated by jealousy, has deliberately spoiled Addie's last moments of life by removing her favorite, Jewel, from the scene. When Anse is uncertain whether to send the brothers on the wood-hauling errand, it is Darl who argues that they should go because they need the three dollars (17). He tells Dewey Dell he knows Addie will die before they get back (28), and he starts taunting Jewel about the impending death as soon as they are on the road (39). How do we reconcile the perpetrator of this nasty maneuver with the sensitive, poetic Darl who drinks from a dipper full of stars (11)? Then we have Addie declaring Anse "dead" at some point over twenty years before the narrative present and starting an affair with Whitfield (173). Her demand to be buried in Jefferson amounts to seeking a posthumous divorce. That is how it goes in the Faulknerian family, perfectly described by Calvin Bedient as "a terrible and frustrating unit of interlocking solitudes, atomic in structure like a molecule" (65).

The interfamily tensions come to a head with the expulsion of Darl. According to Cash's speculation, Dewey Dell has betrayed Darl to Gillespie as the barn-burner (237). We may infer that Gillespie threatened Anse the morning of the Bundrens' departure, and the other adults decided in a brief secret conference that "It wasn't nothing else to do" but declare Darl insane. "It was either send him to Jackson, or have Gillespie sue us . . ." (232). One can suppose that Anse was moved by the threat of losing money, Jewel by his history of antagonism with Darl and Darl's attempt to burn the corpse, Cash by his moral judgment of Darl's crime, and Dewey Dell, if she had a say in the matter, by her resentment of Darl's knowing about her secret pregnancy. Perhaps at this point there was no way to save Darl, but some members of the family actively want to hurt him. It is a gut-wrenching moment when Dewey Dell and Jewel physically attack Darl as the state agents approach to take him away, and Jewel says, "Kill him. Kill the son of a bitch" (238). One might question whether the novel's account of hostilities within the family has enough of the comic about it to qualify as properly grotesque, but this shockingly abnormal and indecorous scene at the cemetery gate clearly justifies invoking the term. After the Bundrens dispose of Addie and Darl, we see a centrifugal movement as Dewey Dell privately pursues her (obviously grotesque) "therapy" while Vardaman sits alone on the curb outside the drugstore, and elsewhere Anse scrambles after his false teeth and prospective new wife. Jewel, though untraced, is probably alone with his demons. Still, at the end, there they are all together, eating bananas, ready to start home with the new Mrs. Bundren in tow.

Insofar as the journey seemed to be a collective effort coura-geously undertaken by the whole family for the whole, involving heroic suffering and heroic action, that perception is undermined by the sudden dismissal of Addie, the expulsion of Darl, and the scurrying aftermath of selfish pursuits. Also, these same corrosive contrasts further dissolve any remaining sense of the funerary ritual as honoring the dead and asserting human dignity. Thus *As I Lay Dying* is a text with very bad manners indeed. It shatters our frames for the social processing of death and the idealization of family. And yet, the overall effect is not purely grim, but rather quite mixed. In addition to the moments of comedy, we cannot forget Addie's intense Romantic self-consciousness, Jewel's instinctive courage, Darl's brilliant perceptiveness, even Cash's stoic self-discipline and devotion to his craft. The crowd in Mottson staring at the rednecks on the wagon had no idea what energies bubbled beneath the shabby surfaces they were observing. Furthermore, the reconstituted Bundren family will survive and continue into the future with the support of an extraordinarily strong and neighborly rural community. *As I Lay Dying* gives readers little guidance as how to evaluate its mixture of ugliness and beauty, despair and affirmation. Yet we are challenged to interpret these contrasts that Bedient suggests seem to generate a "thickness of meaning, the significant indefiniteness of life itself" (63).

WORKS CITED

Bakhtin, Mikhail. *Rabelais and His World.* Trans. Helen Iswolsky. Bloomington: U of Indiana P, 1984.

Bedient, Calvin. "Pride and Nakedness: *As I Lay Dying.*" *MLQ* 29 (1968): 61–76.

Brooks, Cleanth. *William Faulkner: The Yoknapatawpha Country.* New Haven: Yale UP, 1963.

Faulkner, William. *As I Lay Dying: The Corrected Text.* New York: Vintage International, 1990.

Merrill, Robert. "Faulknerian Tragedy: The Example of *As I Lay Dying.*" Mississippi Quarterly 47 (1994): 403–18.

Oates, Joyce Carol. *Haunted: Tales of the Grotesque.* New York: Plume, 1994.

Schroeder, Patricia R. "The Comic World of *As I Lay Dying.*" *Faulkner and Humor: Faulkner and Yoknapatawpha, 1984.* Jackson: UP of Mississippi, 1986: 34–46.

Thomson, Philip. *The Grotesque.* London: Methuen & Co., 1972.

THE BACCHAE
(EURIPIDES)

"The Bacchae"
by Siegfried Melchinger (Trans. Samuel R. Rosenbaum), in *Euripides* (1973)

INTRODUCTION

Providing a detailed analysis of Euripides' play, Siegfried Melchinger asserts that *The Bacchae* is "the tragedy of tragedies," one whose myth "is interpreted as a representation of the contradictions apparent in every era." For Melchinger, the grotesque quality of Dionysus' retribution on Thebes and its ruler, the ever-rational Pentheus, emphasizes the extremities of human nature and the consequences for remaining ignorant of them. The grotesque murder of Pentheus by his own mother results from his refusal to acknowledge the presence and power of the irrational in the city. As Melchinger's analysis of the play makes clear, *The Bacchae*'s grotesque scenes are indispensable to the representation of Dionysus and the contrary drives of the human psyche he holds under his sway.

Melchinger, Siegfried. "*The Bacchae.*" *Euripides.* Trans. Samuel R. Rosenbaum. New York: Frederick Ungar, 1973. 177–89.

Dionysus, the god ever old and ever new—that is, the one who disappeared and returned again—had set out to conquer the world. Asia lies
at his feet. In the south and the north of Hellas, he has established
beachheads. Now he is at the point of subjugating the Hellenes.
Unlucky Thebes is to be the city in which he will start. He chose it not
because he was born there but because it was the city in which he was
insulted. Mythical time is the present time of the play. Cadmus, the
mythical founder of Thebes, is still living. He is the father of Semele,
who was selected by Zeus to be the mother of Dionysus. As god and
begetter, Zeus appeared to her in the guise of a stroke of lightning. So
close did he get to her that she was consumed by its fire. Around the
flame is hallowed ground. A tomb and sanctuary, overgrown with ivy,
stand near the still flaming city.

Semele's sisters disparage their dead sister. It was not Zeus, they
suggest, but a mortal who fathered Dionysus. To avenge this insult,
Dionysus has chosen them, as well as all the women of Thebes, as
his first victims. This is the state of affairs in Thebes when the play
opens.

Young Pentheus is the king. He is the grandson of Cadmus, the
son of Cadmus's oldest daughter, Agave. At a time when Pentheus has
been out of the country, dionysian madness has taken possession of the
women of the city. Leaving hearth and home, they have rushed into
the mountains as, bacchantes, celebrants of Dionysus Bacchus. Moved
by the powers of the god, the older men have also joined them, as has
the patriarch Cadmus.

But the polis is showing resistance. The men, led by Pentheus,
reject the god.

"First the drum of the great mother begins to resound. The drum-
sticks begin their rattle and the resin in the torches of the goddess
begins to glow. Then the host of nymphs rages in. They whirl and
throw themselves around and stamp in ecstatic dance." This is Pindar's
description of the cavalcade of Dionysus and his throng of followers.

The maenads beat their tambourines. Castanets clatter. Their
heads wreathed with ivy leaves, clothed in fawn skins, carrying a
thyrsus in one hand, a torch in the other, the maenads dance wildly
around Dionysus. Dionysus has put on human form. His mask framed
by long locks is that of a girl, as are his clothes. He is not only god and
man, but also both man and woman. At the end of the prologue he
tells the maenads to beat the drum resoundingly so that Thebes will

see what is happening. He himself is going to the mountain to dance with the bacchantes.

The maenads are half women, half creatures, who accompany Dionysus in his triumphal march. They have something strange and wild in them, for, as in every human being, the strange and wild are always latent and will erupt when unleashed. It has manifested itself in the women of Thebes.

The music, the dance, the singing, are barbaric. The new god Dionysus takes no account of any difference between Europe and Asia, between Hellenic and barbarian. He recognizes no difference between Tmolus, near Sardis in Asia Minor, from which he and his throng have come, and Thebes, in which he was born and in which he has now decided to found his cult.

The scene that follows, grotesque and laughable, is meant to be absurd. In bacchante costume, with ivy leaves in his hair, using a thyrsus as a crutch, old blind gray-haired Tiresias the prophet patters in. He is led to the front of the stage and calls to Cadmus. Cadmus emerges in a short cloak, with a fawn skin covering his spindly legs. Tiresias asks where he may dance. The elders have already submitted to the new god, who recognizes no differences in age.

Pentheus, followed by his armed guard, enters the arena. He is angered when he sees these two oldsters leaping and shouting. He wears the mask and costume of a young hero. His manner of speech is lordly, sharp, and, as one of his people says, all too regal. His gestures are rapid and authoritative. His personal courage and intelligence are unquestionable. He is said to be without moderation, but in which respect? Can a king accustomed to ruling his city with common sense be blamed if he refuses to tolerate the lawlessness that has broken out in Thebes?

Perhaps Euripides deliberately offers the scenes in which the older people offend, so that the good sense of the audience will denounce the followers of Dionysus. Where will this lead to if these goings-on are not stopped? And even if a god is behind all this, no polis can survive if such madness prevails. Tiresias and Cadmus, who have accepted Dionysus, have nothing to propose to solve this dilemma. Established civic policies no longer have any relevancy once this divine madness has disrupted the ordinary life of the polis.

Tiresias expounds the credo of Dionysus. The earth was barren, then Dionysus gave it moisture. He gave us wine to have with our bread. He gave us the madness of prophetic vision to add to our understanding, for prophecy is also a form of madness. Tiresias says: Great power has he over Hellas; belief in the power of man does not make for humanity. We men of age join in the god's dances because we are not so insane as to fight against him as you are doing.

Then Cadmus adds another argument that would appeal to every Hellene, no matter how absurd it might seem to us: even if this god turns out not to be a god, it is to the interest of the house and the polis to honor him as if he were a god. He says that whether or not the god be fictional, the worship of him is noble and honorable. So he takes the wreath from his own head and tries to place it on that of Pentheus, inviting him to "Dance with us!"

But Pentheus hisses at his grandfather to keep that wreath away from him. Only respect for the aged and for piety stops him from treating old Cadmus roughly. But the other one, the seer, the seducer—he should be punished. Immediately he orders demolition of the temple of the seer and a police raid on the stranger who has driven the women mad. Death by stoning is the final penalty he commands.

A motive emerges in this scene that will be of decisive significance for the further development of the plot. Pentheus interprets an "orgy" as being what we associate with the word today, as sexual indulgence to excess. The foreigner is leading the women astray, into unchastity! He is desecrating marriage vows.

Pentheus has no other explanation for the events reported to him and that he himself has witnessed on his way into the city. Some hordes of women have already been arrested and thrown into prison. When women have lost all inhibitions, it is only libido that drives them. This attitude is in line with masculine assumptions by which a woman is nothing but an object for satisfying the male's sexual needs. The polis was essentially a male state. The thought that a craving to achieve freedom was expressed in the dionysian revolt of the women probably did not enter the minds of men of the theater of Dionysus. In this opinion there is also something of the bragging of the man for whom a woman is nothing else but a piece of property that exists to serve the satisfaction of his libido.

It would be foolish to maintain that *The Bacchae* represents a kind of early *Doll's House*, a play with a purpose aimed toward the emancipation of women—but one of its basic themes is the conflict between the sexes. It is highlighted by extreme contrasts. On one hand, we are shown the unleashing of the irrational that is believed by some to be more deeply imbedded in women than it is in men. On the other hand, we see the hubris of extreme rationality. Men base their right to power, claiming to be the sole possessors of rationality, and lay claim to the right to rule society on this assumption.

In answer to Pentheus, the chorus asserts the reality of the dionysian credo in the framework of a song of praise to true wisdom. It prefers peace, the company of the muses and the graces, to the boundless self-confidence of arrogant rationality. Dionysus is worshipped here as the god of the common man, the majority, and those who oppose him are not only presumptuous but also lacking in moderation.

The theme is repeated in the development of the plot. True inner peace can be achieved only after the excesses of the dionysian orgies. Once the dark hidden powers have been released and relieved, life under the customary laws of society can return to the golden mean, the balance, the equilibrium. This may well be so, but one must realize that this is not necessarily the point of view of Euripides. It is stated as the view of the dionysian chorus.

The armed guards bring Dionysus in, in fetters. But they do not feel safe with him. He did not offer the least resistance. Beyond that, the maenads they arrested have gone free. The chains that bound them have dropped off, the locks burst open. It is witchcraft.

Pentheus opens the hearing. The answers of the defendant Dionysus as to his person are full of irony. They alternate cheerfully, some coming from Dionysus in his apparently human form, others from him in his actually divine character. The questioning is concentrated on the principal charge of leading women into unchastity. Dionysus repeats the defense Tiresias has already put forward, that a woman's virtue depends on her own character. It does not take an orgy to make a woman immoral. The fact that these rites take place principally at night is quite irrelevant. Vice can prevail equally by day.

Pentheus debates this with Dionysus in a cold fury. He demands to see this god but is rebuked: he cannot see him because he is ungodly. This is too much for Pentheus. Despite Dionysus's warning, Pentheus orders him locked up in the stables. His women are to be sent to the slave market or to the factories. Dionysus, broaching the problem of personal identity, warns him again that he does not know what he is doing or even what he is. The armed guards approach Dionysus cautiously. Smiling indulgently, he goes with them.

The chorus of maenads, surrounded by armed soldiers, weeps loud laments for the disappearance of Dionysus. What follows is a mystery but this is not, as was often later claimed, the entire play.

The sacred section of the play begins now. Its opening measures are ritualistic. It is in keeping with the paradoxical nature of the god that he should die and live again, depart and return, be killed and then resurrected. The maenads raise their lamentation for his disappearance to a lament for the whole world. This weeping rises to a religious ecstasy. At its height they hear the voice of the god from inside his place of confinement calling to them.

The music of their antiphony swells in volume. The earth trembles. Houses are heard collapsing. The flames on Semele's tomb flare up. All are thrown to their knees, maenads and soldiers. Dionysus appears in thunder and lightning. The sacred section of the play has reached its culmination. It is his epiphany. Great glory surrounds the god. Splendor radiates around him triumphantly. He announces in fiery verses what has happened, how Pentheus, first panting with rage, was made a fool of and finally sank in a swoon.

Never was a god's revenge more cruel, contemptuous, and insidious. And never did a man resist a god with greater hubris. Pentheus staggers out of the house with sword in hand. Catching sight of the "stranger," he hurls himself at him. He commands that all doors be locked. A shepherd comes running. He reports miracles on the mountain. He has seen an idyll, full of modesty and morality. Pentheus's unjust suspicions and untruths are given the lie.

It occurs to the shepherds to capture Agave, Pentheus's mother, and bring her into the city in the hope of winning the gratitude of their master. This causes a fight. Like wild animals stirred up by an attack, the rage of the bacchantes is unchained. They begin to tear the cattle apart. They storm down into the valley, pour into the villages like enemy invaders. And when the peasants seize weapons to defend themselves, blood flows not from swords but from blows of the thyrsus. The shepherds beseech their king to accept this god, whoever he may be.

The tearing apart of animals is a ritual of the cult. Like Zagreus in the Orphic myth, who, after being torn to pieces by the Titans, was reborn of Semele, in the person of Dionysus, Dionysus himself is torn apart by the women so he can be born again. The Orphic rites included the tearing apart and eating of animals representing Zagreus, to account for the presence of both divinity and evil in human beings. Thus was the power of the god demonstrated at the same time through an epiphany.

But Pentheus is not yet entirely subdued. He insists on continuing to run amok. He refuses the shepherds' advice. He blusters that this bacchic frenzy is disgracing Thebes in the eyes of all Hellas. He orders his men to mobilize, saying that Theban men will not crawl to the altar of this god in obedience to the terrorizing acts of the bacchantes.

Was he not right? Could he tolerate all this merely because it was instigated by a god? Once more, and for the last time, man's rationality rises up against the irrational terror of the god. Dionysus warns Pentheus in vain that he will die if he raises arms against him. But since warnings do not stop Pentheus, it will take other means to overthrow him. Here the mystery part of the play comes to its ending.

Dionysus displays his power over Pentheus, the mortal, without even needing a miracle. It is the dark side of Pentheus's own character that drives him to his fate. Dionysus awakens it by projecting before Pentheus's eyes a picture that arouses his sexual desires in a wave of perverted lasciviousness. Dionysus promises Pentheus to take him to watch how the bacchantes are carrying on up on the mountain. He will be able to observe everything as a voyeur from a hiding place. Pentheus still calls out for his weapons, but Dionysus, with a cutting exclamation, encourages the self-acting ferment working in Pentheus. Little by little, it destroys Pentheus's reason.

Now Dionysus has him firmly in his hands. His scorn abuses him and puts him to shame. Pentheus, the most masculine of men, must dress in women's clothing, as no man is permitted access to the orgies.

He must put on his head the same wig with flowing locks that he has just been ridiculing Dionysus for wearing. He must throw a fawn skin over his shoulders and carry a thyrsus as a symbol.

As Pentheus objects that all Thebes would laugh at his appearance, Dionysus promises to conduct him through deserted streets. Pentheus darts into the house at once, "into our net," as Dionysus says with mocking laughter before he follows him inside. Dionysus says of himself that though he is the most terrifying of the gods he is also the most merciful. The female clothing will serve Pentheus also as his shroud.

The maenads, now clearly seen as votaries of Dionysus, sing the refrain with real enthusiasm. Man's wisdom counts for little as the dionysian always triumphs, Submission to Dionysus is extolled again, for it brings the happiness of the quiet in the home, of those that live content with what each day brings without yearning for more.

Pentheus staggers to his shocking end. In his women's clothing he dances like a maenad. Dionysus escorts him from the stage in this absurd costume. His madness is clear to all to see, but also its cause: lasciviousness. At last he asks Dionysus to let him parade through the city in his female finery because, he says, he is the only man who would dare do such a thing. Dionysus assures him that he is great indeed, that his fame will rise to heaven after the suffering that he will endure on this expedition to the mountains.

The maenads transfer their mountain orgies to the stage and repeat them. Gruesome become their dancing and singing. They call down death on the godless, the immoral, and the unjust. They will laugh uproariously when Pentheus dies.

A messenger brings news. Euripides does not spare us any of the horror he reports. We see the voyeur avid with eagerness to witness the unchastity of the maenads, hiding in a grove of fir trees. Dionysus himself had bent down a treetop to earth so Pentheus could bounce up on it, so as not to be seen from the ground. Pentheus disappeared out of sight, and a loud voice called out to the bacchantes that the man who mocked their orgies is at hand. And as he spoke, the messenger said, A holy flame leaped up into heaven from the earth. The heavens stood still and the valley was silent. No leaf stirred and no sound of animals could be heard.

Then we see how the maenads tore the tree out of the ground, and, as Pentheus plunges to earth, how they fell upon him, his own mother in the lead, and tore him limb from limb. Each tossed the pieces to the other with her bloody hands. And Pentheus's mother seized the head, torn from the body, to impale it on her thyrsus. She carried it through the forest as though it were that of a lion killed in the hunt.

She is coming to the city. The messenger rushes away, not to see the horrible sight. But the maenads dance and Agave steps into the dance with her son's head on her staff, dancing and exulting with the rest. She comes to invite her father, Cadmus, to the feast. She will nail this captured lion's head up on the wall, so all the world of the polis can see the prize she has taken in the hunt.

The last step is the worst. Agave awakes from her madness. Cadmus comes with the bier on which the severed portions of Pentheus's body have been laid and covered with a black cloth. The raving mother, still radiant, approaches it with the head still on her staff. Now all the cast, even the chorus, falls back from her. She realizes what she has done. Agave is annihilated. So this is the reward for submission to the god, the gratitude of the god. Cadmus whispers that Dionysus has destroyed them.

A gap follows this passage in the surviving manuscripts of the play, but we do have some clues as to how the plot developed. Agave speaks a long lament. She counts over the limbs of the son she bore and murdered. How can she bear to live on after this? Then Dionysus appears ex machina. Some of the god's prophecy has been preserved. All of them—Cadmus, Agave, and her sisters—must leave Thebes and go abroad. In vain Cadmus prays to their ancestor for forgiveness, pleading that angry gods should not act as vindictively as mortals do. The victims, weeping, draw away, taking sad farewell of their country, their noble lineage.

The Bacchae is not like the medieval mystery plays because two mortals rise up against the sacred rituals. The first of them is Pentheus, with his claim for the self-created order of men. Then Agave accuses the gods for punishing minor sins—like the defaming remarks the sisters made about Dionysus's mother, Semele—beyond all measure and with cruel craftiness.

What, then, is *The Bacchae*? It is the tragedy of tragedies. It brings out into the open and examines the old myths that were the stuff of the theater in older times, using the archaic arena, the costumes and forms that were familiar. Gilbert Murray said that it is bound more tightly by form than any Hellenic play we know. It brings together everything the models of previous tragedy contributed and distills out of them what remained relevant to its own day. It is the essence of the human condition as Euripides saw it in 406 BC, after looking back over a long lifetime.

Its myth is interpreted as a representation of the contradictions apparent in every era. Dionysus is not the anti-Apollo that Nietzsche considered him to be. He is in the center between the opposite poles, not the god of metamorphoses, but the god of dichotomy. He is in the middle between man and woman, between Asia and Europe, between Hellas and the barbarian world, between heaven and hell (according to Heraclitus, his other name is Hades), between death and life, between raving and peace (mania and hesychia).

Dionysus is the one who disappears and returns, hunter and hunted, murderer and victim, life and death. The tragedy consists in knowing that these two aspects are different sides of the same manifestation.

Goethe considered *The Bacchae* to be Euripides's most beautiful tragedy. In his last years he was preparing to translate it into "his own beloved German language." But death overtook him before he could do it.

THE BIRDS
(ARISTOPHANES)

"Empire and the Grotesque
in Aristophanes' *The Birds*"
by Khalil M. Habib, Salve Regina University

The Birds (414 BCE), by Aristophanes, is an outlandish story of an ambitious Athenian. Pisthetaerus has abandoned his city in order to supplant the power of the gods and to found his own supposedly democratic and universal empire, with himself as sole ruler. He is, by the end of the play, entirely successful—he creates a universal empire that consists entirely of birds. In his quest, Pisthetaerus himself eventually ceases to be human and becomes a feathered birdman-god. Beneath the buffoonery, *The Birds* is a drama that examines the hope of one bold Athenian to become a god himself by founding a democracy liberated from the shackles of religion and tradition. Pisthetaerus embodies the perfect combination of imperial ambition and extreme impiety. To the ancient Greek mind, this mixture would have represented a truly ludicrous and distorted grotesquery.

Pisthetaerus, whose Greek name translates to "Persuader of his Comrade," skillfully manages to persuade a wide array of pious and provincial birds to turn on the gods and on their particular traditions by convincing them that they themselves, and not the Olympian gods, were the first kings over the world. He proposes a plan to restore these birds to their "original greatness" as gods, a former greatness that predates even their scattered powers as nations. Pisthetaerus awakens in the birds the ambition to rule once again as a mighty bird people, and so the gullible birds enlist their services in Pisthetaerus' revolution against the gods. The birds set out to starve the gods into submission by building a wall between heaven and earth that blocks the smoke of burnt sacrifices from reaching them. With the smoke from sacrifices blocked and prevented from rising to Olympus, the gods waste away, and the Olympians have no choice but to relinquish authority. Aristophanes is implying here that the gods' power and authority depends entirely on belief—on the sacrifices from mortals, without which the gods are but false idols of the mind. As a consequence of this grotesque irreverence, and with the help of Pisthetaerus' military and rhetorical skills, the birds successfully manage to establish a so-called democratic empire, called Cukcoonebulpolis, or Cloud-cuckoo-land. With democracy in his fictional empire of Cloud-cuckoo-land, Aristophanes holds a up mirror to the Athenian experiment. Unsurprisingly, it becomes apparent that Cloud-cuckoo-land is not the democracy promised by its founder and that Pisthetaerus is not the democrat he first pretended to be. Cloud-cuckoo-land turns out to be a tyranny in which Pisthetaerus wields sole title to legitimacy over the birds, the humans, and even the gods. By the end of play, this persuader's disdain for democracy and piety, both religious and familial, becomes obvious to all. Pisthetaerus' grotesque plan to supplant the authority of the gods in the name of freedom was but a pretext to satisfy *his* ambition to rule as a god completely outside of convention and moral restraint.

The Birds begins with two elderly Athenians—Pisthetaerus, our "Persuader of his Comrade," and his friend Euelpides, "Hopeful," who have abandoned their city in order to escape their financial debts and the endless litigation of their fellow Athenians. They have left Athens in order to seek out a life among the birds, where they can spend their remaining days in peace and tranquility, absolving themselves of their civic responsibilities. Under the direction of a Crow and a Jackdaw, Pisthetaerus and Euelpides seek out Tereus the Hoopoe, a mythical king whose tragic story was the subject of a celebrated play by Sophocles (now lost). The men seek Tereus because this wise old Hoopoe Bird was once a human being. Since Tereus was "originally . . . human, just like" them, and "once owed people money" but did not enjoy repaying his debts, Pisthetaerus and Euelpides try to locate him and ask for his advice, hoping he can direct them to a "nice cushy city, soft as woolen blanket, where [they] could curl up and relax" (115–120).

Euelpides requests a city where the worst troubles would be some form of the following:

> A friend appears at my door one morning and says, "Now swear to me by Zeus the Olympian that you and your kids will take a bath and be at my place bright and early for a wedding feast. Now please don't let me down, for otherwise you needn't pay me a visit when I'm in trouble!" (130–135)

By contrast, Pisthetaerus longs for:

> A city where the father of a blooming boy would meet me and complain like this, as if wronged: "It's a dandy way you treat my son, Mr. Smoothy! You met him leaving the gymnasium after his bath, and you did not kiss him, chat him up, or hug him, or fondle his balls—and you my old family friend!" (136–145)

Euelpides seeks the pleasures of the stomach; Pisthetaerus longs for a city with total sexual freedom. Together the two men hope to learn from Tereus and his subject birds of a city free from strife and inhibition, a place of total self-indulgence.

It is fitting that Euelpides and Pisthetaerus should seek their ideals of peace and sexual freedom from Tereus—the old Greek legend of Tereus is a tale of betrayal and vengeance. According to Sophocles and legend, Tereus had once been the king of Thrace and married to the Athenian princess Procne, who bore him a son, Itys. Tereus later raped Procne's sister Philomela and cut out her tongue to silence her. Philomela embroidered the details of the story into cloth, which she sent to her sister, Procne. In revenge, Procne murdered Itys and served up his remains to her husband. Tereus tried to kill both sisters, but the gods intervened and transformed them all into birds. Philomela becomes a swallow, Procne a nightingale (whom we later meet in the *Birds*), and Tereus a hoopoe. Even Itys is revived and becomes a goldfinch.

The gods have chosen to transform this violent family into birds for a reason. Birds are both innocently peaceful and unconsciously incestuous, because neither the awareness of death nor the importance of birth informs their existence. The solution to man's vengeance, betrayal, and endless cycle of violence is a forgetting of eternity and an elimination of the attachments that stem from procreation and sexual desire. No wonder Pisthetaerus sees the potential for his amorous desires to be satisfied in a community of peaceful, naively incestuous birds. Pisthetaerus' comical desire to seek sexual freedom among the birds must be read against this tragic setting of Tereus' legend.

Tereus suggests several cities to Euelpides and Pisthetaerus, but none prove satisfactory to them, for no existing city is so carefree. Euelpides then asks Tereus about life among the birds, which Tereus informs him, "wears quite nicely. To begin with, you must get by without a wallet . . . And in the gardens we feed on white sesame seeds, and myrtle-berries, and poppies, and watermint" (155–106). Euelpides is overjoyed and thinks the birds' easy existence of eating resembles the life of honeymooners (160). Pisthetaerus, however, is unimpressed and unsatisfied by such an existence. He objects to the lack of a unified city. Pisthetaerus has bigger ideas.

Pisthetaerus concocts an amazing plan: he will unite the birds "who fly around aimlessly with [their] beaks agape" into a single, all-powerful bird metropolis. Before he disturbs the order of the birds, however, Pisthetaerus begins to corrupt Tereus. Pisthetaerus enlists Tereus in his grand design by awakening in him a desire for empire. Pisthetaerus tells his host that as soon as the birds settle in one single city and fortify it, "this *site* will instead start being called a *city*." The persuader convinces Tereus that, by forming a single bird metropolis, Tereus could gain a life of power untold. He promises that the birds will "rule over humans as over locusts; and as for the gods, you'll destroy them by Melian famine" (180–185). Pisthetaerus' plan is simple: "Whenever humans sacrifice to the gods, you won't let the aroma of the thigh-bones pass through, unless the gods pay you some tribute" (190). By occupying and fortifying the air (the place of the gods) and earth (the place of human beings), the birds will become rulers of the world. Thus, Pisthetaerus' grotesque ambition for empire drives the action of the play.

Pisthetaerus' ambitious plan depends on the birds overthrowing the gods and erecting a universal empire over which he, Pisthetaerus, can rule. To this end, he promulgates a myth about the birds' origins, designed to appeal to their pride and sense of justice. He seeks to make the birds indignant in order to manipulate them. Pisthetaerus persuades the birds that they were once kings of the earth, telling them: "Yes, you, of all that exists, from yours truly [Pisthetaerus] to

Zeus himself, and born a long time before Cronus, and the Titans, and even the Earth" (465). He convinces them that they do not know this already because they failed to read their Aesop carefully, who

> says in his fable that the Lark was the first of all birds to
> be born, before the Earth and then her father perished of a
> disease, but there being no earth, he'd lain out for four days and
> she did not know what to do, till in desperation she buried her
> father in her own head. (470–475)

Pisthetaerus reasons that, since the birds "were born before the Earth and before the gods, it would follow that the kingship is rightfully theirs by primogeniture!" (480). An excellent persuader, Pisthetaerus offers further "proof" that the birds, and not the gods, once ruled over human beings, claiming that Egypt and Phoenicia were also ruled by birds before they were ruled by kings. Finally, Pisthetaerus adds that Zeus, the present imposter on the throne, wears "an eagle on his head as an emblem of royalty, as does his daughter [Athena] with an owl, and Apollo, *qua* servant, with a hawk" (515). He concludes that the birds were therefore once rulers and can (and ought) to rule again. To add insult to injury, he reminds the birds that they are now only servants and sometimes feasts for humans.

The birds are moved by Pisthetaerus' sermon and impressed by his theological account of their former prominence. Their present state of degradation makes listening to tales of their lost greatness unbearable. They resolve to unite, believing they have nothing to lose but their chains. Naively, they anoint Pisthetaerus their Savior, swearing allegiance to his leadership in gratitude for rediscovering their former royalty and promising to restore them to their rightful place (630–640).

Pisthetaerus resolves to name the new city Cloud-cuckoo-land and anoints the Persian bird, the proud Peacock, as its patron. The greater challenge for Pisthetaerus is, however, to weave the individuals into a harmonious whole. This is particularly important because the birds no longer belong to their former species or tribes but must be united with strange and different birds previously believed to be their rivals. By christening the new city with a name and patron bird, Pisthetaerus appeals to the pride of his followers: he attaches them to their new home, and at the same time, he declares to the world that birds have taken the place of the old gods. The name of the new city and its new patron bird advertise the incredible boast of its founder and followers to have supplanted the gods.

Once in power, Pisthetaerus' true nature surfaces, and his new power goes to his head. He assigns manual labor to the birds and Euelpides. His former cohort, Euelpides, had sought a life of ease when he joined Pisthetaerus on their journey to the birds. Instead, he is given most of the grunt work:

> Come on now, Euelpides, you take off for the sky and make yourself useful to the builders of our walls: take them up gravel, roll up your sleeves and mix some mortar, hand up a trough, fall off the scaffolding, station site watchmen, keep the embers glowing, run a tour with the bell, and bed down right on site. Now send one herald up to the gods above and another herald down to mankind below, and then report to me. (835–845)

Euelpides quickly makes an exit and is not to be seen again. As the action of the play continues, we discover that Pisthetaerus not only controls the building of the great wall, but also all of the decisions involved in ruling the new city, an arrangement he ironically links with "freedom." Pisthetaerus soon discovers that secular power is not sufficient. When he tries to make a sacrifice to the new gods, the birds, trouble ensues. Pisthetaerus ends up dismissing a bothersome priest and takes over the sacrificial services himself. In doing so, he effectively becomes both church and state.

While performing his new sacrificial duties, Pisthetaerus is immediately inundated with five opportunists from Athens, the very city he is seeking to escape (860–1140). The series of five opportunistic parasites comically reveals more about Pisthetaerus and his politics. First, a poor, shivering poet arrives with laudatory poems in honor of the new Cloud-cuckoo-land, begging for a small gift in return. Pisthetaerus gives him a coat left behind by the priest and sends him on his way. One must be careful when handling poets since their writings can subvert political rulers. Before he can return to his sacrifice, Pisthetaerus is again interrupted: a soothsayer approaches him with an oracle that threatens to cause disaster to Pisthetaerus' future rule if he is not paid a considerable sum. Pisthetaerus beats the soothsayer, who barely escapes alive.

Pisthetaerus' sacrifice is then interrupted by Meton, a famous astronomer and geometer, who proceeds to measure the air with a compass in order to lay out the circumference of the new city. He describes an atheistic cosmos, telling Pisthetaerus that the earth is like an oven and that the new city resembles a star. Unlike Pisthetaerus' previous visitors, Meton does not ask for gifts. And unlike the previous visitors, Pisthetaerus is pleased with Meton and admires his education. Neither of the men believe in the authority of gods or tradition. Pisthetaerus tells Meton that although he admires him, he has no need for him in the city, because Cloud-cuckoo-land depends on religious mythology for its political justification. He warns Meton that the citizens would be hostile to his atheistic science just "as in Sparta they're expelling all foreigners, and punches have started to fly pretty thick and fast all over" (1010). When Meton hears of the strong opposition to him from the citizens, he is happy to leave. But in order to reaffirm his own piety, Pisthetaerus publicly beats Meton before letting him escape. The last two visitors, a supervisor and a seller of decrees, are sent by the city of Athens and represent Athenian imperialism. These comical impostors try to impose Athenian influence upon Cloud-cuckoo-land, but Pisthetaerus quickly dispatches them.

Pisthetaerus' tyranny wears on the birds. He is the only truly free person in this land of "freedom." But the birds do not dare rebel, for he saved them from being imprisoned in cages and killed by humans. Their loyalty to Pisthetaerus is based entirely on fear. They begin to realize, however, that they are now instead caged by a tyrannical ruler.

The play's concluding events show the gods brought to their knees by this upstart who, now a bird himself, is depicted lunching on his enemies. A delegation from Olympus consisting of Poseidon, Heracles, and a god from the savage regions of the Triballian arrive in Cloud-cuckoo-land to negotiate a settlement with its ruler, only to discover that Pisthetaerus in one of the play's most grotesque images: Members of an oligarchic plot to overthrow his democracy have been caught, and the birdman Pisthetaerus is about to eat several members of his own species for lunch. Pisthetaerus' sick actions go beyond ordinary cannibalism. Since the birds have become the new gods of the earth, his cannibalism is an act of impiety, not to mention tasteless and vicious.

Pisthetaerus' regime is clearly not the democracy he promised his bird followers, and Pisthetaerus is the opposite of the democrat he first appeared to be. His empire is a democracy in name only, based on a lie and extolling a non-existent "freedom." Although the gods do not punish Pisthetaerus for his impiety, he must live with the choice he made. He began his enterprise in order to free himself from all authority and restraint only to end under the yoke of necessary administrative duties, which take him away from the erotic desire that propelled him in the beginning of his quest. Perhaps the realm of perfection does not reside in politics but in the mind, which exists in relation to the city in an ironic manner. Aristophanes' *The Birds* is meant to be a corrective to democratic imperialism by warning of its worse vices, while revealing to humans the heights to which they can ascend. By getting Athens to laugh at itself, Aristophanes gets away with holding up a mirror to Athenian imperialism, a system that he believes to be a gross perversion of justice. Humans may possess the strength to rival the authority of the gods and govern their own lives, but democracy may also degrade itself if its own power goes unchecked, resulting in a grotesque tyranny capable of devouring its own citizens.

WORKS CITED

Aristophanes. *The Birds*. Henderson, Jeffery, Translated and Edited with Introduction. Newburyport: Focus Classical Library, 1999.

CANDIDE
(VOLTAIRE)

"Optimism"
by Voltaire (Trans. William F. Fleming),
in *Voltaire's Philosophical Dictionary,*
Vol. IV (1910)

INTRODUCTION

In this entry from his *Philosophical Dictionary*, Voltaire elaborates on some of the philosophical and theological issues that *Candide* also raises. Satirically presenting a grotesque world devoid of justice where the idealistic and innocent suffer, *Candide* bears witness to the grotesque horrors of humanity. In the *Philosophical Dictionary*, Voltaire specifically takes issue with a trend of rational idealism present in Enlightenment-era thought, epitomized by the writings of German philosopher Gottfried Wilhelm Leibniz (many consider Dr. Pangloss, Candide's companion and teacher, to be a caricature of Leibniz). According to Leibniz, our world—though filled with suffering—is the best possible world. This is true because if we state that the world is imperfect, we must acknowledge that its creator is imperfect. Since God is perfect by definition, such a conclusion is illogical for Leibniz. Voltaire traces the various manifestations of this type of abstract optimism

Voltaire. "Optimism." *Voltaire's Philosophical Dictionary, Vol. IV*. Trans. William F. Fleming. New York: Lamb Publishing (1903, 1910): 80–89.

and its alternatives in his essay. Never missing an opportunity to highlight the absurdity of each doctrine, Voltaire notes how none of them would console him as he grotesquely describes dying "in frightful torments" from a bladder stone. "Optimism" (also translated as "All Is Well") contains much of the argument that *Candide* satirically pursues, as well as a small demonstration of how Voltaire utilizes grotesque imagery to expose the ignorance of those who attempt to rationalize the world with little regard for its contents. Filled with Voltaire's characteristically sharp wit, this essay suggests that readers approach *Candide* as a grotesque and satirical critique of Enlightenment thought.

⚬⚬⚬

I beg of you, gentlemen, to explain to me how everything is for the best; for I do not understand it. Does it signify that everything is arranged and ordered according to the laws of the impelling power? That I comprehend and acknowledge. Do you mean that every one is well and possesses the means of living—that nobody suffers? You know that such is not the case. Are you of the opinion that the lamentable calamities which afflict the earth are good in reference to God; and that He takes pleasure in them? I credit not this horrible doctrine; neither do you.

Have the goodness to explain how all is for the best. Plato, the dialectician, condescended to allow to God the liberty of making five worlds; because, said he, there are five regular solids in geometry, the tetrahedron, the cube, the hexahedron, the dodecahedron, and the icosahedron. But why thus restrict divine power? Why not permit the sphere, which is still more regular, and even the cone, the pyramid of many sides, the cylinder, etc.?

God, according to Plato, necessarily chose the best of all possible worlds; and this system has been embraced by many Christian philosophers, although it appears repugnant to the doctrine of original sin. After this transgression, our globe was no more the best of all possible worlds. If it was ever so, it might be so still; but many people believe it to be the worst of worlds instead of the best.

Leibnitz takes the part of Plato; more readers than one complain of their inability to understand either the one or the other; and for ourselves, having read both of them more than once, we avow our ignorance according to custom; and since the gospel has revealed nothing on the subject, we remain in darkness without remorse.

Leibnitz, who speaks of everything, has treated of original sin; and as every man of systems introduces into his plan something contradictory, he imagined that the disobedience towards God, with the frightful misfortunes which followed it, were integral parts of the best of worlds, and necessary ingredients of all possible felicity: "*Calla, calla, senor don Carlos; todo che se haze es por su ben.*"

What! to be chased from a delicious place, where we might have lived for ever only for the eating of an apple? What! to produce in misery wretched children, who will suffer everything, and in return produce others to suffer after them? What! to experience all maladies, feel all vexations, die in the midst of grief, and by way of recompense be burned to all eternity—is this lot the best possible? It certainly is not *good* for us, and in what manner can it be so for God? Leibnitz felt that nothing could be said to these objections, but nevertheless made great books, in which he did not even understand himself.

Lucullus, in good health, partaking of a good dinner with his friends and his mistress in the hall of Apollo, may jocosely deny the existence of evil; but let him put his head out of the window and he will behold wretches in abundance; let him be seized with a fever, and he will be one himself.

I do not like to quote; it is ordinarily a thorny proceeding. What precedes and what follows the passage quoted is too frequently neglected; and thus a thousand objections may rise. I must, notwithstanding, quote Lactantius, one of the fathers, who, in the thirteenth chapter on the anger of God, makes Epicurus speak as follows: "God can either take away evil from the world and will not; or being willing to do so, cannot; or He neither can nor will; or, lastly, He is both able and willing. If He is willing to remove evil and cannot, then is He not omnipotent. If He can, but will not remove it, then is He not benevolent; if He is neither able nor willing, then is He neither powerful nor benevolent; lastly, if both able and willing to annihilate evil, how does it exist?"

The argument is weighty, and Lactantius replies to it very poorly by saying that God wills evil, but has given us wisdom to secure the good. It must be confessed that this answer is very weak in comparison with the objection; for it implies that God could bestow wisdom only by allowing evil—a pleasant wisdom truly! The origin of evil has always been an abyss, the depth of which no one has been able to sound. It was this difficulty which reduced so many ancient philosophers and legislators to have recourse to two principles—the one good, the other wicked. Typhon was the evil principle among the Egyptians, Arimanes among the Persians. The Manichaeans, it is said, adopted this theory; but as these people have never spoken either of a good or of a bad principle, we have nothing to prove it but the assertion.

Among the absurdities abounding in this world, and which may be placed among the number of our evils, that is not the least which presumes the existence of two all-powerful beings, combating which shall prevail most in this world, and making a treaty like the two physicians in Molière: "Allow me the emetic, and I resign to you the lancet."

Basilides pretended, with the Platonists of the first century of the church, that God gave the making of our world to His inferior angels, and these, being inexpert, have constructed it as we perceive. This theological fable is laid prostrate by the overwhelming objection that it is not in the nature of a deity all-powerful and all-wise to intrust the construction of a world to incompetent architects.

Simon, who felt the force of this objection, obviates it by saying that the angel who presided over the workmen is damned for having done his business so slovenly, but the roasting of this angel amends nothing. The adventure of Pandora among the Greeks scarcely meets the objection better. The box in which every evil is enclosed, and at the bottom of which remains Hope, is indeed a charming allegory; but this Pandora was made by Vulcan, only to avenge himself on Prometheus, who had stolen fire to inform a man of clay.

The Indians have succeeded no better. God having created man, gave him a drug which would insure him permanent health of body. The man loaded his ass with the drug, and the ass being thirsty, the serpent directed him to a fountain, and while the ass was drinking, purloined the drug.

The Syrians pretended that man and woman having been created in the fourth heaven, they resolved to eat a cake in lieu of ambrosia, their natural food. Ambrosia exhaled by the pores; but after eating cake, they were obliged to relieve themselves in the usual manner. The man and the woman requested an angel to direct them to a water-closet. Behold, said the angel, that petty globe which is almost of no size at all; it is situated about sixty millions of leagues from this place, and is the privy of the universe—go there as quickly as you can. The man and woman obeyed the angel and came here, where they have ever since remained; since which time the world has been what we now find it. The Syrians will eternally be asked why God allowed man to eat the cake and experience such a crowd of formidable ills?

I pass with speed from the fourth heaven to Lord Bolingbroke. This writer, who doubtless was a great genius, gave to the celebrated Pope his plan of "all for the best," as it is found word for word in the posthumous works of Lord Bolingbroke, and recorded by Lord Shaftesbury in his "Characteristics." Read in Shaftesbury's chapter of the "Moralists" the following passage:

"Much may be replied to these complaints of the defects of nature—How came it so powerless and defective from the hands of a perfect Being?—But I deny that it is defective. Beauty is the result of contrast, and universal concord springs out of a perpetual conflict.... It is necessary that everything be sacrificed to other things—vegetables to animals, and animals to the earth.... The laws of the central power of gravitation, which give to the celestial bodies their weight and motion, are not to be deranged in consideration of a pitiful animal, who, protected as he is by the same laws, will soon be reduced to dust."

Bolingbroke, Shaftesbury, and Pope, their working artisan, resolve their general question no better than the rest. Their "all for the best" says no more than that all is governed by immutable laws; and who did not know that? We learn nothing when we remark, after the manner of little children, that flies are created to be eaten by spiders, spiders by swallows, swallows by hawks, hawks by eagles, eagles by men, men by one another, to afford food for worms; and at last, at the rate of about a thousand to one, to be the prey of devils everlastingly.

There is a constant and regular order established among animals of all kinds—a universal order. When a stone is formed in my bladder, the mechanical process is admirable; sandy particles pass by small degrees into my blood; they are filtered by the veins; and passing the urethra, deposit themselves in my bladder; where, uniting agreeably to the Newtonian attraction, a stone is formed, which gradually increases, and I suffer pains a thousand times worse than death by the finest arrangement in the world. A surgeon, perfect in the art of Tubal-Cain, thrusts into me a sharp instrument; and cutting into the perineum, seizes the stone with his pincers, which breaks during the endeavors, by the necessary laws of mechanism; and owing to the same mechanism, I die in frightful torments. All this is "for the best," being the evident result of unalterable physical principles, agreeably to which I know as well as you that I perish.

If we were insensitive, there would be nothing to say against this system of physics; but this is not the point on which we treat. We ask if there are not physical evils, and whence do they originate? There is no absolute evil, says Pope in his "Essay on Man"; or if there are particular evils, they compose a general good. It is a singular general good which is composed of the stone and the gout—of all sorts of crime and sufferings, and of death and damnation.

The fall of man is our plaister for all these particular maladies of body and soul, which you call "the general health"; but Shaftesbury and Bolingbroke have attacked original sin. Pope says nothing about it; but it is clear that their system saps the foundations of the Christian religion, and explains nothing at all.

In the meantime, this system has been since approved by many theologians, who willingly embrace contradictions. Be it so; we ought to leave to everybody the privilege of reasoning in their own way upon the deluge of ills which overwhelm us. It would be as reasonable to prevent incurable patients from eating what they please. "God," says Pope, "beholds, with an equal eye, a hero perish or a sparrow fall; the destruction of an atom, or the ruin of a thousand planets; the bursting of a bubble, or the dissolution of a world."

This, I must confess, is a pleasant consolation. Who does not find a comfort in the declaration of Lord Shaftesbury, who asserts, "that God will not derange His general system for so miserable an animal as man?" It must be confessed at least that this pitiful creature has a right to cry out humbly, and to endeavor, while bemoaning himself, to understand why these eternal laws do not comprehend the good of every individual.

This system of "all for the best" represents the Author of Nature as a powerful and malevolent monarch, who cares not for the destruction of four or five hundred thousand men, nor of the many more who in consequence spend the rest of their days in penury and tears, provided He succeeds in His designs.

Far therefore from the doctrine—that this is the best of all possible worlds—being consolatory, it is a hopeless one to the philosophers who embrace it. The question of good and evil remains in irremediable chaos for those who seek to fathom it in reality. It is a mere mental sport to the disputants, who are captives that play with their chains. As to unreasoning people, they resemble the fish which are transported from a river to a reservoir, with no more suspicion that they are to be eaten during the approaching Lent, than we have ourselves of the facts which originate our destiny.

Let us place at the end of every chapter of metaphysics the two letters used by the Roman judges when they did not understand a pleading. N. L. *non liquet*—it is not clear. Let us, above all, silence the knaves who, overloaded like ourselves with the weight of human calamities, add the mischief of their calumny; let us refute their execrable imposture by having recourse to faith and Providence.

Some reasoners are of opinion that it agrees not with the nature of the Great Being of Beings for things to be otherwise than they are. It is a rough system, and I am too ignorant to venture to examine it.

DON QUIXOTE
(MIGUEL DE CERVANTES)

"Heine on Cervantes and the *Don Quixote*"
by Heinrich Heine, in *Temple Bar* (1876)

INTRODUCTION

Don Quixote, which some refer to as the first novel in the Western world, is a massive creation filled with grotesqueries. Heinrich Heine argues that Cervantes uses grotesque imagery and outlandish comedy to critique the chivalric romances popular at the time. According to Heine, Cervantes was so successful with his critique that chivalric romances went out of favor. For Heine, *Quixote* is a grotesque satire filled with absurd character types that, ironically, actually populate the world.

The Life and Deeds of the Ingenious Knight, Don Quixote de la Mancha, by Miguel Cervantes de Saavedra, was the first book that I read after I had reached an intelligent age, and knew something of the world of letters. I still remember well enough that childish time when, early one morning, I stole away from home and hastened to the Palace Garden to read *Don Quixote* undisturbed. It was a lovely May-day;

Heine, Heinrich. "Heine on Cervantes and the *Don Quixote*." *Temple Bar*, Vol. XLVIII (October 1876), 235–49.

blooming Spring lay in the quiet morning light listening to his praise chaunted by his sweet flatterer the nightingale, who sang her song of praise so caressingly gently, with such melting enthusiasm, that the most shamefaced buds sprang open, and the wanton grasses and the perfumed sunbeams kissed each other more eagerly, and trees and Bowers trembled with pure rapture. As for me, I placed myself on an old massy stone seat in the so-called Avenue of Sighs, near the waterfall, and delighted my small heart with the great adventures of the bold Knight.

In my childish simplicity I took everything in good earnest; whatever comical antics were played by fate with the poor hero, I supposed it must be so; that being laughed at, belonged as much to heroism as being wounded, and I felt as much vexation at the one as sympathy in my soul with the other. I was a child, and did not know the irony that the Creator had woven into the world, and which the great poet had imitated in his printed microcosm, and I could have found it in my heart to shed the bitterest tears when the noble Knight, for all his nobleness, received only ingratitude and blows. As I, little practised in reading, spoke each word aloud, birds and trees, brook and flowers, all were able to hear; and as such innocent things of nature, like children, know nothing of the irony of the world, they, too, took it all in good earnest, and wept with me at the sufferings of the poor Knight; indeed, an old veteran oak sobbed, and the waterfall shook his white beard more passionately, and seemed to chide the wickedness of the world. We felt that the Knight's heroism does not deserve less admiration, if the lion, not caring to fight, turned his back on him, and that his deeds are the more deserving of praise, the weaker and more dried up his body, the more rotten his armour, and the more wretched the jade which carried him. We despised the low rabble that, decked with gay silk mantles, elegant turns of phrase and ducal titles, ridiculed a man so far their superior in mind and noble feeling.

Dulcinea's Knight rose the higher in my esteem and won more of my love the longer I read the wonderful book, and that happened daily in the same garden, so that by autumn I reached the end—and I shall never forget the day when I read of the sad combat in which the Knight so ignominiously succumbed.
[...]

It is now eight years ago that I wrote for the *Reisebilder* these lines, in which I described the impression made on my mind long before by reading *Don Quixote*. Heavens! how the years go. It seems to me that it was only yesterday that I finished the book in the Avenue of Sighs, in the palace garden at Düsseldorf, and that my heart is still stirred with admiration of the deeds and sufferings of the great Knight. Has my heart remained unchanged all this time, or has it returned, after a wondrous cycle, to the feelings of childhood? Probably the latter is the case, for I remember that in each lustrum of my life I have read *Don Quixote* with alternating feelings. When I bloomed into youth, and thrust my inexperienced hands into the rose-bushes of life, and climbed to the top of the highest crag to be nearer the sun, and night after night dreamed of nothing but eagles and pure maidens—at that time I found *Don Quixote* a very unreal book, and if it lay in my way I pushed it angrily aside. Later, when I ripened into manhood, I became somewhat reconciled with Dulcinea's unlucky champion, and I began to laugh at him. "The man is a fool," I said. Yet in a curious way the shadowy figures of the haggard Knight and the fat Squire followed me in all the paths of my life, especially when I arrived at some critical crossroad. Thus I remember, on going to France, that, awaking one morning in the carriage from a feverish doze, I saw in the early mist two well-known figures riding by me, the one to my right hand being Don Quixote de la Mancha on his ethereal Rozinante, and the other, to my left, Sancho Panza, on his very material Dapple. We had just reached the French frontier. The noble Manchegan Knight bowed his head with reverence before the tricoloured flag which fluttered towards us from the high frontierstaff. The good Sancho saluted with somewhat cooler nod the first French gens-d'armes that made their appearance. At last both friends rode fast in advance. I lost sight of them, and only heard at times Rozinantes inspired neigh and the responsive yeighing of the donkey.

At that time I thought that the absurdity of Quixotism lay in this, that the noble Knight wished to recall to life a long-since outlived past, and his poor limbs, especially his back, came into painful contact with the realities of the present. Alas! I have found since that it is just as fruitless a form of folly to try to bring the future too soon into the present, if in such an attack on the ponderous interests of the day one has only a very sorry jade, very rotten armour, and a body itself in as bad repair. The wise shake their sagacious heads as much at one as at the other kind of Quixotism. But still Dulcinea del Toboso is the fairest woman in the world, albeit I lie miserably in the dust. Never will I retract that assertion. I cannot help myself. Strike home with your lances, O knights of the silver moon, O barbers' men in disguise!

What was the thought of the great Cervantes when he wrote his great book? Was his object only the overthrow of the romance of chivalry, the reading of which in his time so raged in Spain that spiritual and temporal ordinances were powerless against it? Or was it his intention to bring into ridicule all manifestation of human enthusiasm in general, and above all the heroism of the men of the sword?

Evidently he intended only a satire on the romances in question, which he wished, by throwing light on their absurdities, to hand over to public scorn, and consequently to oblivion. And in this he met with brilliant success, for what neither the exhortations of the pulpit, nor the threats of the municipality could effect, was done by a poor author with his pen. He so radically uprooted the tales of chivalry that soon after the appearance of *Don Quixote* the taste for such books died out all through Spain, and not one more was printed. But the pen of the man of genius is always greater than himself—it always reaches far beyond his actual intentions, and Cervantes, without clearly knowing it, wrote the greatest satire on human enthusiasm. He never suspected it, he, the hero who had spent the greater part of his life in knightly combats, and in his old age often rejoiced that he, too, had fought in the battle of Lepanto, though he had paid for that glory with the loss of his left hand.

[...]

We find as few anti-absolutist as anti-Catholic tones in *Don Quixote*. Critics who detect such are evidently in error. Cervantes was the son of a school that had even poetically idealised unconditional obedience to the rules, and that ruler was the King of Spain at a time when his Majesty outshone the whole world. The common soldier became conscious of himself when touched by the rays of that majesty, and willingly sacrificed his individual freedom for such gratification of Castilian national pride.

The political greatness of Spain at that time must have not a little raised and widened the character of its men of letters. In the mind of a Spanish poet, as in the empire of Charles V., the sun never set. The fierce combats with the Moors were at an end, and as the scent of flowers is strongest after a thunder-storm, poetry always blooms in greatest splendour after a civil war. This phenomenon we see in England in Elizabeth's reign, and there, at the same time as in Spain, a school of poets arose that provokes remarkable comparisons. There we see Shakespeare, here Cervantes, as the flower of the school. The English poets in the reign of Elisabeth have a certain family likeness, as have the Spanish under the three Philips; and neither Shakespeare nor Cervantes can lay claim to originality in our sense of the word. They do not stand out among their contemporaries in any way through different modes of thinking and feeling, or through a special kind of expression, but only by greater depth, warmth, tenderness, and power; their poems are more penetrated and surrounded by the aether of poesy.

But each poet was not merely the flower of his time; each was also a root of the future. As Shakespeare must be regarded as the founder of the later dramatic art through the influence of his works, especially on Germany and the France of to-day, we must in the same way reverence in Cervantes the founder of the modern novel. On this point I will allow myself a few passing remarks.

The older novel, the so-called romance of chivalry, took its rise in the poetry of the middle ages; it was at first a prose form of those epic poems, the heroes of which belonged to the mythic cycle of Charlemagne and of the Holy Grail. Their subject-matter consisted always of knightly adventures. It was the novel of the nobility, and the characters which appeared in it were either fabulous creations of the imagination or knights with golden spurs. Nowhere was there a trace of the people. These romaunts, which degenerated into the most absurd excesses, Cervantes overthrew by his *Don Quixote*. But in writing a satire which destroyed the old romance he himself gave the type for a new species of poetry which we call the modern novel. That is what great poets always do. They found something new while they destroy the old. They never deny without affirming something. Cervantes founded the modern novel by introducing into the knightly romance the faithful delineation of the lower classes—by giving the life of the people a place in it. The tendency to describe the doings of the commonest populace, of the most abject rabble, belongs not merely to Cervantes, but to all his literary contemporaries, and is found in the painters as well as in the poets of that time. A Murillo, who stole the divinest colours from heaven to paint his beautiful Madonnas, copied also with the same love the filthiest beings on earth. It was perhaps the very enthusiasm for art that made these noble Spaniards feel the same delight in the faithful portraiture of a beggar boy lousing himself as in producing the figure of the most Blessed Virgin. Or was it the charm of contrast that drove the highest nobles—a trim courtier like Quevedo, or a powerful minister like Mendoza—to write their tales of rogues and tattered beggars? Perhaps they wished to transfer themselves by their imagination from the monotonous surroundings of their rank into the opposite sphere of life, as we find the same need in many German writers, who fill their novels with descriptions only of the elegant world, and always make their heroes counts and barons. In Cervantes we do not find this one-sided tendency to describe the ignoble quite apart—he mingles the ideal with the common; the one serves as light or shade to the other, and the noble element is just as strong in it as the popular.

[. . .]

To the spirit of Cervantes and the influence of his works I have been able to make but few allusions. I can still less dwell here on the true artistic worth of his romance, as explanations would occur which would descend much too far into the domain of aesthetics. I can only draw attention generally to the form of his romance, and to its two central figures. The form is that of a description of travels, always the most natural form for that kind of writing. I will here recall only the *Golden Ass* of Apuleius, the first romance of antiquity. Later poets have tried to avoid the monotony of this form by that which we now call the plot of a novel. But through poverty of invention most novelists have been led to borrow their plots from each other, at least with a few modifications; and through the perpetual recurrence of the same characters, situations, and events, the public at length has become somewhat wearied of this kind of literature. Then, to escape from the tediousness of hackneyed plots, recourse was had for some time to the ancient original form of "travels." But this, too, is thrust aside so soon as an original writer appears with new fresh novel plots. In literature, as in politics, everything moves in obedience to the law of action and reaction. Now as to the two figures, Don Quixote and Sancho Panza, which constantly parody each other, and yet complete each other so wonderfully that they form the true hero of the tale, they bear witness in equal measure to the poet's sense of art and to his depth of mind. Whilst other authors, in whose novels the hero goes through the world only as a solitary person, are obliged to have recourse to soliloquy, letters, or diaries in order to make known the thoughts and feelings of the hero, Cervantes' can everywhere let a natural dialogue arise; and as the one figure always parodies what the other says, the author's meaning becomes all the more evident. Many imitations have been made since then of that double figure which gives so artistic a naturalness to Cervantes' novel, and from whose character, like a giant Indian tree, unfolds, as from a single seed, the whole romance, with all its wild foliage, its perfumed blossoms, gleaming fruits, and the monkeys and magic birds that rock themselves in its branches.

But it would be unjust to lay everything here to the account of slavish imitation—the introduction of two such figures as Don Quixote and Sancho Panza so easily suggests itself, of whom one, the poetical, seeks adventures, and the other, half from attachment, half from self-interest, runs behind, through sunshine and shower, such as we ourselves have often met in life. To recognise the pair, be it in art or in actual life under the most various disguises, one must, it must be admitted, particularly attend of course to the essential point—their intellectual stamp, and not to the accidents of their outward appearance. I could give countless examples. Do we not discover Don Quixote and Sancho Panza quite as much under the forms of Don Juan and Leporello as perchance in the person of Lord Byron and his servant Fletcher? Do we not recognise the same types and their mutual relation in the forms of the Knight of Waldsee and of his Kaspar Larifari, as well as in the forms of many an author and his bookseller, of whom the latter perceives very clearly the follies of his author, but, nevertheless, in order to gain material advantage from them, follows him faithfully in all his knight-errantries? And Publisher Sancho, if he sometimes only gains cuffs in the transaction, yet always remains fat while the noble Knight daily grows thinner and thinner. But I have found the types of Don Quixote and his Squire among women as well as men. I particularly remember a beautiful Englishwoman, a sentimental, romantic blonde, who, with her friend, had ran away from a London boarding-school, and wished to travel over the whole world, seeking a man's heart as noble as she had dreamed of on soft, moonlight nights. Her friend, a plump brunette, hoped that the opportunity would give her for her share, if not something quite specially ideal, at least a good-looking husband. I see her still—the slender figure, with her love-sick blue eyes, as, on the Brighton shore, she sent out her longing soul across the swelling sea to France. Meanwhile her friend cracked nuts, enjoyed the sweet kernel, and threw the shells into the water.

However, neither in the masterpiece of other artists, nor in nature
itself, do we find the two types in question as completely developed in
their mutual relations as in Cervantes. Every feature in the character
and appearance of the one answers here to an opposed and yet allied
feature in the other. Here every detail has a parodic meaning. Nay,
there is the same ironical parallel between Rozinante and Sancho's
donkey as between the Knight and his Squire, and the two animals are
in some degree the symbolical representatives of the same ideas.

In their language, as in their mode of thought, master and servant
show the most remarkable contrasts, and here I cannot refrain from
mentioning the difficulties which the translator had to overcome
who turned honest Sancho's home-baked, knotty, vulgar idiom into
German. By his fragmentary, not seldom inelegant proverbs honest
Sancho quite reminds us of King Solomon's fools of Markulf, whose
short sayings in opposition to a pathetic idealism also give expression
to that knowledge which the common people gain by experience. Don
Quixote, on the other band, uses the language of culture of the higher
classes, and represents even by the *grandeza* of his rounded periods
the high-born Hidalgo. Sometimes these periods are too much spun
out, and the Knight's style is like a haughty court lady in a puffed-out
silk dress, with long rustling train. But the Graces, disguised as pages,
smiling, carry the train, and the long sentences close with the most
charming turns.

We sum up the character of Don Quixote's and Sancho Panza's
language in these words: the former, when he speaks, seems always to
sit on his tall horse, the other talks as if he were astride his humble
donkey.

EDGAR ALLAN POE'S SHORT STORIES
(EDGAR ALLAN POE)

"The Grotesque in the Age of Romanticism: Tales of the Grotesque and Arabesque"
by Wolfgang Kayser (Trans. Ulrich Weisstein),
in *The Grotesque in Art and Literature*, (1981)

INTRODUCTION

In his landmark study of the grotesque, Wolfgang Kayser discusses how Edgar Allan Poe's concept of the grotesque is related to the fiction of German novelist E.T.A. Hoffman and the critical thought of Walter Scott and William Hazlitt. After discussing the possible influence of these sources on Poe's fiction, Kayser cites passages from "The Masque of Red Death" and "The Murders in the Rue Morgue," both of which explicitly deal with the grotesque as an aesthetic term. Kayser concludes that the word "grotesque" had "two different levels of meaning [for Poe]: to describe a concrete situation in which chaos prevails, and to indicate the tenor of entire stories concerned with terrible, incomprehensible, inexplicable, bizarre, fantastic, and nocturnal happenings."

Kayser, Wolfgang. "The Grotesque in the Age of Romanticism: Tales of the Grotesque and Arabesque." The Grotesque in Art and Literature. Trans. Ulrich Weisstein. New York: Columbia UP, 1981. First edition 1963: 76–81.

Edgar Allan Poe followed E. T. A. Hoffmann in developing a type of story that is suffused with grotesque elements and that just as strongly affected the fiction of subsequent ages. Poe called the first collection of twenty-five of his stories *Tales of the Grotesque and Arabesque* (1840). While formerly Poe was generally thought to have been strongly dependent on Hoffmann, some recent scholars tend to belittle or deny such a connection. All such assertions, however, are vague and meaningless so long as the two authors' stories are not stylistically, structurally, and conceptually analyzed in such a way as to dissolve the crude concepts of influence and dependence. Poe was, of course, familiar with the works of his German predecessor. In his preface to the *Tales* he betrays a familiarity even with second-rate German tellers of horror stories by declaring: "Let us admit, for the moment, that the 'phantasy-pieces' [he probably alludes to Hoffmann's *Phantasiestücke*] now given, are Germanic or what not. Thus Germanism is 'the vein' for the time being. Tomorrow I may be anything but German, as yesterday I was everything else." But he was perfectly right when he added, "If in many of my productions terror has been the thesis, I maintain that terror is not of Germany, but of the soul." Nor must one forget that neither of the two masters invented the tale of terror. They had forerunners and found the magazines of their day replete with all sorts of horror stories.[1] The way for the genre was especially paved by the Gothic novel. Just as Hoffmann, in his tales, refers to Schiller's *Geisterseher* (Visionary) and Grosse's *Genius*, Edgar Allan Poe occasionally mentions Mrs. Ann Radcliffe, and both were, of course, familiar with the *Castle of Otranto* by Horace Walpole, the eminently successful inventor of the "tales of terror."

It is probably in emulation of Walter Scott, who may have trans-mitted the word and the concept of the grotesque to him, that Poe uses grotesque and arabesque synonymously in the title of his collec-tion. In his essay "The Novels of E. T. A. Hoffmann" (*Foreign Review*, July, 1827), Scott had called Hoffmann the first outstanding artist to represent the fantastic or supernatural grotesque in his compositions. In the same passage Scott attempts a definition of the grotesque:

> In fact, the grotesque in his compositions partly resembles the arabesque in painting, in which are introduced the most strange and complicated monsters, resembling centaurs, griffins, sphinxes, chimeras, rocs, and all other creatures of romantic

imagination, dazzling the beholder as it were by the unbounded fertility of the author's imagination, and sating it by the rich contrast of all the varieties of shape and colouring, while there is in reality nothing to satisfy the understanding or inform the judgment.

Scott also regretted that Hoffmann confused the supernatural with the absurd and that, by his taste and temperament, he was pushed too far in the direction of the grotesque and the fantastic.

Scott's definition of the grotesque is noteworthy insofar as the term is used to denote a literary category, and one can see how he arrives at the definition by way of the arabesque in painting. This usage was as yet unknown in English. To be sure, apart from the ornamental grotesque it had long been possible to call a figure grotesque, which, according to French seventeenth-century usage, meant distorted and caricatural. When applied to landscapes, the word indicated a lack of order as well as a somber and ominous mood.[2] The famous critic William Hazlitt was the first to extend the meaning when in 1820 he spoke of English literature as being Gothic and grotesque.[3] By so doing, he detached the word from its tangible context (whether ornament, figure, or landscape) and made it a general category. As the conjunction with Gothic implies, emphasis is laid on the ominous and somber aspects of the phenomenon. The word serves as a rather vague designation of the atmosphere or mood of a work, or the impression which it makes upon the reader. Scott, however, did not only use it to characterize the nature of the impression but also to denote a well-defined structure of literary, or pictorial, reality. Its emotional correlate was no longer a somber mood but rather a feeling of helplessness and disparagement before an increasingly absurd and fantastically estranged world.

What first strikes one in the title of Poe's collection is the fact that, contrary to the then current usage, the word "grotesque" is no longer meant derogatorily, as was still true of Walter Scott. One further notes that the arabesque is also drawn into the realm of literature as category (in Germany Friedrich Schlegel had done the same around 1800).[4] Moreover, the word, as it appears in the title of Poe's book seems to be more closely related to Hazlitt's impressionistic than to Scott's structural use of it. Poe's preface begins with the sentence, "The epithets 'Grotesque' and 'Arabesque' will be found to indicate with sufficient precision the prevalent tenor of the tales here published." And Poe further underscored his intentions by using the words "gloom" and "Germanism."

But Poe employed the word "grotesque" in still another sense, which was more closely related to that which Scott preferred. In 1841, the latter's essay on E. T. A. Hoffmann had been published (for the first time in America) in Philadelphia, which was then Poe's residence, in the second volume of his critical writings. One must assume that, now at least, Poe became acquainted with the piece. (The essay also enabled Poe to deepen his understanding of the German author; for Scott furnished detailed summaries and partial translations of the novellas *Das Majorat* [The Entail] and *Der Sandmann*. The influence of both works can be seen in the stories which Poe authorized at this time.) The novella *The Masque of the Red Death* (1842), for instance, contains an interpretive description of the phenomenon that goes much beyond Scott and is perhaps the most complete and authoritative definition any author has given of the grotesque. In trying to escape the plague, the Italian Prince Prospero and his guests have withdrawn into an abbey. The Prince has ordered the seven halls, which had been built according to his own eccentric taste, to be decorated for a splendid ball and given instructions as to the kind of masks to be worn by the participants:

> Be sure they were grotesque. There were much glare and glitter and piquancy and phantasm—much of what has been since seen in *Hernani*. There were arabesque figures with unsuited limbs and appointments. There were delirious fancies such as the madman fashions. There was much of the beautiful, much of the wanton, much of the bizarre, something of the terrible, and not a little of that which might have excited disgust. To and fro in the seven chambers there stalked, in fact, a multitude of dreams. And these—the dreams—writhed in and about, taking hue from the rooms, and causing the wild music of the orchestra to seem as the echo of their steps.

The distortion of all ingredients; the fusion of different realms; the coexistence of beautiful, bizarre, ghastly, and repulsive elements; the merger of the parts into a turbulent whole; the withdrawal into a phantasmagoric and nocturnal world (Poe used to speak of his "daydreams")—all these features have here entered into the concept of the grotesque. This world is well prepared for the intrusion of the deadly nocturnal powers personified by Death in his red mask.

In another tale, *The Murders in the Rue Morgue*, Poe characterizes the appearance of the room in which the double murder has taken place by calling it "a *grotesquerie* in horror absolutely alien from humanity." Poe thus uses the word "grotesque" on two different levels of meaning: to describe a concrete situation in which chaos prevails and to indicate the tenor of entire stories concerned with terrible, incomprehensible, inexplicable, bizarre, fantastic, and nocturnal happenings. In these stories Poe makes use of a considerable number of motifs made familiar by E. T. A. Hoffmann and the literature of horror in general: the double (which, in *The Black Cat*, is extended to a terrifying animal); artistry consummated in a work that causes the artist's death; the mysterious presence of past and distant things, which drives sensitive souls to their death, etc. Yet no one will confuse the author of the *Nachtgeschichten* with that of the *Tales of the Grotesque*. Poe's work, for one thing, shows a marked preference for repulsive, ghastly, and criminal phenomena. Written in 1841 or 1842 and published in 1843, *The Black Cat* somewhat resembles Hoffmann's *Sandman*, which Poe must have known at least through Scott's summary of it. While in the latter story the world is estranged for the narrator by the mysterious figure of the sandman (Coppelius), the uncanny cat effects the estrangement in the former. Both characters offend against the apparition, and in both the estrangement is heightened by the baffling return of the hostile principle, which precipitates the catastrophe. But instead of the madness which causes Nathanael's death in Hoffmann's story, Poe uses the protagonist's cruel murder of his wife. The detailed description of the deed, burial of the corpse, and its discovery are so compelling that the grotesque seems to be quenched by the horror. In the grotesqueries of the Rue Morgue, too, the horror of the crime prevails; here Dupin's intelligence triumphantly solves the crime, which was so inhuman as to seem altogether inexplicable. Still another difference between Poe and Hoffmann comes to light in this connection. Hoffmann confronts the sinister elements with an average intelligence unable to cope with them, while Poe, in a number of his stories, counters them with an amazing talent for combination. The ominous has thus been transformed into a puzzle capable of being solved by a sharp-witted individual. In *The Purloined Letter*, the criminal minister proves himself superior to all investigations by the police because he is both mathematician and poet, while the police work solely on the basis of their past experience. Dupin, however, is a match for the minister and thus able to outwit him. Both figures personify the higher gift of poetic combination. Poetic combination is also embodied in the speaker of "The Philosophy of Composition" who gives an account of the alleged genesis of "The Raven." By turning the crime into a puzzle that can be solved, and by letting an ingenious detective find the solution, Poe originated the genre of the detective story. Stories of this kind, however, no longer belong to the *Tales of the Grotesque*. Still, some of the characters in the latter book can trace their extraordinary power of deduction to this source; just as the proclivity to direct all elements to the denouement may be an outgrowth of the technique used in the detective story. Here we touch upon a third difference between Poe and Hoffmann. In Poe, the concentration on the denouement frequently impedes the creation of independent scenes of masterful construction at which Hoffmann excels.

"What is your conclusion?", Dupin asks after having called the condition of the room in which the murder took place a *grotesquerie*. In *The Black Cat*, the horror inspired by the fact that the imprint of the cat appears on the only remaining wall section of the burned-out house—the cat itself being dead—is soothed by the narrator's ingeniously contrived explanation. And the previously quoted excerpt from *The Masque of the Red Death* is a short summarizing description rather than an actual scene; for with the following sentence the action continues and hastens to its end. As far as their size, their structure, and the narrative technique employed in them are concerned, Poe's *Tales* are strikingly different from Hoffmann's *Nachtgeschichten*. The younger writer, no doubt, was inspired by the older one. But in assimilating these influences, Poe turned them into something new and unique that was to acquire its own historical sphere of influence.[5]

NOTES

1. The stories included in the *Gespensterbuch*, which A. Apel and F. Laun (Fr. A. Schulze) began editing in 1814, are often of a fairly high quality. Fouque was one of the subsequent editors of the publication, which was later called *Wunderbuch*. Here Poe's stories, which had originally been published in American

magazines, appeared side by side with other tales of horror, and in Hawthorne and Washington Irving Poe had prominent predecessors.

2. The same usage is found in German; for instance, in the opening passage of Lenz' *Waldbruder*: "Grotesquely piled up mountains."

3. The *New English Dictionary* (Oxford, 1901) lists the earlier instances of grotesque but fails to quote Scott and Poe and the change of meaning they brought about.

4. Arthur H. Quinn, *Edgar Allan Poe: A Critical Biography* (New York, 1941), comes to the conclusion that Poe uses the word "arabesque" to denote a "powerful imagination," whereas "grotesque" signifies a "burlesque or satiric trait." But Poe's language does not seem to confirm this.

5. See H. H. Kiihnelt, *Die Bedeutung E.A. Poes fur die englische Literatur* (Innsbruck, 1949); Pierre Cambiaire, *The Influence of E. A. Poe in France* (New York, 1927); Leon Lemonnier, *E. Poe et les Conteurs Français* (Paris, 1947).

FRANKENSTEIN
(MARY SHELLEY)

"Elements of the Grotesque
in Mary Shelley's *Frankenstein*"
by Robert C. Evans,
Auburn University at Montgomery

Opening the pages of Mary Shelley's *Frankenstein*, many have sought in vain the usual exaggerations and grotesque conventions of the horror film. Why? Because most of us know films the novel has spawned and not the book itself. We encounter the vintage 1931 Boris Karloff movie (and the various sequels, imitations, and parodies thereof) long before we read Shelley's novel, and Karloff's monster—with his gigantic frame, green skin, lumbering gait, stitched, square forehead, and electrodes protruding from his neck—makes an indelible impression. So, too, does Dr. Frankenstein's eerie laboratory, ensconced in a gigantic mountaintop castle and featuring a huge operating table, massively vaulted ceilings, weird electrical devices, and stormy, light-ning-filled weather. And, of course, no one can forget Frankenstein's demented if somewhat incompetent assistant, a hunchback (with a bad haircut) named Fritz, who helps his master illegally collect and assemble the body parts needed to create the monster, including the all-important (if defective) brain.

Almost none of these memorable details appear in the novel, nor does the book feature any compensating emphasis on other horrific elements. Thrill-seeking readers often find themselves disappointed by the book, and teachers often report that students are initially bored by Shelley's novel. Shelley's original version of the Frankenstein story offers, of course, many other sources of appeal, including a strikingly thoughtful, impressively intelligent, and unusually well-read monster (or "Creature") who ruminates at length—and in highly articulate and philosophical language—on his strange origins, pathetic life, and heartfelt disappointments and desires. He feels, thinks, and speaks like a nineteenth-century gentleman, and he thus makes a striking contrast with the nearly mute and primitive monster played by Karloff. Indeed, in depicting her creature and giving him such a thoughtful and sensitive voice, Shelley often goes out of her way to create empathy. She contrasts her creature's physical ugliness—usually mentioned rather than described in detail—with his emotional and intellectual refinement. She seems to have wanted to create a monster that was far less monstrous than he easily could have been, and in this, she succeeded.

But, Mary Shelley's *Frankenstein* does contain numerous grotesque elements and many more opportunities for grotesque descriptions. The entire premise of the book—of breathing life into a dead body—is grotesque almost by definition, and certainly Victor Frankenstein himself is at least partially grotesque in his secret motives, unethical conduct, and perverse achievements. Moreover, Shelley herself, in her "Introduction" to the revised, 1831 edition (in which she describes the genesis of the novel) seems to promise grotesque scenes in abundance. Thus, she explains that she had intended to write a book "which would speak to the mysterious fears of our nature and awaken thrilling horror—one to make the reader dread to look around, to curdle the blood, and quicken the beatings of the heart" (22). She describes how her "imagination, unbidden, possessed and guided" her to an "acute mental vision" of a:

> pale student of unhallowed arts kneeling beside the thing he had put together. I saw the hideous phantasm of a man stretched out, and then, on the working of some powerful engine, show signs of life, and stir with an uneasy, half vital motion. Frightful must it be . . . . His success would terrify the artist; he would rush away from his odious handywork, horror-stricken. . . . He sleeps; but he is awakened; he opens

his eyes; behold the horrid thing stands at his bedside, opening his curtains, and looking on him with yellow, watery, but speculative eyes. (22-23)

Shelley's phrasing here sounds almost like a trailer for the Karloff film, but the novel she actually produced emphasizes grotesque effects far less forcefully than does the Introduction. By examining her book with a view toward determining the ways and degrees to which it both is and is not grotesque, we can come to a better understanding of the kind of work Shelley actually created.

One of the earliest passages in the novel to show grotesque potential is the one in which Victor Frankenstein describes his youthful familiarity with "the natural decay and corruption of the human body. In my education," he explains, "my father had taken the greatest precautions that my mind should be impressed with no supernatural horrors" (53). Victor has been trained *not* to respond to—or take any special notice of—matters that most people might consider grotesque, and this early training perhaps helps explain why his narrative emphasizes grotesque details much less fully than one might have anticipated. Thus, he mentions his relative indifference to graveyards (53), whereas a different sort of narrator might have dwelt on such places by describing them in grim detail. He *does* mention, in passing, how bodies "become food for the worm," but that phrasing seems stale and conventional. Also, he does mention that he was "forced to spend days and nights in vaults and charnel-houses," and he does report that his "attention was fixed upon every object the most insupportable to the delicacy of the human feelings" (54). His language here, however, is general and abstract. A writer who was more concerned with emphatically grotesque effects than Shelley would have seized this opportunity to dwell at length on disgusting and horrible details of rotting corpses and decaying flesh. Instead, Victor Frankenstein is, mostly, politely restrained: "I saw how the fine form of man was degraded and wasted; I beheld the corruption of death succeed the blooming cheek of life; I saw how the worm inherited the wonders of the eye and brain" (54). Only in that last clause—with its splendidly incongruous verb "inherited"—does Victor come close to achieving a truly grotesque effect. Otherwise, his description seems too abstract and generic to achieve the shock, disgust, horror, and sense of absurdity often associated with the genuinely grotesque.

Another passage from the novel—a passage that might easily have been far more grotesque than it is—is the one in which Victor describes how:

> the moon gazed on my midnight labours, while, with unrelaxed and breathless eagerness, I pursued nature to her hiding-places. Who shall conceive the horrors of my secret toil, as I dabbled among the unhallowed damps of the grave, or tortured the living animal to animate the lifeless clay? . . . I collected bones from charnel-houses; and disturbed, with profane fingers, the tremendous secrets of the human frame. . . . I kept [a] workshop of filthy creation: my eye-balls were starting from their sockets in attending to the details of my employment. The dissecting room and the slaughter-house furnished many of my materials; and often did my human nature turn with loathing from my occupation . . . . (56)

Some aspects of this passage do achieve a truly grotesque effect— especially the reference to "tortur[ing] the living animal to animate the lifeless clay." It is, after all, one thing to attempt to revive the dead, but it is another (and far more grotesque) thing altogether to torture the living. In just those few words, Frankenstein hints at a capacity for evil, for sadism, and for indifference to suffering that is both shocking and disgusting, but mostly the rest of the passage seems rather tame, at least by modern standards. Thus, Frankenstein tells us how his "eyeballs were starting from their sockets" as he looked upon his activities, but he fails to make our own eyeballs react in anything like the same way, partly because he fails to make us *see* the actual, vivid details of his work. His phrasing is remarkably restrained and decorous, and he tends to tell (rather than explicitly show) the details of his work.

The narrative comes closer to achieving more fully grotesque effects when Victor describes the actual coming-to-life of "the lifeless thing" on which he has been working (57). He sets a suitably gothic scene by describing a dark, rainy, "dreary night of November" as the actual birthday of the Creature, and he achieves a nicely grotesque detail when he recounts how "the dull yellow eye" (almost the eye of a lizard or snake) "of the creature opened" (58). Similarly grotesque is

the combination of beauty and ugliness when Frankenstein describes
in more detail the Creature's physical appearance:

His limbs were in proportion, and I had selected his features as
beautiful. Beautiful!—Great God! His yellow skin scarcely covered
the work of muscles and arteries beneath; his hair was of a lustrous
black, and flowing; his teeth of a pearly whiteness; but these luxuri-
ances only formed a more horrid contrast with his watery eyes, that
seemed almost of the same colour as the dun white sockets in which
they were set, his shriveled complexion and straight black lips. (58)

If all of *Frankenstein* were written in this sort of highly specific
language, featuring so many gruesome and gross details and with such
a striking emphasis on weird contrasts, the novel would be grotesque
through and through. However, the passage just quoted offers one of
the fullest physical descriptions of the Creature that is ever given. A
different sort of author might have gone on for page after page in a
similar vein, but Shelley, mostly, had different interests and different
intentions. She does, to be sure, soon offer a description of a strangely
grotesque dream in which Victor imagines kissing Elizabeth, the
woman he intends to marry:

. . . as I imprinted the first kiss on her lips, they became livid
with the hue of death; her features appeared to change, and I
thought that I held the corpse of my dead mother in my arms; a
shroud enveloped her form, and I saw the graveworms crawling
in the folds of the flannel. (58)

This passage does achieve a genuinely grotesque effect, not only
because of the highly specific imagery of the worms but also because of
the bizarre confusion of mother and lover in Victor's tormented mind.
Also, when Victor awakes in a fright from this dream, he happens
to see the Creature standing next to his bed, fixing his monstrous
yellow eyes on his terrified creator. The ensuing sentence could easily
have come from the screenplay of a Karloff film: "His jaws opened,
and he muttered some inarticulate sounds, while a grin wrinkled his
cheeks . . . [and] one hand was reached out, seemingly to detain me,
but I escaped, and rushed down the stairs" (58). That brief reference
to the Creature's "grin" is one of the most vividly grotesque moments
in the entire novel. It reflects, if only for a moment, the combination
of the comic and horrific that seems so specifically characteristic of

the grotesque, and it certainly adds a quick hint of mystery and even of possible malevolence to the Creature. Why is he grinning? Has he enjoyed watching Frankenstein suffer during his sleep? Does he take pleasure in his creator's terror upon seeing him? Is he grinning because he pathetically assumes that Frankenstein will be happy to see him? Shelley's brief reference to the Creature's "grin" raises numerous unanswerable questions, and for that reason alone, it verges on the truly grotesque.

The Creature now disappears from the text for two years and many pages. Frankenstein does spot him briefly while walking near a lake in Switzerland, but both his and our views of the generically described "filthy daemon" and "depraved wretch" are indistinct (72-73). Later still, while walking in the mountains, Frankenstein again encounters the Creature. This time, instead of depicting the grotesque physical horror of the monster, Victor instead uses vague language to describe the encounter: the Creature is described as "the figure of a man," as a "shape," as a "wretch," as a "Devil," and even (a bit more surprisingly) as a "vile insect" (89-90). Admittedly, the Creature is capable of moving "with superhuman speed," and its size seems to "exceed that of a man," and Frankenstein even calls it a "sight tremendous and abhorred" and says that its "unearthly ugliness rendered it almost too horrible for human eyes" (89-90). The ugliness and horror, however, are never made very specific or concrete, and so the Creature never seems as visibly and memorably grotesque in this passage as he might have seemed in the hands of a different kind of writer with a different set of intentions.

Moreover, when the Creature actually speaks—as he now does, for page after articulate and thoughtful page—any potential resemblance between him and a genuinely grotesque and repulsive monster mostly disappears. Shelley makes this Creature sympathetic in every sense of the word. Although physically repulsive, he is spiritually attractive and appealing. He reveals himself a creature far more sinned against than sinning, but to the extent that he wins our affection and regard, he ceases to be fully grotesque. As he tells his lengthy tale, he comes to resemble a kindly neighbor and diligent student rather than a repulsive monster. Occasionally, Shelley does remind us of the Creature's ugliness (95, 113, 117), but generally these passages make him seem more a beleaguered victim than a malevolent ogre. As the Creature continues to face rejection, his soul darkens: Shelley creates the possibility that it is the Creature's continual maltreatment that leads him to kill. And it is in the description of this killing—and its immediate aftermath—that Shelley creates perhaps the most sustained passage of truly grotesque writing in the entire novel.

Several factors combine to make this extended episode genuinely grotesque. The most important of these factors is that the Creature's first victim is a child. The Creature, in fact, describes him as "a beautiful child, who came running . . . with all the sportiveness of infancy" (122). As it turns out, this beautiful, sportive child is none other than William Frankenstein, the young brother of Victor, although the Creature does not yet know this fact. In any case, when the Creature spots the boy, he is taken by the idea that the youngster is "unprejudiced, and had lived too short a time to have imbibed a horror of deformity. If, therefore, I could seize him, and educate him as my companion and friend, I should not be so desolate in this peopled earth" (122). Yet, the boy screams and shields his eyes when the Creature grabs him, and when the Creature tries to reassure and calm the boy, the youth responds with insults: "'monster! ugly wretch! you wish to eat me, and tear me to pieces—You are an ogre—Let me go, or I will tell my papa'" (123).

Up until this point it is possible to feel genuine sympathy for both the Creature and the frightened youngster, but a more macabre and grotesque tone enters the narrative when the Creature explains, "Boy, you will never see your father again; you must come with me'" (123). Suddenly the Creature, for perhaps the first time in the book, seems recognizably evil and even perverse, and the fact that his intended victim is a child makes his motives and behavior seem all the more repulsive. Surely, Shelley intended this scene to shock her readers, and she achieved her intended effect, for the Creature now begins to behave—and speak—as if he is the very ogre the child imagines him to be. The Creature starts to metamorphose from a sympathetic being into the very sort of grotesque monster the child feared. Although the Creature's appearance doesn't change, our understanding and perception of his conduct does. An attempt to kidnap anyone would have made him seem criminal, but an attempt to kidnap a child and keep that child permanently from his parents makes the Creature seem demented and depraved. It isn't difficult to sympathize with the boy, then, when he exclaims, "Hideous monster! let me go" (123).

The grotesquerie continues when the boy next asserts, "My papa is a Syndic—he is M. Frankenstein—he will punish you. You dare not keep me" (123). This moment unveils a grotesque irony: Of all the children the Creature could possibly have encountered, the Creature stumbles across the one child whose family he has an intense reason to hate. Suddenly, the child's situation is even more dangerous than it had been a second earlier, and so the suspense of the scene is heightened. Moreover, the effect of the scene becomes even more complicated because of the smug arrogance of the boy, who automatically assumes that his family's lofty status will protect him from harm. Ironically, the very fact that he assumes will ensure his safety has immediately increased his danger, and when the Creature instantly declares "you shall be my first victim," the monster suddenly seems unequivocally monstrous—and undeniably grotesque—for the very first time. Even now, however, Shelley complicates the effect of the scene, for she leaves it tantalizingly unclear whether the Creature deliberately kills the boy or whether the youth's death is an unfortunate accident. The Creature explains that the "child still struggled, and loaded me with epithets which carried despair to my heart; I grasped his throat to silence him, and in a moment he lay dead at my feet" (123). The actual death, then, may easily have been unintended. Moreover, even in the moment of the boy's killing, Shelley manages to suggest some sympathy for the Creature by having him mention his "despair." The murder of William Frankenstein is, then, the first truly grotesque episode in the Creature's career.

Even more grotesque than the actual murder is the Creature's immediate response: "I gazed on my victim," he reports, and the verb "gazed" suggests not disgust or regret but fascination and even obsession (123). (Other verb phrases—such as "glanced at" or "forced myself to look upon"—would have had entirely different effects.) He reports that as he gazed, he noted that "my heart swelled with exultation and hellish triumph: clapping my hands, I exclaimed, 'I, too, can create desolation; my enemy [i.e., Victor Frankenstein] is not invulnerable; this death will carry despair to him, and a thousand other miseries shall torment and destroy him'" (123). Killing the child was grotesque in itself, but exulting in the child's death (and in the pain it will cause another) makes the Creature seem even more monstrous. At this point in the book, he has become a far more complicated and perplexing creature than he had seemed even just a short while before, and by killing the child he has clearly killed part of his own innocence. By committing the murder, he has become a more "mature" or "adult" being in some respects, but he has clearly regressed in others.

Shelley heightens the grotesque effects of this episode even further by letting the Creature next describe his response to "the portrait of a most lovely woman" that he discovers (apparently in some kind of locket or necklace) hanging from the boy's neck. "For a few moments," he notes, "I gazed with delight on her dark eyes, fringed by deep lashes, and her lovely lips; but presently my rage returned: I remembered that I was for ever deprived of the delights that such beautiful creatures could bestow" (123). Thus, no sooner does the Creature kill for the first time than he also becomes sexually aroused. His reference, in particular, to the woman's "lovely lips" and to the "delights that such beautiful creatures could bestow" clearly implies that he is no longer seeking merely the kind of friendly companionship and genial conversation he sought from the boy. Yet, his sexual longings—and the realization he could repulse any woman with his appearance—soon fill him with "rage" (123). The Creature's identity now seems grotesquely unstable and unpredictable. One moment he is the impulsive killer (perhaps unintentionally) of an innocent (if somewhat smug and conceited) child; the next moment he hellishly exults in his murder; then he becomes sexually aroused; and, finally, he is full of violent anger at all mankind.

What follows next is, however, perhaps the most grotesque moment in the entire book—a moment that makes even the murder of the boy pale a bit in comparison. Leaving the scene of the murder, the Creature comes upon a barn in which an attractive young woman is sleeping. Bending over her and contemplating her beauty, he whispers, "Awake, fairest, thy lover is near—he who would give his life but to obtain one look of affection from thine eyes: my beloved, awake!" (123-24). In such a tense, suspense-filled moment, questions arise: what will happen if the woman awakes? Will she be the next murder victim? What are the Creature's intentions? Does he plan to kidnap her? Does he plan to kill her? Or does he, perhaps, intend (most grotesquely) to rape her and then kill her? At least the boy had a chance to resist and possibly even escape, but the woman seems entirely vulnerable. The apparent sarcasm (and even comic cynicism) of the Creature's words makes his conduct here seem even more grotesque, and the whole episode brims with ugly tension.

Fortunately, the Creature decides neither to rape the sleeping woman nor to kill her. Instead, with careful calculation, he plants the necklace on her body so she will be suspected of the child's murder. Eventually, she is indeed suspected, tried, convicted, and executed, and so the Creature grotesquely manages to make an innocent person pay for his own crime. And from this point on the Creature engages in other grotesque behavior or expresses other grotesque desires. Thus, he requests that Frankenstein make him a female companion—"a creature of another sex, but as hideous as myself" (125), and it is clear from the terms of his request that he desires not merely a friend but a grotesque sexual partner. Much later in the book, Frankenstein again encounters the creature and notices how a grotesque, "ghastly grin wrinkled his lips as he gazed on me" while Frankenstein worked on constructing the hideous she-creature (141). Later still, after Frankenstein has decided to abandon that project, the Creature grotesquely threatens him by saying, "I shall be with you on your wedding-night" (142). Then, in fulfillment of that vow, the Creature does indeed kill Victor's new bride, and it is Victor himself who not only discovers the body (163) but also glimpses the Creature immediately afterwards: "A grin was on the face of the monster; he seemed to jeer, as with his fiendish finger he pointed toward the corpse of my wife" (164). It is such grinning and jeering—the taking of such obvious comic pleasure in others' pain—that finally makes the Creature truly grotesque.

WORKS CITED

Barash, Frances. "Grotesque." *Dictionary of Literary Themes and Motifs*. Ed. Jean-Charles Seigneuret. 2 vols. Westport, CT: Greenwood, 1988. 1: 559–71.

Harmon, William. *A Handbook to Literature*. 10th ed. Upper Saddle River, NJ: Pearson, Prentice Hall, 2006.

Kayser, Wolfgang. *The Grotesque in Art and Literature*. Trans. Ulrich Weisstein. Bloomington: Indiana UP, 1963.

Shelley, Mary. *Frankenstein*. Ed. Johanna M. Smith. Boston: Bedford, 1992.

Thomson, Philip. *The Grotesque*. London: Methuen, 1972.

"Good Country People"
(Flannery O'Connor)

"A Sharp Eye for the Grotesque in Flannery O'Connor's 'Good Country People'"
by Robert C. Evans,
Auburn University at Montgomery

"My own feeling is that writers who see by the light of their Christian faith will have, in these times, the sharpest eyes for the grotesque, for the perverse, and for the unacceptable."

—Flannery O'Connor, *Collected Works* 805

Practically anyone who has read Flannery O'Connor's fiction would agree that it is frequently "grotesque," and indeed for many readers its grotesqueness is a huge part of its appeal or fascination. The word "grotesque" appears repeatedly in printed commentary on O'Connor's writings: a numbered list of the hundreds of articles and books mentioning the term takes up more than a page in R. Neill Scott's huge and splendid *Reference Guide*, and it is difficult to find an analyst of O'Connor who has *not* used the word at some point in trying to describe the effects of her fiction. O'Connor herself, in attempting to explain her work, wrote one of her own best essays—a typically wry and ironic piece titled "Some Aspects of the Grotesque in Southern Fiction" (*Collected* 813-21)—and her personal comments on the grotesque are also scattered throughout her lively and thoughtful collection of letters, *The Habit of Being*. At least three books on O'Connor (by Gilbert Muller, Marshall Bruce Gentry, and Anthony

Di Renzo) include the word "grotesque" in their titles or subtitles, and the articles and book chapters on O'Connor that employ that term in their titles are far too numerous to cite.

Nearly everyone, then (including O'Connor herself), agrees that her fiction is often "grotesque," but what, exactly, does the term mean? Not surprisingly for a word so widely used, definitions abound. A standard handbook on literature begins by noting that "grotesque" is a:

> term applied to a decorative art in sculpture, painting, and architecture, characterized by fantastic representations of human and animal forms often combined into formal distortions to the point of absurdity, ugliness, or caricature. It was so named after the ancient paintings and decorations found in the underground chambers (*grotte*) of Roman ruins. By extension, *grotesque* is applied to anything having the qualities of *grotesque* art: bizarre, incongruous, ugly, unnatural, fantastic, abnormal. (Harmon 244)

Other discussions of the grotesque emphasize its typically incongruous "mingling of the fantastic and the ideal, the sordid and the real, [and] the comic and the horrific" (Barash 562), while still other commentators have stressed its focus on suddenness, surprise, and estrangement (Kayser 185) and its often violent juxtapositions of laughter and disgust, "the animate and inanimate, and the human and nonhuman" (Houlahan 339).

Anthony Di Renzo, in one of the best book-length treatments of O'Connor and the grotesque, discusses the grotesque effects of her fiction by pointing to her "violent slapstick," her "penchant for distorting the human figure," and the "prevalence of caricature" in her writings, and he also notes how her emphasis on the ugly motivates, in some readers, "a mixture of [both] outrage and fascination" (3). He argues that O'Connor's grotesque art "expresses the repressed," and that it "crosses borders, ignores boundaries, and overspills margins" (5). He finds, in her works, a frequent focus on "the stupid, the obscene, [and] the banal" (7) as well as a repeated emphasis on "marginal characters" (13). He asserts O'Connor "insists on paradox, on double vision, [and] on the interpenetration of opposites" (106), claiming her work often depends on techniques of "caricature, parody, and irony" (107). He finds that a "remarkable compression" of divergent effects is "one of

[O'Connor's] strengths as a writer and is a hallmark of the grotesque" (108), and he contends that her best grotesque writing blends the comic and tragic (109), the demonic and the holy (133), the real and surreal (229), and "low humor and high seriousness" (169).

It is that last trait, in fact—the combination of often bizarre comedy with a profound interest in moral and spiritual truth—that distinguishes O'Connor's use of the grotesque from the way it is used by many other artists, especially many other modern writers. Whereas many recent authors have used the grotesque merely to emphasize the ugly, absurd, bizarre, and seemingly pointless aspects of existence, O'Connor's use of such a style is always grounded in a vision of values by which she measures the shortcomings of modern life. Her use of the grotesque, in other words, is never gratuitous or self-indulgent. She does not focus on the disgusting, ludicrous, and repulsive merely for the sake of seeming outrageous, cynical, sophisticated, or clever. Although her work is rarely, if ever, sentimental (and indeed, one function of the grotesque in her writing is precisely to sabotage any hint of sentimentality), neither is her writing ever nihilistic. She never describes the ugly, the violent, the repulsive, or the meaningless because she doubts the genuine possibility of beauty, kindness, the appealing, or the meaningful. For O'Connor, in fact, the universe is quite literally *full* of meaning, but its meanings can only be judged by reference to her firm belief in the reality of the Christian God, whom she regards as the source, guarantor, and judge of everything (and everyone) that exists. Her use of the grotesque, then, is ultimately satirical, corrective, and therapeutic: she wants to shock us into realizing the shortcomings of our lives so that we can begin to appreciate something higher, better, and more holy.

No one, in fact, has more succinctly explained O'Connor's use of the grotesque than O'Connor herself. In the essay already mentioned, she wittily remarks that any writing "that comes out of the South is going to be called grotesque by the Northern reader, unless it is grotesque, in which case it is going to be called realistic" (*Collected* 815). O'Connor, however, is interested in the deeper realism of deliberately grotesque writing, in which "the writer has made alive some experience which we are not accustomed to observe everyday, or which the ordinary man may never experience in his ordinary life." The characters in such works "lean away from typical social patterns, toward mystery and the unexpected" (815). To the writer interested in this sort of grotesqueness, "what he sees on the surface will be of interest to him only as he can go through it into an experience of mystery itself. . . . Such a writer will be interested in what we don't understand rather than in what we do." O'Connor is careful to emphasize that such a writer cannot afford to ignore the real, mundane, or concrete, but she argues that "the kind of writer I am describing will use the concrete in a more drastic way. His way will much more obviously be the way of distortion." The sort of fiction that results from this kind of grotesque technique "is almost of necessity going to be violent and comic, because of the discrepancies it seeks to combine" (816). Although "the writer who produces grotesque fiction may not consider his characters any more freakish than ordinary fallen man usually is, his audience is going to," and that audience will usually assume that the purpose of creating such characters is for the sake of showing them "compassion" (816). For O'Connor, however, "when the grotesque is used in a legitimate way, the intellectual and moral judgments implicit in it will have the ascendancy over feeling" (816–17). O'Connor's use of the grotesque, in other words, is intended to be anything but mawkish or sentimental.

Just when she seems to be verging toward seeming overly-solemn, however, O'Connor cracks one of her typically serious jokes: "Whenever I'm asked why Southern writers particularly have a penchant for writing about freaks, I say it is because we are still able to recognize one. To be able to recognize a freak, you have to have some conception of the whole man, and in the South the general conception of man is still, in the main, theological" (817). The "freak," in this sense, is a symbol of "our essential displacement"—our fundamental separation, through pride, sin, and imperfection, from God (818). If many of O'Connor's stories describe freaks and freakish behavior, it is not because she mocks freaks *per se* but because she considers all humans (herself included) fools and freaks in the eyes of God. Her purpose in writing is less to mirror society (since "a literature which mirrors society would be no fit guide for it" [819]) than to help jar and jolt society awake by using a style that is sometimes violent, sometimes comic, and sometimes both at once. As she memorably put it in another fine essay:

> The novelist with Christian concerns will find in modern life distortions which are repugnant to him, and his problem will

be to make these appear as distortions to an audience which is used to seeing them as natural; and he may well be forced to take ever more violent means to get his vision across to this hostile audience. When you can assume that your audience holds the same beliefs as you do, you can relax a little and use more normal ways of talking to it; when you have to assume that it does not, then you have to make your vision apparent by shock—to the hard of hearing you shout, and for the almost blind you draw large and startling figures. (805-06)

In many stories, O'Connor did her level best to shout and startle. In "A Good Man Is Hard to Find" (perhaps her best single work), an entire family—including a doddering grandmother, two bland parents, two pugnacious children, and an innocent infant—are all slaughtered by a homicidal gang of escaped convicts. (And yet, in spite of everything, the story arguably has a happy ending.) In "The Displaced Person," the title character is run over and killed by a runaway tractor, much to the satisfaction of some of his co-workers. In "Everything That Rises Must Converge," an aging white mother dies of a heart attack after being tormented psychologically by her son and then struck in the face by an enraged black woman. In "The Comforts of Home," another son accidentally shoots and kills his own mother while struggling with a girl he considers a slut, while in "Greenleaf" a smug female farmer is gored to death by a marauding bull. The list of violently bizarre (or bizarrely violent) deaths in O'Connor's fiction could easily be extended, and yet all of the stories just mentioned—as well as most of O'Connor's writings—contain ample doses of equally bizarre humor. By now it should be clear that her intention is often to use such unexpected juxtapositions in order to shock her readers into a new awareness, particularly by depicting sudden, comic and often deadly twists of plot.

Compared to the stories just mentioned, "Good Country People" seems almost tame. In this justly famous work, O'Connor depicts yet another mother, Mrs. Hopewell, who lives on a farm with two tenant workers named Mr. and Mrs. Freeman, the proud parents of teenaged daughters with the absurd names of Glynese and Carramae. Mrs. Hopewell is herself the mother of a thirty-two-year-old daughter named Joy, who still lives at home and who possesses a Ph.D. in philosophy, a surly disposition, and a wooden leg. Her original leg "had been literally blasted off" (as O'Connor delicately puts it) during a hunting accident when the girl was only ten (267), and the incident has helped darken Joy's personality: she treats her mother and Mrs. Freeman with contempt, she believes in literally nothing (a philosophical stance known as "nihilism"), she is certain of her superiority to most other people, and, partly to torment a parent she considers annoyingly positive, she has legally changed her name from Joy to Hulga.

When a young traveling Bible salesman with the wonderfully ridiculous name of Manley Pointer shows up at the Hopewell farm one day, he manages to persuade Mrs. Hopewell to invite him to stay for dinner. True to form, Hulga regards him with disdain, but she also agrees to meet him privately the next day for an intimate picnic. She intends to seduce him—philosophically and perhaps also sexually—and she also plans to disabuse him of his innocence, including his innocent, ignorant Christian faith. When Pointer takes an intense interest in her wooden leg, Hulga begins to imagine that he is as obsessed with her as she herself is, and when Pointer—having convinced her to climb into the hayloft of a remote barn—asks if he can remove the leg, Hulga is both bewildered and somewhat flattered. Pointer, she assumes, is perhaps able to appreciate her sublime uniqueness. Only after the leg has been removed and some messy kisses have been exchanged does Hulga discover his true intentions: opening a hollowed-out Bible, he removes a flask of whiskey, a pack of obscene playing cards, and a condom, and he refuses Hulga's frantic pleas that he return her leg. For a moment it almost appears that Hulga will be raped, but eventually Pointer dismisses her with the same kind of contempt she herself has so often shown to others. He makes it clear that his religious faith was just an act, and he undercuts Hulga's intellectual pride with a withering final comment: "you ain't so smart. I been believing in nothing ever since I was born!" (283). When we last see Hulga, she has been left both literally and figuratively without a leg to stand on.

The grotesque aspects of "Good Country People" begin with its very first sentence, which describes the tenant worker, Mrs. Freeman, as if she were a machine: "Besides the neutral expression that she wore when she was alone, Mrs. Freeman had two others, forward and reverse, that she used for all her human dealings" (263). This combination of the human and the mechanical (of living being and dead matter) makes Mrs. Freeman seem less than fully human, and what makes her character seem especially grotesque is the fact that she freely *chooses* to behave like a machine. In fact, she is *determined* to be less than a fully rounded, complex character (a choice that contributes, paradoxically, to her odd complexity), and this emphasis on the grotesqueness of the kind of limitation that results from proud and self-willed choice is, indeed, a key to this work. Mrs. Freeman and other characters in the story—especially Hulga—repeatedly and willfully sacrifice their God-given potential for freedom and flexibility, choosing instead to adopt rigid, inflexible postures in their thinking, their conduct, and their treatment of others. It is largely this deliberate sacrifice of their full potential as beings originally made in the image of God that makes them both grotesque and funny; their rigidity is at times ugly, at times frightening, at times pitiable, and at times quite laughable. It is, in large part, precisely this sort of complex combination of effects that makes such characters "grotesque."

Examples of such behavior abound in "Good Country People": the story is full of characters who not only treat others as things (rather than as complex souls) but who, paradoxically, often seem to think of themselves with the same simple-minded and limiting rigidity. Usually the mechanical inflexibility O'Connor describes is deeply grounded in her characters' pride, arrogance, and self-centeredness. As a Christian, O'Connor believed, of course, that this sort of vanity was the root of all human sin; part of what makes the characters in this story grotesque is their utter lack of humility. Their pride is ugly and comic—ugly because they cheat themselves of their potential moral and spiritual beauty, comic because they take themselves far more seriously than O'Connor does. Thus "Mrs. Freeman could never be brought to admit herself wrong on any point" (263), while Hulga, "whose constant outrage had obliterated every expression from her face," is described as having "the look of someone who has achieved blindness by an act of will and means to keep it" (264-65). Hulga's wooden leg is just the most obvious symbol of the fact that she is spiritually maimed, emotionally crippled, inflexibly rigid, and lacking in the sort of rich and full vitality her Creator intended her to have. Yet we are not meant to pity Hulga; after all, she has *chosen* to think and act as she does. She has made *herself* ugly—and laughable—and that is why the joke, finally, is on her.

Thus, when Hulga stands "square and rigid-shouldered with her neck thrust slightly forward" and tells her mother, "If you want me, here I am—LIKE I AM" (266), her inflexible physical posture perfectly matches her equally inflexible egotism, and both the posture and the arrogance make her seem both unattractive and ridiculous. Little wonder, then, that Hulga and many of the other characters— who share a selfish pride by which they alienate themselves from each other and from God (Whom O'Connor considered the source of all life)—are often described as non-living or mechanical. Hulga resembles "the broad blank hull of a battleship" and responds to her mother's continued use of the name "Joy" "in a purely mechanical way" (266); Mrs. Freeman has "beady steel-pointed eyes" (267); even Manley Pointer later is described as having "eyes like two steel spikes" (282), and it is ironically appropriate that the one thing that most fascinates him about Hulga is not her soul, character, personality, or feelings, but her wooden leg. Having already reduced herself (through her egotism and belligerence) to something mechanical and not completely alive, Hulga ultimately is valued as nothing more than a piece of dead wood. And, since she is a philosophical materialist, her fate seems ironically appropriate.

For a frightening moment, of course, it looked as if Pointer might also value her as nothing more than a body—as a piece of flesh to be selfishly used and then disposed. The use of persons in such ways is, to say the least, inherently grotesque, and yet part of the point of the story seems to be that when human beings neglect—or deliberately ignore or suppress—their spiritual dimensions, they can hardly expect to be treated as much more than physical bodies. Repeatedly, indeed, O'Connor mocks the flesh in this story—not because she disrespects bodies *per se* but because she wants to suggest that the flesh, when divorced from the soul and over-valued for its own sake, can seem both ugly and laughable. This emphasis on the comic (but also unattractive) aspects of the body begins quickly in "Good Country People." Thus, Mrs. Freeman is eager to share the details of how often her fifteen-year-old pregnant daughter, Carramae, has "vomited since the last report" (264), and she later proudly says of this daughter that "'She thrown up four times after supper'" (269). Manley Pointer claims that his own father had been crushed under a tree when Pointer himself was eight year[s] old," and then, in keeping with the story's emphasis on grotesque physical details, he helpfully elaborates: "He had been crushed very badly, in fact, almost cut in two and was practically not recognizable" (272). Later, of course, we suspect that this is just a dramatic tale invented to play on Hulga's sympathies, but even when we first hear it, it seems typical of the way O'Connor refuses to take the human body seriously. Oddly enough, our impulse is not to wince when we read such a sentence, but to laugh, partly because it is hard to think of any of these people as being real in the usual sense of that word. Having reduced themselves to the level of caricatures, they resemble cartoon figures. To say this, however, is not at all to criticize O'Connor; instead it is to praise her as a master satirist who implicitly, consistently (but rarely overtly) judges her characters against an ideal standard and lets them reveal their self-imposed limitations. As pieces of flesh, she refuses to take them seriously; as souls and personalities with moral and spiritual dimensions and responsibilities, she takes them very seriously indeed.

It is, in fact, when detailing the ethical and spiritual lapses of her characters that O'Connor's writing can seem most truly grotesque (in the darker senses of that word). Sometimes the moral shortcomings of the characters can seem relatively minor, as when Hulga thinks of Glynese and Carramae as being merely "useful" when they distract her mother, occupying "attention that might otherwise have been directed" at Hulga herself (266). Sometimes the characters' inconsiderate treatment of each other can even seem funny, as when Hulga at first thinks that she "could not stand Mrs. Freeman for she had found that it was not possible to be rude to her" (266). There are times, however, when the characters' disregard of others' full humanity (and thereby of their own) seems almost perverse or evil. One of the most shocking moments in the story, for instance, occurs when the narrator reports that

> Mrs. Freeman had a special fondness for the details of secret infections, hidden deformities, assaults upon children. Of diseases, she preferred the lingering or incurable. Hulga had heard Mrs. Hopewell give her the details of the hunting accident, how the leg had been literally blasted off, how she [Joy/Hulga] had never lost consciousness. Mrs. Freeman could listen to it any time as if it had happened an hour ago. (267)

Mrs. Freeman's reactions here seem almost sadistic in their morbid indifference to (or, more accurately, in their bizarre interest in) the pain and suffering of others. Although some hostile critics might claim that O'Connor herself shared some of Mrs. Freeman's strange obsessions, O'Connor would no doubt respond that their shared interests were differently motivated: O'Connor was interested in the darkly grotesque aspects of human existence precisely because she wanted to shock her readers into an awareness of something higher and better, whereas Mrs. Freeman (like Hulga and Manley Pointer as well) seems incapable of imagining anything above and beyond the material and mundane.

In moments such as the one just quoted, "Good Country People" can seem deeply disturbing. For the most part, however, this is actually one of O'Connor's consistently *comic* tales. Its grotesque aspects—such as its awful puns about Hulga "lumber[ing] into the bathroom" or "stump[ing] into the kitchen" (263; 267) serve the welcome purpose of encouraging us to take Hulga, Mrs. Hopewell, Mrs. Freeman, and indeed humans in general, far less seriously than they tend to take themselves. From the largest possible perspective (O'Connor seems to suggest), all humans and most fallen human behavior can seem comically grotesque. Humans who cut themselves off from God are (from O'Connor's point of view) at least as crippled as Hulga, and in the final analysis O'Connor is much less interested in what happens to Hulga's leg than in what has happened, and may yet happen, to her soul.

WORKS CITED OR CONSULTED

Barash, Frances. "Grotesque." *Dictionary of Literary Themes and Motifs*. Ed. Jean-Charles Seigneuret. 2 vols. Westport, CT: Greenwood, 1988. 1: 559–71.

Di Renzo, Anthony. *Flannery O'Connor and the Medieval Grotesque*. Carbondale: Southern Illinois UP, 1993.

Gentry, Marshall Bruce. *Flannery O'Connor's Religion of the Grotesque*. Jackson: U Press of Mississippi, 1986.

Harmon, William. *A Handbook to Literature*. 10th ed. Upper Saddle River, NJ: Pearson, Prentice Hall, 2006.

Houlahan, Mark. "The Grotesque." *Reader's Guide to Literature in English*. Ed. Mark Hawkins-Dady. London: Fitzroy Dearborn, 1996: 339–40.

Kayser, Wolfgang. *The Grotesque in Art and Literature.* Trans. Ulrich Weisstein. Bloomington: Indiana UP, 1963.

Muller, Gilbert. *Nightmares and Visions: Flannery O'Connor and the Catholic Grotesque.* Athens: U of Georgia P, 1972.

O'Connor, Flannery. *Collected Works.* Ed. Sally Fitzgerald. New York: The Library of America, 1988.

———. *The Habit of Being.* Ed. Sally Fitzgerald. New York: Farrar, Straus, Giroux, 1979.

Scott, R. Neil. *Flannery O'Connor: An Annotated Reference Guide to Criticism.* Milledgeville, GA: Timberlane Books, 2002.

GULLIVER'S TRAVELS
(JONATHAN SWIFT)

"The Political Significance of *Gulliver's Travels*"
by C. H. Firth,
in *The Proceedings of the British Academy* (1919)

INTRODUCTION

In his work on the political significance of *Gulliver's Travels*, C. H. Firth explains "hints, parallels, and characters" in the novel, finding a sharp social commentary and arguing that Swift's novel is "not merely a literary exercise" but "an instrument with which he sought to effect a definite end." Thus, for Firth, Swift's monstrous creation with its grotesque characters, such as the Lilliputians, standing just under six inches tall, holds up a kind of distorted looking-glass or mirror for the world, as in Swift's famous definition of satire given in his "Preface" to *The Battle of the Books*: "Satire is a sort of glass wherein beholders do generally discover everybody's face but their own, which is the chief reason so few are offended by it."

Firth, C. H. *The Political Significance of* Gulliver's Travels *from The Proceedings of the British Academy Vol. IX*. Norwood, PA: Norwood Editions, 1977 (read 10 December 1919).

A critic who seeks to explain the political significance of *Gulliver's Travels* may be guilty of too much ingenuity, but he cannot fairly be charged with exaggerated curiosity. He is searching for a secret which Swift tells us is hidden there, and endeavouring to solve riddles which were intended to exercise his wits. Swift loved to mystify the public; he often preferred to speak in parables when there was no reason for doing so. In this case there was good reason for his preference. At that time, and for many years later, it was dangerous to write plainly about public affairs, or to criticize public men with any freedom.

When Swift wrote his *History of the Last Four Years of the Queen* he proposed to prefix to it characters of the party leaders of that period in order to make it more intelligible. In 1738 he contemplated the publication of this *History.* Though it was about five-and-twenty years after the events described, he was warned by his friend Erasmus Lewis, that if the characters he had drawn were published as they stood 'nothing could save the author's printer and publishers from some grievous punishment'.[1] Accordingly it was not published till 1758, thirteen years after Swift's death.

Authors who wrote about public affairs immediately after they had happened and about ministers of state while they were actually in office were obliged to use literary artifices of various kinds in order to express their opinions with impunity. But it was not without some compensating advantage, for to be allusive and indirect, while it protected the author, stimulated the curiosity of the reader.

In *Gulliver's Travels* many figures which seem to be imaginary are meant to depict real personages, or at all events are drawn from them. Swift says in one of his earlier writings: 'In describing the virtues and vices of mankind, it is convenient, upon every article, to have some eminent person in our eye, from whence we copy our description.' Again he says: 'I have thought of another expedient, frequently practised with great safety and success by satirical writers; which is that of looking into history for some character bearing a resemblance to the person we would describe; and with the absolute power of altering, adding, or, suppressing what circumstances we please, I conceive we must have very bad luck or very little skill to fail.' He admitted that this method of writing had one serious drawback. 'Though the present age may understand well enough the little hints we give, the parallels we draw, and the characters we describe, yet this will all be

lost to the next. However, if these papers should happen to live till our grandchildren are men, I hope they may have curiosity enough to consult annals and compare dates, in order to find out.'[2]
[. . .]

Political allusions abound in the *Travels*. Some are to the events of the end of Queen Anne's reign, others to events in the reign of George I. Naturally those events which happened during the five years in which the *Travels* were completed left most traces on the work. In England at the beginning of the period there was the South Sea Bubble (1720), which was followed by the return of Walpole to office (1721) and by the return of Bolingbroke from exile (1723), by the ejection of Carteret from the English cabinet (1724), and by the supremacy of Walpole in it (1725). In Ireland during the same period the struggle over Wood's patent began and ended (1722–5).

These references to public events and public personages are most frequent in the First and Third Voyages. Each of these Voyages consists of a part which was written about 1714, as Pope's statement proves, and internal evidence confirms. Each of these Voyages also contains other parts written later, as Swift's letters indicate, and the contents of the additions show. Moreover, there are signs in the text itself, such as repetitions, explanations, and alterations, which show where the matter was added.

Let us begin by examining the Voyage to Lilliput. The first part of it, which contains the story of Gulliver's shipwreck, and of his early adventures among the pigmies, has no political significance. It is simply what Shakespeare terms 'very gracious fooling'. This no doubt represents the part written in 1714. On the other hand, the account of the laws and customs of Lilliput contained in Chapter VI was probably written later. It seems to be an afterthought, because in Chapter IV Gulliver had announced that he proposed to reserve 'for a greater work' the very subjects treated of in Chapter VI.[3] There is also a distinct change of tone; a serious didactic purpose becomes apparent. The institutions of Lilliput are described for the instruction of Swift's fellow countrymen, just as Sir Thomas More described the institutions of Utopia. 'There are some laws and customs in this empire very peculiar,' says Gulliver; 'and if they were not so directly contrary to those of my own dear country, I should be tempted to say a little in their justification.'[4] Thus he directs the attention of his readers to the impunity of certain crimes in England and the shortcomings of English education.

By a curious contradiction, as soon as Swift turns to describe the politics of Lilliput it ceases to be Utopia and becomes England itself, instead of being an example to England. 'We labour', says Gulliver's informant, 'under two mighty evils: a violent faction at home and the danger of an invasion by a most potent enemy from abroad.'[5]

In Lilliput there are two struggling parties called 'Tramecksan and Slamecksan, from the high and low heels on their shoes, by which they distinguish themselves.'[5] These typify the High Church and Low Church parties, or the Tories and Whigs. The potent enemy abroad is the island of Blefuscu, which typifies France, engaged in an obstinate struggle with its neighbour for a whole generation. The conversion of Lilliput into England marks the change of plan made by Swift when he took up the half-finished story of the First Voyage again, about 1720, and turned his story into a political allegory. This change involved other changes. The majestic Emperor of Lilliput of the second chapter, with his 'Austrian lip and arched nose',[6] was a purely conventional monarch, not representing George I or any other real king. It was now necessary to convert this personage into George I, which was effected by making him a Whig 'determined to make use of only Low Heels in the administration of the government', and wearing himself heels lower than any of his court. The parallel was emphasized by making the heir to the throne show an inclination to the High Heels, as the Prince of Wales did to the Tories.[7] Finally Swift inserted an ironical passage on the lenity and mercy of the King, intended to call to the minds of his readers the executions which had taken place after the rebellion in 1715, and the encomiums on the King's mercy which the Government had published at the time.[8]

The King was not the only personage who underwent a sort of transformation when Swift took his half-told story in hand again. Gulliver is changed too. At first Gulliver to a certain extent represented Swift himself—that is, certain incidents in Gulliver's adventures were an allegorical representation of certain incidents in Swift's life. Editors of *Gulliver's Travels* rightly agree in their interpretation of the story of Gulliver's extinction of the fire in the palace at Lilliput, and of the resentment of the Empress in consequence. Sir Walter Scott says: 'It is perhaps a strained interpretation

of this incident to suppose that our author recollected the preju-
dices of Queen Anne against the indecency and immorality of his
own satirical vein, though it was so serviceable to the cause of her
ministry.'[9] Mr. Dennis says: 'Queen Anne was so much disgusted
with the *Tale of a Tub* that in spite of Swift's political services she
could never be induced to give him preferment in the Church.'[10] J.
F. Waller and W. C. Taylor, in their editions of *Gulliver*, interpret
the incident in a similar fashion. It is not an unreasonable interpretation, for it is clear that Swift's satirical writings stood in the way
of his promotion. He failed to obtain the Irish bishopric he hoped
to get in 1708,[11] and it was with great difficulty that he obtained a
deanery in 1713.[12]

The tradition is that the first failure was due to the influence of
Dr. Sharp, the Archbishop of York, who showed the Queen the *Tale
of a Tub*.[13] The second, it is alleged, was due to the influence of the
Duchess of Somerset, incensed by Swift's *Windsor Prophecy*, written
in December 1711.[14] Swift believed that this was the case, and in the
lines entitled 'The Author on Himself', written in 1714, he mentioned
both causes, and spoke of Queen Anne as 'a royal prude', whose opposition to his preferment was due to the efforts of his enemies. In that
poem he names firstly the Duchess of Somerset and the Archbishop
of York, and secondly the Earl of Nottingham and Robert Walpole as
the enemies in question.

In *Gulliver's Travels* the captain's chief enemy is a certain lord
named Bolgolam, who was pleased, says Gulliver, 'without provoca-
tion to be my mortal enemy. . . . That minister was Galbet, or Admiral
of the Realm, very much in his master's confidence, and a person well
versed in affairs, but of a morose and sour complexion.' He is referred
to later as Gulliver's 'mortal enemy', and his 'malice' is mentioned and
insisted upon.[15]

This person is clearly intended to represent the Earl of
Nottingham. The 'morose and sour complexion' attributed to
Bolgolam at once suggests the identification. In one of his pamphlets
Swift says that Nottingham's 'adust complexion disposeth him to
rigour and severity', and time after time he refers to him by his
nickname of 'Dismal'. 'Dismal, so men call him from his looks',
explains Swift to Stella.[16] The earl had long been Swift's personal
enemy. In 1711, when Nottingham joined the Whigs in their
attack on the foreign policy of the Government, Swift wrote two

ballads against him, 'An Orator Dismal from Nottinghamshire' and 'Toland's Invitation to Dismal'.[17] Nottingham retaliated by using whatever private influence he possessed at court to stop Swift's preferment, and finally by an open and bitter attack upon him in Parliament. On June 1, 1714, when the Schism Act was debated in the House of Lords, Nottingham opposed the bill, saying that it was dangerous because it gave too much power to the bishops, 'though now they had the happiness of having so worthy bishops, yet it possibly might happen that a person who wrote lewdly, nay, even atheistically, might by having a false undeserved character given him be promoted to a bishopric by her Majesty.'[18] Another version makes Nottingham say: 'I own I tremble when I think that a certain divine who is hardly suspected of being a Christian, is in a fair way of being a Bishop.'[19] More than any other statesman of the period, he might be described with justice as Swift's 'mortal enemy'. On the other hand, it is more difficult to explain why Nottingham should be designated 'High Admiral'. There was no Lord High Admiral in England after 1709, and the different noblemen who held the post of First Lord of the Admiralty between 1709 and 1726 were none of them enemies of Swift. One reason for the designation can be suggested. Nottingham had been First Lord from February 1680 to May 1684, and ever afterwards 'piqued himself upon understanding sea affairs'. In William III's reign, when he was Secretary of State, he was continually interfering in the management of the fleet. 'All men', says Lord Dartmouth, 'that had been bred to that profession unanimously agreed that he was totally ignorant in their science, and were highly provoked when he pretended to contradict or give them directions.'[20] To term Nottingham 'High Admiral' may be an ironical reference to this notorious foible.

Nottingham was President of the Council in the first Ministry of George I, and held that post till February 29, 1716, when he was dismissed because he pressed for the pardon of the leaders of the late rebellion.[21] This attack upon him under the character of Bolgolam must have been written in the summer of 1714, when his offences against Swift were fresh and Swift's anger against him was hot. The prose character is the counterpart of the verses entitled 'The Author on Himself', which belong to the same summer. It is not likely that it was written after 1716, when Nottingham's clemency had led to his fall from office.

When Swift, in 1719 or 1720, took up his unfinished story again, and converted it into a political allegory, he changed his plan, developed, as we have seen, the character of the Emperor, and shadowed forth under the misfortunes of Gulliver the fate of Bolingbroke. That statesman must have been much in Swift's mind about that time. He had resumed his correspondence with his exiled friend in February 1719, at which time there was some prospect of Bolingbroke's pardon and his return to England, though the hope was not realized till 1723. During that period several long letters passed between them. It was towards the end of 1721 that Swift seems to have mentioned his *Travels* to Bolingbroke. 'I long to see your *Travels*', wrote the latter, answering on January 1, 1722, a letter from Swift dated September 29, 1721.[22]

The parallel between the fate of Bolingbroke and that of Gulliver was very close. Like Gulliver, Bolingbroke had brought a great war to an end and concluded a peace 'upon conditions very advantageous' to his country, but was denounced by his political opponents for not prosecuting the war to the complete subjugation of the enemy. He was accused of treasonable intercourse with the ambassadors of France, as Gulliver was with those of Blefuscu. Gulliver fled from Lilliput because he felt that he could not obtain a fair trial, 'having in my life', says he, 'perused many state trials, which I ever observed to terminate as the judges thought fit to direct,' and because he knew that powerful enemies sought his life. Bolingbroke declared that he fled from England because 'I had certain and repeated information from some who are in the secret of affairs, that a resolution was taken by those who have power to execute it to pursue me to the scaffold. My blood was to have been the cement of a new alliance; nor could any innocence be any security, after it had once been demanded from abroad. and resolved on at home, that it was necessary to cut me off.'[23]

[…]

But was it simply blind wrath against the human race which inspired Swift? Isolated expressions lend some colour to the theory. 'Expect no more from man than such an animal is capable of producing,' wrote Swift to Sheridan, 'and you will every day find my description of Yahoos more resembling';[24] and again: 'I hate and detest that animal called man, though I heartily love John, Peter, Thomas, and so forth.'[25] 'I tell you after all that I do not hate mankind: it is you others who hate them because you would have them reasonable animals, and are angry for being disappointed. I have always rejected that definition, and made another of my own.' His definition of man was not *animal rationale* but *animal rationis capax*.[26]

[...]

Seeking to explain the hints, parallels, and characters in *Gulliver's Travels*, I have followed Swift's own advice, 'to consult annals and compare dates'. The history of the years 1713–26 gives the events which might be reflected in Swift's romance. The other writings of Swift show which of those events interested him. If at a given time his pamphlets, his sermons, his verses, and his letters are all full of one idea it will not be absent from his mind when he depicts imaginary countries. *Gulliver's Travels* show plainly that when Swift began to write them England and English politics filled his mind, and that when he completed them Ireland and Irish affairs were his absorbing interest. As he passed from one subject to another his tone altered, his satire ceased to be playful and became serious and bitter.

Satire was not to him merely a literary exercise: it was an instrument with which he sought to effect a definite practical end. He had the restless temperament of the reformer. 'My notion is', he wrote in 1714, 'that if a man cannot mend the public he should mend old shoes, if he can do no better.'[27] He described himself in the *Modest Proposal* as 'wearied out for many years with offering vain, idle, visionary thoughts, and at length utterly despairing of success'.[28] In *Gulliver's Travels* he denounced projectors, but confessed that he had been himself 'a sort of projector' in his younger days. It was folly, he said now, and of all projectors those were most irrational who proposed schemes for teaching ministers to consult the public good and princes to know their true interest.[29] In his later letters he spoke with some scorn of his own 'foolish zeal in endeavouring to save this wretched island',[30] and disclaimed any right to the title of patriot: 'What I do is owing to perfect rage and resentment, and the mortifying sight of slavery, folly, and baseness.'[31] And again: 'What I did for this country was from a perfect hatred at tyranny and oppression. . . . We are slaves and knaves and fools.'[32] Thus he raged on paper, but in reality he was a charitable and public-spirited misanthropist who, in spite of ingratitude and disappointment,

> Kept the tenor of his mind
> To merit well of human-kind.[33]

Notes

1. *Correspondence*, edited by F. Elrington Ball, vi. 78.
2. *Works*, edited by Temple Scott, ix. 81, 101, 110; cf. also 271 and v. 297.
3. *Gulliver's Travels*, pp. 48, 59. The edition referred to throughout this paper is that edited by Mr. G. R. Dennis in 1899, forming volume viii of the *Prose Works of Swift*, edited by Temple Scott.
4. Ibid., p. 59.
5. Ibid., p. 48.
6. Ibid., p. 29.
7. Ibid., pp. 48–9.
8. Ibid., p. 74.
9. *Works*, ed. 1824, xi. 74.
10. *Gulliver's Travels*, p. 57.
11. Craik, *Life of Swift*, 1882, pp. 145, 184
12. Craik, p. 259; *Correspondence*, ii. 22.
13. Craik, p, 114; *Correspondence*, i. 73, 152, ii. 212; Johnson, *Lives of the Poets*, ed. Hill, iii. 10, 68.
14. Poems, ed. W. E. Browning, 1910, ii. 150; Orrey's *Remarks*, 48, *Correspondence*, ii. 212; *Works*, v. 463.
15. *Gulliver's Travels*, pp. 43, 69, 72, 73.
16. *Works*, ii. 294; x. 29.
17. *Poems*, ii. 148, 156.
18. *Wentworth Papers*, p. 385.
19. Mahon, *History of England*, i. 82.
20. Burnet, *History of My Own Time*, ii. 95, ed. 1833.
21. Torrens, *History of Cabinets*, 1894. i. 116–18; Tindal, iv, 487.
22. *Correspondence*, iii. 24–32, 40, 88, 109, 170.
23. Sichel, *Life of Bolingbroke*, 1901, i, 523.
24. *Correspondence*, iii. 267.

25. Ibid. iii. 277.
26. Ibid. iii. 277, 293.
27. *Correspondence*, ii, 265.
28. *Works*, vii. 215.
29. *Gulliver's Travels*, pp. 185, 195.
30. *Correspondence*, iv. 331.
31. Ibid. iv. 34.
32. Ibid. v. 64.
33. *Poems*, i. 259.

HENRY IV, PART 1
(WILLIAM SHAKESPEARE)

"The Grotesque in *Henry IV, Part 1*"
by John Kerr,
Saint Mary's University of Minnesota

A testament to the largeness of Shakespeare's creation of Jack Falstaff is that he looms larger in our cultural memory than any of the other characters in *Henry IV, Part 1*. In Shakespeare's own time, Falstaff was a primary attraction for playgoers. Scholars since Shakespeare's day have repeatedly trumpeted Falstaff as the greatest achievement of the play, and often as the greatest comic character in the history of drama.

Moreover, Falstaff has come to stand as a key figure in the history of the literary grotesque. The grotesque involves primarily an excessive or distorted experience of the body. Falstaff—the gluttonous, alcoholic, thieving wit—embodies this concept in many ways. His corpulence, mentioned repeatedly throughout *Henry IV, Part 1*, visibly depicts his embracing of the delights of the flesh. Falstaff prominently displays the excesses of the festive life. But the grotesque also incorporates the ugly and the bizarre, the diseased and horrific processes of decay and death. Falstaff avoids acknowledgment of his own mortality, and so these darker elements of the grotesque remain mostly on the edge of his consciousness, although they come fully into the audience's awareness.

More broadly, the grotesque functions as an avenue for social critique. In *Henry IV, Part 1*, Falstaff's earthiness allows the audience a wider slice of life than would be possible if the play remained centered on the King and his court. From the heady affairs of state that plague Henry IV at his palace, we descend into an atmosphere of wine, sex, and crime at the tavern. Shakespeare accents the distance between these higher and lower social strata through the linguistic medium he chooses for each. At the palace and on the battlefield, the nobles speak in verse; in the tavern and on the highway (during a robbery) the characters speak in prose. On this social level, the grotesque operates counter-culturally in two ways. First, in his rejection of noble duty, Falstaff raises questions about high-flown moral values. He remains suspicious about abstractions such as "honor," which depend in large part upon a denial of the body's value. Second, the audience witnesses the characters with supposedly "higher" values acting with no greater moral compass than Falstaff possesses. The King himself has usurped the throne; Henry Hotspur, the admirably passionate military leader, dies as a traitor. Ultimately, the petty intrigues at the lower end of society serve to mirror the deeper and more insidious intrigues of the court.

To get a fuller sense of the literary grotesque in *Henry IV, Part 1*, a quick sketch of the medieval currents that fed into Shakespeare's time will be helpful. In the church-regulated culture of the Christian Middle Ages, the soul officially took priority over the body. The body was corrupt and would go to the grave, whereas the soul would live on. In many ways, people were asked to hide or deny impulses of the flesh. At the same time, a focus on the shortcomings of the body could lead to graphic displays of the bizarre and horrific. For instance, gargoyles and other creatures combining human and bestial forms haunted cathedrals. Similarly, *mementi mori*—images intended to remind observers of death—included bodies in various stages of decay. While such objects carried a message for the soul's salvation, they could create fascination regarding the bodily grotesque for its own sake.

Medieval drama provided another outlet for the grotesque. Reaching the largely illiterate audience at a public performance was made easier by bursts of slapstick, obscene language, and an occasional tirade against dominating wives or the current political leadership. Moreover, characters such as "Vice" that depicted immoral tendencies helped plays incorporate the less acceptable (but certainly real) behaviors of the culture.

More directly challenging Christian morality, ribald songs and stories embraced the desire to eat, drink, and be merry. The Goliards, for instance, praised the merits of drink and sex in songs like the following:

> If a boy and a girl hang out together in the cellar,
> the union is a happy one. With love arising,
> and with boredom banished from their midst,
> there begins an inexpressible game with limbs, shoulders and
>   lips.
> (translation mine)

Fabliaux—brief comic tales—provided another venue for the sexual and bodily vulgar. "The Miller's Tale," from Geoffrey Chaucer's *Canterbury Tales,* stands as a wonderful late-medieval example of this tradition. In the tale's ridiculously funny climax, an old man is cheated on by his wife and her lover; a second lover serenading through the window receives a fart in the face (big as a thunderstroke); the first lover gets branded on the buttocks with a red hot tool; and the old husband cracks his head as he falls from the ceiling in a ludicrous but complex parody of the Judaeo-Christian Flood story.

Though necessarily brief, this glimpse of the medieval grotesque emphasizes some important trends that carried into Shakespeare's more refined theatrical environment. First, the grotesque contains elements of what we might now call "gross" (such as bodily elimina-tions and noises) as well as bodily excesses and deficiencies (whether in appearance or desire). Second, while most literally tied to the body, the grotesque can serve more broadly to undermine our attempts to reduce the world to a strict sense of order. (Shakespeare frequently portrays the bodily monstrous as a threat to civil order, as with Caliban in *The Tempest* and Richard in *Richard III.* On a contemporary note, one might think of rock musicians who adorn and distort their bodies or clothing as a badge of resistance to the status quo.) Third, art provides a medium not only for *capturing* the countercultural energy of the grotesque, but also for *displaying* that vitality in a public forum. Dramatic performance holds a special status in this regard, especially for a largely illiterate public; theatre becomes a communal venue for observing and living out those elements which social norms may attempt to suppress.

As suggested earlier, Falstaff anchors the grotesque in *Henry IV,*
Part 1, but he does so in a restricted way: while he embraces the body,
he rejects the body's destiny. He has been likened to the pleasure-
seeking, wine-guzzling Roman god Silenus. He is all life force and
holiday. When Falstaff opens his performance by asking the time of
day, Prince Henry's response sets the tone for the course of the play:

> Thou art so fat-witted, with drinking of old sack and unbuttoning
> thee after supper and sleeping upon benches after noon,
> that thou hast forgotten to demand that truly which thou
> wouldst truly know. What a devil hast thou to do with the
> time of the day? Unless hours were cups of sack and minutes
> capons and clocks the tongues of bawds and dials the signs of
> leaping-houses and the blessed sun himself a fair hot wench in
> flame-colored taffeta, I see no reason why thou shouldst be so
> superfluous to demand the time of the day. (1.2.2-11)

This portrayal of Falstaff's indulgence in the flesh will be
confirmed throughout the remainder of *Henry IV, Part 1*. While
hiding from the sheriff in Act 2, Falstaff falls asleep behind a
tapestry in the tavern. Henry has him searched, and Peto pulls from
his pocket the following bill:

> Item, A capon,. . 2s. 2d.
> Item, Sauce,. . . 4d.
> Item, Sack, two gallons, 5s. 8d.
> Item, Anchovies and sack after supper, 2s. 6d.
> Item, Bread, ob. (2.4.509-13)

The barroom banter always returns to Falstaff's large belly. Henry
refers to his hefty senior as a "fat-kidneyed rascal" (2.2.5), "fat-guts"
(2.2.29), "clay-brained guts . . . whoreson, obscene, grease tallow-catch"
(2.4.215-17), "a sanguine coward . . . bed-presser . . . horseback-breaker
. . . huge hill of flesh" (2.4.229-31). This carnally indulgent sensibility
bespeaks a holiday sensibility. Indeed, unless we include drinking and
trading insults, Falstaff performs no real action in the early scenes
other than robbing a group of pilgrims. Even here, he complains about
having to forego his horse and travel on foot: "Eight yards of uneven
ground is threescore and ten miles afoot with me" (2.4.23-4).

When, for a gag, Henry and Poins disguise themselves and steal from Falstaff what he has taken from the travelers, Falstaff runs away without putting up a fight. Later in the tavern, in one of the play's most famous scenes, Falstaff retells the events (drinking all the while) in such a way as to suggest that he bravely fought off the attackers, first claiming that he held off two men, then four, and so on up to eleven (as with his diet, his lies are excessive). When Henry reveals the truth, Falstaff has a response ready at hand: he really knew that it was Henry, and did not attack him out of instinct:

> Why, hear you, my masters: was it for me to kill the heir-
> apparent? should I turn upon the true prince? why, thou
> knowest I am as valiant as Hercules: but beware instinct; the
> lion will not touch the true prince. Instinct is a great matter; I
> was now a coward on instinct. (2.4.254-58)

With a few biting jabs, Henry lets Falstaff off the hook, as the audience is likely to, for the shortcomings are essentially harmless, and there is something admirable in Falstaff's quick invention to suit the circumstances. For the time being, Old Jack remains a pleasant and amusing fool in comic circumstances. He brings forth the festive side of the bodily grotesque, but the darker forces remain at bay.

Meanwhile, in scenes that alternate with these comic ones, sobering trouble comes to a head on the political landscape. Harry Percy (Hotspur), angry that King Henry IV has imprisoned his uncle, refuses to turn over prisoners of war that rightfully belong to the king. Some of the king's leading nobles join forces with Hotspur, as does the Welsh leader Owen Glendower. In contrast with Falstaff's avoidance of responsibility, this upper-class milieu rages internally to establish order. At the same time, whereas Falstaff blots out any recognition of his mortality, the nobles frankly confront the likelihood of death in battle. As audience, we get a glimpse of the horrific aspects of the bodily grotesque even in the opening mention of war's carnage. Relaying news about losses against the Welsh, Westmoreland reports to Henry IV not merely the death, but also the mutilation of the thousand fallen bodies:

> Upon whose dead corpse there was such misuse,
> Such beastly shameless transformation,

By those Welshwomen done as may not be
Without much shame retold or spoken of. (1.1.43-6)

The world of the court recognizes what Falstaff resists: the body will come to devastation. Conversely, Falstaff in his pursuit of pleasure sees through the illusion of grandeur that attends the nobles' willingness to die for their cause.

Hotspur in particular gains a tragic perspective on the bodily grotesque in the play's finale. Mortally wounded in battle by Prince Henry, he desperately laments the loss of his glory as he passes from this world:

> [Hotspur:] O, Harry, thou hast robb'd me of my youth!
> I better brook the loss of brittle life
> Than those proud titles thou hast won of me;
> They wound my thoughts worse than sword my flesh:
> But thought's the slave of life, and life time's fool;
> And time, that takes survey of all the world,
> Must have a stop. O, I could prophesy,
> But that the earthy and cold hand of death
> Lies on my tongue: no, Percy, thou art dust
> And food for—
> [Henry:] For worms, brave Percy. (5.4.76-86)

All the drive and spark in the fiery Hotspur has been put out. Despite his privileged social status, he too returns to dust, his corpse serving as nourishment for the lowliest of creatures. The terrible beauty of Hotspur's ambition gives way to recognition—in an incomplete final gasp—of the horror of the flesh. The attempt to control England's history fails; Hotspur ironically fails to write even his own story's ending.

Rather than dancing on the treasonous Hotspur's not so proverbial grave, Prince Henry proceeds with a generous eulogy:

> Fare thee well, great heart!
> Ill-weaved ambition, how much art thou shrunk!
> When that this body did contain a spirit,
> A kingdom for it was too small a bound;
> But now two paces of the vilest earth

Is room enough: this earth that bears thee dead
Bears not alive so stout a gentleman.
If thou wert sensible of courtesy,
I should not make so dear a show of zeal:
But let my favors hide thy mangled face;
And, even in thy behalf, I'll thank myself
For doing these fair rites of tenderness.
Adieu, and take thy praise with thee to heaven!
Thy ignominy sleep with thee in the grave,
But not remember'd in thy epitaph! (5.4.86-100)

Henry initially confirms Hotspur's realization of the bodily grotesque. The largeness of Hotspur's ambition can now be contained in "two paces of the vilest earth." In the end, though, Henry upholds the Christian distinction between body and soul: he asks that Hotspur's ambition die with the body and his honor rise with his sprit to heaven. Thus, while Hotspur has come to a tragic understanding of the bodily in its full impact, Henry adopts the value system that claims to transcend the body.

This body/soul dichotomy continues as Henry's eye next lights on what he takes to be Falstaff's dead body (Falstaff, echoing his cowardly behavior during the robbery in Act 2, actually fakes his death to avoid being killed in battle). In contrast with his parting words to Hotspur, here Henry offers no hint of an afterlife. Rather, Falstaff's large corpus signifies the meager fate of a life devoted to the body:

What, old acquaintance! could not all this flesh
Keep in a little life? Poor Jack, farewell!
I could have better spared a better man:
O, I should have a heavy miss of thee,
If I were much in love with vanity!
Death hath not struck so fat a deer to-day,
Though many dearer, in this bloody fray.
Embowell'd will I see thee by and by:
Till then in blood by noble Percy lie. (5.4.101-109)

The contrast with Hotspur could not be clearer. There are many dead "dearer" than Falstaff; there are none alive "more stout" than

Hotspur. Harry proclaims no legacy for Falstaff. His old friend has become a mere mound of flesh, and horrifically so: he will be "Embowell'd," and in the meantime lie "in blood."

We see in Henry's valediction to Hotspur and his dismissal of Falstaff a choice between different visions of reality. Henry has been aware of this divide, and of the path he will choose, from the beginning of the play. In Act 1, Scene 2, Henry reveals his intention to move out of obscurity and shine as the true heir to the throne:

> Yet herein will I imitate the sun,
> Who doth permit the base contagious clouds
> To smother up his beauty from the world,
> That, when he please again to be himself,
> Being wanted, he may be more wonder'd at,
> By breaking through the foul and ugly mists
> Of vapors that did seem to strangle him. (1.2.185-191)

From the outset, Henry has been joining the ranks of the day world, the realm of duty and order. Falstaff, on the other hand, enlists himself in the troops of night:

> Marry, then, sweet wag, when thou art king, let not us that are
> squires of the night's body be called thieves of the day's beauty:
> let us be Diana's foresters, gentlemen of the shade, minions of
> the moon; and let men say we be men of good government,
> being governed, as the sea is, by our noble and chaste mistress
> the moon, under whose countenance we steal. (1.2.2-11)

The reference to the moon's governance here is significant, for in Shakespeare's day the moon was linked with the never-ending turns of Fortune, as Henry's response to Falstaff makes clear: "Thou sayest well, and it holds well too; for the fortune of us that are the moon's men doth ebb and flow like the sea, being governed, as the sea is, by the moon" (1.2.28-30). In opposition to the solidity that the royal political structure strives to enforce, the tides of the ocean shift constantly, reflecting the unceasing metamorphosis of the human condition.

This destabilization of reality extends beyond events themselves to the level of our very perceptions. The nighttime provides cover for illusion and deception. Falstaff's men disguise themselves to commit the theft, Henry and Poins disguise themselves to rob Falstaff, and all the while Henry has failed to reveal to the others his true intentions regarding his role as future king. In particular, Falstaff's labeling of his band as "foresters" under Diana's reign opens up some reality-questioning, for the forest is a place where things may appear one way but be another. Shakespeare's comedy *A Midsummer Night's Dream* provides a good context for the unsettling experience of the forest. The four lovers in that play enter the woods to escape the legal restrictions of Athens; they wind up falling in and out of love with each other; the waxing and waning of their affections build to a pitch of hate and threatened violence that includes abandonment, fighting, murder, and rape. What appears to be reality in Athens (civilization, "gentlemanly" conduct, monogamous marriage, friendship) gives way to other possibilities (disorder, open desire for premarital sex and forced violation, pursuit of additional sexual partners, duels between sisterly companions). The night-shrouded forest comes to symbolize the chaotic forces that perpetually gnaw at the margins of our rational attempts to create meaning.

In Shakespeare's plays, the logic of the day is always subsumed by the night, at least for a time. We witness the surrounding dark in the horror of tragedy, as when Othello prepares to murder his innocent wife Desdemona, first snuffing out the candle, then her life: "Put out the light, and then put out the light" (*Othello* 5.2.7). Macbeth utters a similar sentiment when he hears the news of his wife's death: "all our yesterdays have lighted fools / The way to dusty death. Out, out, brief candle!" (*Macbeth* 5.22-3). These are men become monstrous. Their grotesquerie provides a window into the devouring night of death whose ravenous belly Romeo, too, acknowledges as he enters the mausoleum to join Juliet:

> Thou detestable maw, thou womb of death,
> Gorged with the dearest morsel of the earth,
> Thus I enforce thy rotten jaws to open,
> And, in despite, I'll cram thee with more food! (5.3.45-8)

Night and death hover close at hand in the comedies as well. In *Much Ado About Nothing*, Leander is deceived at night into thinking his beloved has had sex with another man; his ensuing rejection of his fiancée leads her to undergo a pseudo-death, much like Juliet's.

And, as epigrammatic of Shakespeare's perception of the human position in the universe, we may take the words of Lysander in *A Midsummer Night's Dream*. First listing the forces that keep lovers apart, Lysander goes on to suggest that even the rare union of true lovers will at best be

> Swift as a shadow, short as any dream;
> Brief as the lightning in the collied night,
> That, in a spleen, unfolds both heaven and earth,
> And ere a man hath power to say 'Behold!'
> The jaws of darkness do devour it up. (1.1.144-48)

Love, life—our very awareness of what is good and beautiful—is but a brief flash; we do not have time to speak about it properly ("Behold!") before the enveloping "jaws of darkness" consume it.

Thus, while Falstaff's self-perception remains limited, he becomes for the audience a remarkable figure of the grotesque. Not in love with the illusions that our daytime consciousness insists to be reality, he plays with life. He does not let himself be seduced into thinking war amounts to more than a collision of bodies. As he and Henry survey the dismal troops over which Falstaff has charge in the concluding battle, Falstaff assures Henry that they are "good enough to toss; food for powder, food for powder; they'll fill a pit as well as better" (4.2.62-64). He resists the temptation of a higher moral code that would belittle the experience of the flesh:

> Can honor set to a leg? no: or an arm? no: or take away the
> grief of a wound? no. Honor hath no skill in surgery, then? no.
> What is honor? a word. What is in that word honor? What is
> that honor? air. (5.1.131-34)

In his grotesque attachment to carnal reality, Falstaff offers a critique of our abstract values. Though he tiptoes around acceptance of his own mortality, he always brings us back to the body as flesh, indeed as flesh that will be food in turn. He refers to people as "bacons" (2.2.82), "toasts-and-butter" (4.2.20), and "food for powder" (4.2.63). Imagining an unintended encounter with Hotspur, Falstaff says to himself, "let him make a carbonado [steak] of me" (5.3.57).

While the tragic breathes over the corpses of the battlefield, the comic winks at us and scuttles out of the scene. Unlike Juliet, Falstaff rises from his artificial death. To be sure, he will have his day of reckoning (a pathetic one in *Henry V*), but for now he has accomplished his goal of living and enjoying another day: "I like not such grinning honor as Sir Walter hath: give me life: which if I can save, so; if not, honor comes unlooked for, and there's an end" (5.3.57-60). Falstaff is dishonorable, ridiculous, even pathetic; but he is alive. Hotspur, meanwhile, lies with a "mangled face" (not even "grinning honor"), a premature death in a treacherous cause.

Shakespeare builds us to the highest of heights, marveling at the human ability to construct profound worlds of relationship, meaning, and art. But, over and over, he reminds us that we build our reality out of "airy" words. When Romeo prepares for death in *Romeo and Juliet*, he says goodbye to his lips—"the doors of breath"—that allowed him to co-create his love with Juliet. With this same breath, Romeo also helped to make civil brawls through nothing more than "an airy word." Shakespeare presents us with the body's full scope: the same powers that allow creation lead to destruction. And he always brings us back to the possibility that, when the flesh fails, all else may fail too. The jaws of darkness will devour us and then, like the upper class Hotspur, like the slumming Falstaff, like the waiter in the tavern, we will be food for worms.

INFERNO
(DANTE ALIGHIERI)

"Grotesque Renaissance,"
by John Ruskin,
in *The Stones of Venice, Volume the Third:*
The Fall (1880)

INTRODUCTION

In this excerpt from *Stones of Venice*, John Ruskin, an influential nineteenth-century art critic, discusses the nature of the grotesque, citing Dante's *Inferno* as one of the "most perfect portraitures of fiendish nature." Noting the importance of representing the "degradation of the body" when depicting vice, Ruskin attributes the success of Dante's grotesque portrayals to his "mingling of extreme horror . . . with ludicrous actions and images." Following his discussion of Dante, Ruskin goes on to explore the grotesque's relation to beauty, claiming that if the same objects rendered by art as grotesque were perceived in their "true light," they would cease to disturb and become "altogether sublime." For Ruskin, "the fallen human soul," limited in its ability to grasp an infinite world, distorts the objects of its contemplation the farther it reaches. Though highly speculative, Ruskin's remarks provide insight into Dante's project and how his use of the grotesque

---

Ruskin, John. "Grotesque Renaissance." *The Stones of Venice, Volume the Third: The Fall*. New York: John Wiley & Sons, 1880: 112–65.

may be related to the enormity of his vision, a vision so remote
from and incongruous with lived experience.

∞

[. . . Nothing] is so refreshing to the vulgar mind as some exercise of
[satire or humor], more especially on the failings of their superiors;
and that, wherever the lower orders are allowed to express themselves
freely, we shall find humor, more or less caustic, becoming a principal
feature in their work. The classical and Renaissance manufacturers
of modern times having silenced the independent language of the
operative, his humor and satire pass away in the word-wit which has
of late become the especial study of the group of authors headed by
Charles Dickens; all this power was formerly thrown into noble art,
and became permanently expressed in the sculptures of the cathedral.
It was never thought that there was anything discordant or improper
in such a position: for the builders evidently felt very deeply a truth
of which, in modern times, we are less cognizant; that folly and sin
are, to a certain extent, synonymous, and that it would be well for
mankind in general, if all could be made to feel that wickedness is as
contemptible as it is hateful. So that the vices were permitted to be
represented under the most ridiculous forms, and all the coarsest wit
of the workman to be exhausted in completing the degradation of the
creatures supposed to be subjected to them.

Nor were even the supernatural powers of evil exempt from this
species of satire. For with whatever hatred or horror the evil angels
were regarded, it was one of the conditions of Christianity that they
should also be looked upon as vanquished; and this not merely in their
great combat with the King of Saints, but in daily and hourly combats
with the weakest of His servants. In proportion to the narrowness
of the powers of abstract conception in the workman, the nobleness
of the idea of spiritual nature diminished, and the traditions of the
encounters of men with fiends in daily temptations were imagined
with less terrific circumstances, until the agencies which in such
warfare were almost always represented as vanquished with disgrace,
became, at last, as much the objects of contempt as of terror.

The superstitions which represented the devil as assuming various
contemptible forms of disguises in order to accomplish his purposes
aided this gradual degradation of conception, and directed the study

of the workman to the most strange and ugly conditions of animal form, until at last, even in the most serious subjects, the fiends are oftener ludicrous than terrible. Nor, indeed, is this altogether avoidable, for it is not possible to express intense wickedness without some condition of degradation. Malice, subtlety, and pride, in their extreme, cannot be written upon noble forms; and I am aware of no effort to represent the Satanic mind in the angelic form, which has succeeded in painting. Milton succeeds only because he separately describes the movements of the mind, and therefore leaves himself at liberty to make the form heroic; but that form is never distinct enough to be painted. Dante, who will not leave even external forms obscure, degrades them before he can feel them to be demoniacal; so also John Bunyan: both of them, I think, having firmer faith than Milton's in their own creations, and deeper insight into the nature of sin. Milton makes his fiends too noble and misses the foulness, inconstancy, and fury of wickedness. His Satan possesses some virtues, not the less virtues for being applied to evil purpose. Courage, resolution, patience, deliberation in council, this latter being eminently a wise and holy character, as opposed to the "Insania" of excessive sin: and all this, if not a shallow and false, is a smooth and artistical, conception. On the other hand, I have always felt that there was a peculiar grandeur in the indescribable, ungovernable fury of Dante's fiends, ever shortening its own powers, and disappointing its own purposes; the deaf, blind, speechless, unspeakable rage, fierce as the lightning, but erring from its mark or turning senselessly against itself, and still further debased by foulness of form and action. Something is indeed to be allowed for the rude feelings of the time, but I believe all such men as Dante are sent into the world at the time when they can do their work best; and that, it being appointed for him to give to mankind the most vigorous realization possible both of Hell and Heaven, he was born both in the country and at the time which furnished the most stern opposition of Horror and Beauty, and permitted it to be written in the clearest terms. And, therefore, though there are passages in the *Inferno* which it would be impossible for any poet now to write, I look upon it as all the more perfect for them. For there can be no question but that one characteristic of excessive vice is indecency, a general baseness in its thoughts and acts concerning the body,[1] and that the full portraiture of it cannot be given without marking, and that in the strongest lines, this tendency to corporeal degradation; which, in the time of Dante, could be done frankly, but cannot now. And, therefore, I think the twenty-first and twenty-second books of the *Inferno* the most perfect portraitures of fiendish nature which we possess; and at the same time, in their mingling of the extreme of horror (for it seems to me that the silent swiftness of the first demon, "con l' ali aperte e sovra i pie leggier," cannot be surpassed in dreadfulness) with ludicrous actions and images, they present the most perfect instances with which I am acquainted of the terrible grotesque. But the whole of the *Inferno* is full of this grotesque, as well as the *Faerie Queen*; and these two poems, together with the works of Albert Durer, will enable the reader to study it in its noblest forms, without reference to Gothic cathedrals. [. . .]

The reader is always to keep in mind that if the objects of horror, in which the terrible grotesque finds its materials, were contemplated in their true light, and with the entire energy of the soul, they would cease to be grotesque, and become altogether sublime; and that therefore it is some shortening of the power, or the will, of contemplation, and some consequent distortion of the terrible image in which the grotesqueness consists. Now this distortion takes place [. . .] in three ways: either through apathy, satire, or ungovernableness of imagination. It is this last cause of the grotesque which we have finally to consider; namely, the error and wildness of the mental impressions, caused by fear operating upon strong powers of imagination, or by the failure of the human faculties in the endeavor to grasp the highest truths.

The grotesque which comes to all men in a disturbed dream is the most intelligible example of this kind, but also the most ignoble; the imagination, in this instance, being entirely deprived of all aid from reason, and incapable of self government. I believe, however, that the noblest forms of imaginative power are also in some sort ungovernable and have in them something of the character of dreams; so that the vision, of whatever kind, comes uncalled, and will not submit itself to the seer, but conquers him, and forces him to speak as a prophet, having no power over his words or thoughts. Only, if the whole man be trained perfectly, and his mind calm, consistent and powerful, the vision which comes to him is seen as in a perfect mirror, serenely, and in consistence with the rational powers; but if the mind be imperfect and ill trained, the vision is seen as in a broken mirror, with strange distortions and discrepancies, all the passions of the heart breathing upon it in cross ripples, till hardly a trace of it remains unbroken. So that, strictly speaking, the imagination is never governed; it is always the ruling and Divine power: and the rest of the man is to it only as an instrument which it sounds, or a tablet on which it writes; clearly and sublimely if the wax be smooth and the strings true, grotesquely and wildly if they are stained and broken. And thus the *Iliad*, the *Inferno*, the *Pilgrim's Progress*, the *Faerie Queen*, are all of them true dreams; only the sleep of the men to whom they came was the deep, living sleep which God sends, with a sacredness in it, as of death, the revealer of secrets.

Now, observe in this matter, carefully, the difference between a dim mirror and a distorted one; and do not blame me for pressing the analogy too far, for it will enable me to explain my meaning every way more clearly. Most men's minds are dim mirrors, in which all truth is seen, as St. Paul tells us, darkly: this is the fault most common and most fatal; dullness of the heart and mistiness of sight, increasing to utter hardness and blindness; Satan breathing upon the glass, so that if we do not sweep the mist laboriously away, it will take no image. But, even so far as we are able to do this, we have still the distortion to fear, yet not to the same extent, for we can in some sort allow for the distortion of an image, if only we can see it clearly. And the fallen human soul, at its best, must be as a diminishing glass, and that a broken one, to the mighty truths of the universe round it; and the wider the scope of its glance, and the vaster the truths into which it obtains an insight, the more fantastic their distortion is likely to be, as the winds and vapors trouble the field of the telescope most when it reaches farthest.

Note

1. Let the reader examine, with special reference to this subject, the general character of the language of Iago.

KING LEAR
(WILLIAM SHAKESPEARE)

"*King Lear* and the Comedy of the Grotesque"
by G. Wilson Knight,
in *Twentieth Century Interpretations of King Lear:*
A Collection of Critical Essays, (1978)

INTRODUCTION

"The comic and the tragic," according to G. Wilson Knight, "rest both on the idea of incompatibilities, and are also, themselves, mutually exclusive: therefore to mingle them is to add to the meaning of each; for the result is then but a new sublime incongruity." Informed by this conception of the comic and the tragic, Knight discusses the comic aspects of *King Lear*, noting, along with the Fool, "humorous potentialities in the most heart-wrenching of incidents." Such a reading, for Knight, allows us to appreciate the importance of absurdity in our perception of the tragic. Knight claims that the grotesque incidents in *King Lear* incite a profoundly conflicted response in readers, one in which we are pulled between the sublime

---

Knight, G. Wilson "*King Lear* and the Comedy of the Grotesque." *Twentieth Century Interpretations of King Lear: A Collection of Critical Essays*. Ed. Janet Adelman. Englewood Cliffs, NJ: Prentice Hall, 1978. p. 34–49. First published as a chapter of Knight's book (*The Wheel of Fire*. London: Methuen & Co., 1949. p.160–76).

and the ridiculous, suffering and joy, Lear's madness and the
Fool's penetrating laughter.

෧෴෧

It may appear strange to search for any sort of comedy as a primary
theme in a play whose abiding gloom is so heavy, whose reading of
human destiny and human actions so starkly tragic. Yet it is an error
of aesthetic judgement to regard humour as essentially trivial. Though
its impact usually appears vastly different from that of tragedy, yet
there is a humour that treads the brink of tears, and tragedy which
needs but an infinitesimal shift of perspective to disclose the varied
riches of comedy. Humour is an evanescent thing, even more difficult
of analysis and intellectual location than tragedy. To the coarse mind
lacking sympathy an incident may seem comic which to the richer
understanding is pitiful and tragic. So, too, one series of facts can be
treated by the artist as either comic or tragic, lending itself equiva-
lently to both. Sometimes a great artist may achieve significant effects
by a criss-cross of tears and laughter. Chekhov does this, especially
in his plays. A shifting flash of comedy across the pain of the purely
tragic both increases the tension and suggests, vaguely, a resolution
and a purification. The comic and the tragic rest both on the idea of
incompatibilities, and are also, themselves, mutually exclusive: therefore to mingle them is to add to the meaning of each; for the result is
then but a new sublime incongruity.

    King Lear is roughly analogous to Chekhov where *Macbeth* is
analogous to Dostoievsky. The wonder of Shakespearian tragedy is
ever a mystery—a vague, yet powerful, tangible, presence; an interlocking of the mind with a profound meaning, a disclosure to the
inward eye of vistas undreamed, and fitfully understood. *King Lear*
is great in the abundance and richness of human delineation, in the
level focus of creation that builds a massive oneness, in fact, a universe,
of single quality from a multiplicity of differentiated units; and in a
positive and purposeful working out of a purgatorial philosophy. But
it is still greater in the perfect fusion of psychological realism with
the daring flights of a fantastic imagination. The heart of a Shakespearian tragedy is centered in the imaginative, in the unknown; and
in *King Lear*, where we touch the unknown, we touch the fantastic.
The peculiar dualism at the root of this play which wrenches and splits

the mind by a sight of incongruities displays in turn realities absurd, hideous, pitiful. This incongruity is Lear's madness; it is also the demonic laughter that echoes in the *Lear* universe. In pure tragedy the dualism of experience is continually being dissolved in the masterful beauty of passion, merged in the sunset of emotion. But in comedy it is not so softly resolved—incompatibilities stand out till the sudden relief of laughter or its equivalent of humour: therefore incongruity is the especial mark of comedy. Now in *King Lear* there is a dualism continually crying in vain to be resolved either by tragedy or comedy. Thence arises its peculiar tension of pain: and the course of the action often comes as near to the resolution of comedy as to that of tragedy. So I shall notice here the imaginative core of the play, and, excluding much of the logic of the plot from immediate attention, analyse the fantastic comedy of *King Lear*.

From the start, the situation has a comic aspect. It has been observed that Lear has, so to speak, staged an interlude, with himself as chief actor, in which he grasps expressions of love to his heart, and resigns his sceptre to a chorus of acclamations. It is childish, foolish—but very human. So, too, is the result. Sincerity forbids play-acting, and Cordelia cannot subdue her instinct to any judgement advising tact rather than truth. The incident is profoundly comic and profoundly pathetic. It is, indeed, curious that so storm-furious a play as *King Lear* should have so trivial a domestic basis: it is the first of our many incongruities to be noticed. The absurdity of the old King's anger is clearly indicated by Kent:

> Kill thy physician, and the fee bestow
> Upon the foul disease. (I. i. 166)

The result is absurd. Lear's loving daughter Cordelia is struck from his heart's register, and he is shortly, old and grey-haired and a king, cutting a cruelly ridiculous figure before the cold sanity of his unloving elder daughters. Lear is selfish, self-centered. The images he creates of his three daughters' love are quite false, sentimentalized: he understands the nature of none of his children, and demanding an unreal and impossible love from all three, is disillusioned by each in turn. But, though sentimental, this love is not weak. It is powerful and firm-planted in his mind as a mountain rock embedded in earth. The tearing out of it is hideous, cataclysmic. A tremendous soul is, as it were, incongruously geared to a puerile intellect. Lear's senses prove his idealized love-figments false, his intellect snaps, and, as the loosened drive flings limp, the disconnected engine of madness spins free, and the ungeared revolutions of it are terrible, fantastic. This, then, is the basis of the play: greatness linked to puerility. Lear's instincts are themselves grand, heroic-noble even. His judgement is nothing. He understands neither himself nor his daughters:

> *Regan.* 'Tis the infirmity of his age: yet he hath ever but slenderly known himself.
> *Goneril.* The best and soundest of his time hath been but rash ... (I. i. 296)

Lear starts his own tragedy by a foolish misjudgement. Lear's fault is a fault of the mind, a mind unwarrantably, because selfishly, foolish. And he knows it:

> O Lear, Lear, Lear!
> Beat at this gate that let thy folly in,
> And thy dear judgement out! (I. iv. 294)

His purgatory is to be a purgatory of the mind, of madness. Lear has trained himself to think he cannot be wrong: he finds he is wrong. He has fed his heart on sentimental knowledge of his children's love: he finds their love is not sentimental. There is now a gaping dualism in his mind, drawn asunder by incongruities, and he endures madness. So the meaning of the play is embodied continually into a fantastic incongruity, which is implicit in the beginning—in the very act of Lear's renunciation, retaining the 'title and addition' of King, yet giving over a king's authority to his children. As he becomes torturingly aware of the truth, incongruity masters his mind, and fantastic madness ensues; and this peculiar fact of the Lear-theme is reflected in the *Lear* universe:

> *Gloucester.* These late eclipses in the sun and moon portend no good to us: though the wisdom of nature can reason it thus and thus, yet nature finds itself scourged by the sequent effects: love cools, friendship falls off, brothers divide: in

cities, mutinies; in countries, discord; in palaces, treason; and the bond cracked 'twixt son and father. This villain of mine comes under the prediction; there's son against father: the King falls from bias of nature; there's father against child. We have seen the best of our time: machinations, hollowness, treachery, and all ruinous disorders, follow us disquietly to our graves. (I. ii. 115)

Gloucester's words hint a universal incongruity here: the fantastic incongruity of parent and child opposed. And it will be most helpful later to notice the Gloucester-theme in relation to that of Lear.

From the first signs of Goneril's cruelty, the Fool is used as a chorus, pointing us to the absurdity of the situation. He is indeed an admirable chorus, increasing our pain by his emphasis on a humour which yet will not serve to merge the incompatible in a unity of laughter. He is not all wrong when he treats the situation as matter for a joke. Much here that is always regarded as essentially pathetic is not far from comedy. For instance, consider Lear's words:

> I will have such revenges on you both
> That all the world shall—I will do such things—
> What they are, yet I know not; but they shall be
> The terrors of the earth. (II. iv. 282)

What could be more painfully incongruous, spoken, as it is, by an old man, a king, to his daughter? It is not far from the ridiculous. The very thought seems a sacrilegious cruelty, I know: but ridicule is generally cruel. The speeches of Lear often come near comedy. Again, notice the abrupt contrast in his words:

> But yet thou art my flesh, my blood, my daughter;
> Or rather a disease that's in my flesh,
> Which I must needs call mine: thou art a boil,
> A plague-sore, an embossed carbuncle,
> In my corrupted blood. But I'll not chide thee ... (II. iv. 224)

This is not comedy, nor humour. But it is exactly the stuff of which humour is made. Lear is mentally a child; in passion a titan. The absurdity of his every act at the beginning of his tragedy is contrasted with the dynamic fury which intermittently bursts out, flickers—then flames and finally gives us those grand apostrophes lifted from man's stage of earth to heaven's rain and fire and thunder:

> Blow, winds, and crack your cheeks! rage! blow!
> You cataracts and hurricanoes, spout
> Till you have drench'd our steeples, drown'd the cocks! (III. ii. 1)

Two speeches of this passionate and unrestrained volume of Promethean curses are followed by:

> No, I will be the pattern of all patience;
> I will say nothing. (III. ii. 37)

Again we are in touch with potential comedy: a slight shift of perspective, and the incident is rich with humour. A sense of self-directed humour would have saved Lear. It is a quality he absolutely lacks.

Herein lies the profound insight of the Fool: he sees the potentialities of comedy in Lear's behaviour. This old man, recently a king, and, if his speeches are fair samples, more than a little of a tyrant, now goes from daughter to daughter, furious because Goneril dares criticize his pet knights, kneeling down before Regan, performing, as she says, 'unsightly tricks' (II. iv. 159)—the situation is excruciatingly painful, and its painfulness is exactly of that quality which embarrasses in some forms of comedy. In the theatre, one is terrified lest some one laugh: yet, if Lear could laugh—if the Lears of the world could laugh at themselves—there would be no such tragedy. In the early scenes old age and dignity suffer, and seem to deserve, the punishments of childhood:

> Now, by my life,
> Old fools are babes again; and must be used
> With checks as flatteries. (I. iii. 19)

The situation is summed up by the Fool:

> *Lear.* When were you wont to be so full of songs, sirrah?
> *Fool.* I have used it, nuncle, ever since thou madest thy

daughters thy mother: for when thou gavest them the rod, and put'st down thine own breeches. . . . (I. iv. 186)

The height of indecency in suggestion, the height of incongruity. Lear is spiritually put to the ludicrous shame endured bodily by Kent in the stocks: and the absurd rant of Kent, and the unreasonable childish temper of Lear, both merit in some measure what they receive. Painful as it may sound, that is, provisionally, a truth we should realize. The Fool realizes it. He is, too, necessary. Here, where the plot turns on the diverging tugs of two assurances in the mind, it is natural that the action be accompanied by some symbol of humour, that mode which is built of unresolved incompatibilities. Lear's torment is a torment of this dualistic kind, since he scarcely believes his senses when his daughters resist him. He repeats the history of Troilus, who cannot understand the faithlessness of Cressida. In *Othello* and *Timon of Athens* the transition is swift from extreme love to revenge or hate. The movement of Lear's mind is less direct: like Troilus, he is suspended between two separate assurances. Therefore Pandarus, in the latter acts of *Troilus and Cressida*, plays a part similar to the Fool in *King Lear*: both attempt to heal the gaping wound of the mind's incongruous knowledge by the unifying, healing release of laughter. They make no attempt to divert, but rather to direct the hero's mind to the present incongruity. The Fool sees, or tries to see, the humorous potentialities in the most heart-wrenching of incidents:

> *Lear.* O me, my heart, my rising heart! but, down!
> *Fool.* Cry to it, nuncle, as the cockney did to the eels when she put 'em i' the paste alive; she knapped 'em o' the coxcombs with a stick, and cried 'Down, wantons, down!' 'Twas her brother that, in pure kindness to his horse, buttered his hay. (II. iv. 122)

Except for the last delightful touch—the antithesis of the other—that is a cruel, ugly sense of humour. It is the sinister humour at the heart of this play: we are continually aware of the humour of cruelty and the cruelty of humour. But the Fool's use of it is not aimless. If Lear could laugh he might yet save his reason.

But there is no relief. Outside, in the wild country, the storm grows more terrible:

> *Kent.* . . . Since I was man
> Such sheets of fire, such bursts of horrid thunder,
> Such groans of roaring wind and rain, I never
> Remember to have heard . . . (III. ii. 45)

Lear's mind keeps returning to the unreality, the impossibility of what has happened:

> Your old kind father, whose frank heart gave all—
> O, that way madness lies; let me shun that;
> No more of that. (III. iv. 20)

He is still self-centered; cannot understand that he has been anything but a perfect father; cannot understand his daughters' behaviour. It is

> as this mouth should tear this hand
> For lifting food to't . . . (III. iv. 15)

It is incongruous, impossible. There is no longer any 'rule in unity itself'.[1] Just as Lear's mind begins to fail, the Fool finds Edgar disguised as 'poor Tom'. Edgar now succeeds the Fool as the counterpart to the breaking sanity of Lear; and where the humour of the Fool made no contact with Lear's mind, the fantastic appearance and incoherent words of Edgar are immediately assimilated, as glasses correctly focused to the sight of oncoming madness. Edgar turns the balance of Lear's wavering mentality. His fantastic appearance and lunatic irrelevancies, with the storm outside, and the Fool still for occasional chorus, create a scene of wraithlike unreason, a vision of a world gone mad:

> . . . Bless thy five wits! Tom's a-cold—O, do de, do de, do de.
> Bless thee from whirlwinds, star-blasting, and taking! Do
> poor Tom some charity, whom the foul fiend vexes: there
> could I have him now—and there—and there again, and there.
> (III. iv. 57)

To Lear his words are easily explained. His daughters 'have brought him to this pass'. He cries:

> *Lear.* Is it the fashion that discarded fathers
> Should have thus little mercy on their flesh?
> Judicious punishment! 'twas this flesh begot
> Those pelican daughters.
> *Edgar.* Pillicock sat on Pillicock-hill:
> Halloo, halloo, loo, loo!
> *Fool.* This cold night will turn us all to fools and madmen. (III.
> iv. 71)

What shall we say of this exquisite movement? Is it comedy? Lear's profound unreason is capped by the blatant irrelevance of Edgar's couplet suggested by the word 'pelican'; then the two are swiftly all but unified, for us if not for Lear, in the healing balm of the Fool's conclusion. It is the process of humour, where two incompatibles are resolved in laughter. The Fool does this again. Lear again speaks a profound truth as the wild night and Edgar's fantastic impersonation grip his mind and dethrone his conventional sanity:

> *Lear.* Is man no more than this. Consider him well. Thou owest
> the worm no silk, the beast no hide, the sheep no wool, the cat
> no perfume. Ha! Here's three on's are sophisticated! Thou art
> the thing itself: unaccommodated man is no more but such a
> poor, bare, forked animal as thou art. Off, off, you lendings!
> come unbutton here. (*Tearing off his clothes.*)
> *Fool.* Prithee, nuncle, be contented; 'tis a naughty night to swim
> in. (III. iv. 105)

This is the furthest flight, not of tragedy, but of philosophic comedy. The autocratic and fiery-fierce old king, symbol of dignity, is confronted with the meanest of men: a naked lunatic beggar. In a flash of vision he attempts to become his opposite, to be naked, 'unso-phisticated'. And then the opposing forces which struck the light-ning-flash of vision tail off, resolved into a perfect unity by the Fool's laughter, reverberating, trickling, potent to heal in sanity the hideous unreason of this tempest-shaken night: 'tis a naughty night to swim in'. Again this is the process of humour: its flash of vision first bridges the positive and negative poles of the mind, unifying them, and then expresses itself in laughter.

This scene grows still more grotesque, fantastical, sinister. Gloucester enters, his torch flickering in the beating wind:

> *Fool*: . . . Look, here comes a walking fire.
> (*Enter* Gloucester, with a *torch*.)
> *Edgar*. This is the foul fiend Flibbertigibbet: he begins at curfew and walks till the first cock . . . (III. iv. 116)

Lear welcomes Edgar as his 'philosopher', since he embodies that philosophy of incongruity and the fantastically-absurd which is Lear's vision in madness. 'Noble philosopher', he says (III. iv. 176), and 'I will still keep with my philosopher' (III. iv. 180). The unresolved dualism that tormented Troilus and was given metaphysical expression by him (*Troilus and Cressida*, V. ii. 134–57) is here more perfectly bodied into the poetic symbol of poor Tom: and since Lear cannot hear the resolving laugh of foolery, his mind is focused only to the 'philosopher' mumbling of the foul fiend. Edgar thus serves to lure Lear on: we forget that he is dissimulating. Lear is the centre of our attention, and as the world shakes with tempest and unreason, we endure something of the shaking and the tempest of his mind. The absurd and fantastic reign supreme. Lear does not compass for more than a few speeches the 'noble anger' (II. iv. 279) for which he prayed, the anger of Timon. From the start he wavered between affection and disillusionment, love and hate. The heavens in truth 'fool' (II. iv. 278) him. He is the 'natural fool of fortune' (IV. vi. 196). Now his anger begins to be a lunatic thing, and when it rises to any sort of magnificent fury or power it is toppled over by the ridiculous capping of Edgar's irrelevancies:

> *Lear*. To have a thousand with red burning spits
> Come hissing in upon 'em—
> *Edgar*. The foul fiend bites my back. (III. vi. 17)

The mock trial is instituted. Lear's curses were for a short space terrible, majestic, less controlled and purposeful than Timon's but passionate and grand in their tempestuous fury. Now, in madness, he flashes on us the ridiculous basis of his tragedy in words which emphasize the indignity and incongruity of it, and make his madness something nearer the ridiculous than the terrible, something which moves our pity, but does not strike awe:

> Arraign her first; 'tis Goneril. I here take my oath before this honourable assembly, she kicked the poor king her father. (III. vi. 49)

This stroke of the absurd—so vastly different from the awe we experience in face of Timon's hate—is yet fundamental here. The core of the play is an absurdity, an indignity, an incongruity. In no tragedy of Shakespeare does incident and dialogue so recklessly and miraculously walk the tight-rope of our pity over the depths of bathos and absurdity.

This particular region of the terrible bordering on the fantastic and absurd is exactly the playground of madness. Now the setting of Lear's madness includes a sub-plot where these same elements are presented in stark nakedness, with no veiling subtleties. The Gloucester-theme is a certain indication of our vision and helps us to understand, and feel, the enduring agony of Lear. As usual, the first scene of this play strikes the dominant note. Gloucester jests at the bastardy of his son Edmund, remarking that, though he is ashamed to acknowledge him, 'there was good sport at his making' (I. i. 23). That is, we start with humour in bad taste. The whole tragedy witnesses a sense of humour in 'the gods' which is in similar bad taste. Now all the Lear effects are exaggerated in the Gloucester theme. Edmund's plot is a more Iago-like, devilish, intentional thing than Goneril's and Regan's icy callousness. Edgar's supposed letter is crude and absurd:

> . . . I begin to find an idle and fond bondage in the oppression of aged tyranny . . . (I. ii. 53)

But then Edmund, wittiest and most attractive of villains, composed it. One can almost picture his grin as he penned those lines, commending them mentally to the limited intellect of his father. Yes—the Gloucester theme has a beginning even more fantastic than that of Lear's tragedy. And not only are the Lear effects here exaggerated in the directions of villainy and humour: they are even more clearly exaggerated in that of horror. The gouging out of Gloucester's eyes is a thing unnecessary, crude, disgusting: it is meant to be. It helps to provide an accompanying exaggeration of one element—that of cruelty—in the horror that makes Lear's madness. And not only horror: there is even again something satanically comic bedded deep in it. The sight of physical torment, to the uneducated, brings laughter. Shakespeare's England delighted in watching both physical torment and the comic ravings of actual lunacy. The dance of madmen in Webster's *Duchess of Malfi* is of the same ghoulish humour as Regan's plucking Gloucester by the beard: the groundlings will laugh at both. Moreover, the sacrilege of the human body in torture must be, to a human mind, incongruous, absurd. This hideous mockery is consummated in Regan's final witticism after Gloucester's eyes are out:

> Go, thrust him out at gates, and let him smell
> His way to Dover. (III. vii. 93)

The macabre humoresque of this is nauseating: but it is there, and integral to the play. These ghoulish horrors, so popular in Elizabethan drama, and the very stuff of the *Lear* of Shakespeare's youth, *Titus Andronicus*, find an exquisitely appropriate place in the tragedy of Shakespeare's maturity which takes as its especial province this territory of the grotesque and the fantastic which is Lear's madness. We are clearly pointed to this grim fun, this hideous sense of humour, at the back of tragedy:

> As flies to wanton boys are we to the gods;
> They kill us for their sport. (IV. i. 36)

This illustrates the exact quality I wish to emphasize: the humour a boy—even a kind boy—may see in the wriggles of an impaled insect. So, too, Gloucester is bound, and tortured, physically; and so the mind of Lear is impaled, crucified on the cross-beams of love and disillusion.

There follows the grim pilgrimage of Edgar and Gloucester towards Dover Cliff: an incident typical enough of *King Lear*—

> 'Tis the times' plague when madmen lead the blind. (IV. i. 46)

They stumble on, madman and blind man, Edgar mumbling:

... five fiends have been in poor Tom at once; of lust, as
Obidicut; Hobbididance, prince of dumbness; Mahu, of
stealing; Modo, of murder; Flibbertigibbet, of mopping and
mowing, who since possesses chambermaids and waiting-
women ... (IV. i. 59)

They are near Dover. Edgar persuades his father that they are
climbing steep ground, though they are on a level field, that the sea
can be heard beneath:

> *Gloucester.* Methinks the ground is even.
> *Edgar.* Horrible steep
> Hark, do you hear the sea?
> *Gloucester.* No, truly.
> *Edgar.* Why, then your other senses grow imperfect
> By your eyes' anguish. (IV. vi. 3)

Gloucester notices the changed sanity of Edgar's speech, and remarks
thereon. Edgar hurries his father to the supposed brink, and vividly
describes the dizzy precipice over which Gloucester thinks they
stand:

> How fearful
> And dizzy 'tis to cast one's eyes so low!
> The crows and choughs that wing the midway air
> Show scarce so gross as beetles: half way down
> Hangs one that gathers samphire, dreadful trade! ... (IV. vi. 12)

Gloucester thanks him, and rewards him; bids him move off; then
kneels, and speaks a prayer of noble resignation, breathing that
stoicism which permeates the suffering philosophy of this play:

> O you mighty gods!
> This world I do renounce, and, in your sights,
> Shake patiently my great affliction off:
> If I could bear it longer, and not fall
> To quarrel with your great opposeless wills,
> My snuff and loathed part of nature should
> Burn itself out. (IV. vi. 35)

Gloucester has planned a spectacular end for himself. We are given these noble descriptive and philosophical speeches to tune our minds to a noble, tragic sacrifice. And what happens? The old man falls from his kneeling posture a few inches, flat, face foremost. Instead of the dizzy circling to crash and spill his life on the rocks below—just this. The grotesque merged into the ridiculous reaches a consummation in this bathos of tragedy: it is the furthest, most exaggerated, reach of the poet's towering fantasticality. We have a sublimely daring stroke of technique, unjustifiable, like Edgar's emphasized and vigorous madness throughout, on the plane of plot-logic, and even to a super-ficial view somewhat out of place imaginatively in so dire and stark a limning of human destiny as is *King Lear;* yet this scene is in reality a consummate stroke of art. The Gloucester-theme throughout reflects and emphasizes and exaggerates all the percurrent qualities of the Lear-theme. Here the incongruous and fantastic element of the Lear-theme is boldly reflected into the tragically-absurd. The stroke is auda-cious, unashamed, and magical of effect. Edgar keeps up the deceit; persuades his father that he has really fallen; points to the empty sky, as to a cliff:

> . . . the shrill-gorged lark
> Cannot be heard so far . . . (IV. vi. 59)

and finally paints a fantastic picture of a ridiculously grotesque devil that stood with Gloucester on the edge:

> As I stood here below, methought his eyes
> Were two full moons; he had a thousand noses,
> Horns whelk'd and waved like the enridged sea;
> It was some fiend . . . (IV. vi. 70)

Some fiend, indeed. There is masterful artistry in all this. The Gloucester-theme has throughout run separate from that of Lear, yet parallel, and continually giving us direct villainy where the other shows cold callousness; horrors of physical torment where the other has a subtle mental torment; culminating in this towering stroke of the grotesque and absurd to balance the fantastic incidents and speeches that immediately follow. At this point we suddenly have our first sight of Lear in the full ecstasy of his later madness. Now, when our imaginations are most powerfully quickened to the grotesque and incongruous, the whole surge of the Gloucester-theme, which has just reached its climax, floods as a tributary the main stream of our sympathy with Lear. Our vision has thus been uniquely focused to understand that vision of the grotesque, the incongruous, the fantastically-horrible, which is the agony of Lear's mind:

> (*Enter* Lear, *fantastically dressed with wild flowers.*) (IV. vi. 81)

So runs Capell's direction. Lear, late 'every inch a king', the supreme pathetic figure of literature, now utters the wild and whirling language of furthest madness. Sometimes his words hold profound meaning. Often they are tuned to the orthodox Shakespearian hate and loathing, especially sex-loathing, of the hate-theme. Or again, they are purely ludicrous, or would be, were it not a Lear who speaks them:

> ... Look, look, a mouse! Peace, peace; this piece of toasted cheese will do't ... (IV. vi. 90)

It is certainly as well that we have been by now prepared for the grotesque. Laughter is forbidden us. Consummate art has so forged plot and incident that we may watch with tears rather than laughter the cruelly comic actions of Lear:

> *Lear:* I will die bravely, like a bridegroom.[2] What!
> I will be jovial: come, come; I am a king,
> My masters, know you that?
> *Gentleman.* You are a royal one, and we obey you.
> *Lear:* Then there's life in't. Nay, if you get it, you shall get it with running. Sa, sa, sa, sa. (IV. vi. 203)

Lear is a child again in his madness. We are in touch with the exquisitely pathetic, safeguarded only by Shakespeare's masterful technique from the bathos of comedy.

This recurring and vivid stress on the incongruous and the fantastic is not a subsidiary element in *King Lear*: it is the very heart of the play. We watch humanity grotesquely tormented, cruelly and with mockery impaled: nearly all the persons suffer some form of crude indignity in the course of the play. I have noticed the major themes of Lear and

Gloucester: there are others. Kent is banished, undergoes the disguise of a servant, is put to shame in the stocks; Cornwall is killed by his own servant resisting the dastardly mutilation of Gloucester; Oswald, the prim courtier, is done to death by Edgar in the role of an illiterate country yokel—

> ... keep out, che vor ye, or ise try whether your costard or my ballow be the harder ... (IV. vi. 247)

Edgar himself endures the utmost degradation of his disguise as 'poor Tom', begrimed and naked, and condemned to speak nothing but idiocy. Edmund alone steers something of an unswerving tragic course, brought to a fitting, deserved, but spectacular end, slain by his wronged brother, nobly repentant at the last:

> *Edmund.* What you have charged me with, that have I done;
> And more, much more; the time will bring it out:
> 'Tis past, and so am I. But what art thou
> That hast this fortune on me? If thou'rt noble, I do forgive thee.
> *Edgar.* Let's exchange charity.
> I am no less in blood than thou art, Edmund;
> If more, the more thou hast wrong'd me.
> My name is Edgar ... (V. iii. 164)

The note of forgiving chivalry reminds us of the deaths of Hamlet and Laertes. Edmund's fate is nobly tragic: 'the wheel has come full circle; I am here' (V. iii. 176). And Edmund is the most villainous of all. Again, we have incongruity; and again, the Gloucester-theme reflects the Lear-theme. Edmund is given a noble, an essentially tragic, end, and Goneril and Regan, too, meet their ends with something of tragic fineness in pursuit of their evil desires. Regan dies by her sister's poison; Goneril with a knife. They die, at least, in the cause of love—love of Edmund. Compared with these deaths, the end of Cordelia is horrible, cruel, unnecessarily cruel—the final grotesque horror in the play. Her villainous sisters are already dead. Edmund is nearly dead, repentant. It is a matter of seconds—and rescue comes too late. She is hanged by a common soldier. The death which Dostoievsky's Stavrogin singled out as of all the least heroic and picturesque, or rather, shall we say, the most hideous and degrading: this is the fate that grips the white innocence and resplendent love-strength of Cordelia. To be hanged, after the death of her enemies, in the midst of friends. It is the last hideous joke of destiny: this—and the fact that Lear is still alive, has recovered his sanity for this. The death of Cordelia is the last and most horrible of all the horrible incongruities I have noticed:

> Why should a dog, a horse, a rat have life,
> And thou no breath at all? (V. iii. 308)

We remember: 'Upon such sacrifices, my Cordelia, the gods themselves throw incense' (V. iii. 20). Or do they laugh, and is the *Lear* universe one ghastly piece of fun?

We do not feel that. The tragedy is most poignant in that it is purposeless, unreasonable. It is the most fearless artistic facing of the ultimate cruelty of things in our literature. That cruelty would be less were there not this element of comedy which I have emphasized, the insistent incongruities, which create and accompany the madness of Lear, which leap to vivid shape in the mockery of Gloucester's suicide, which are intrinsic in the texture of the whole play. Mankind is, as it were, deliberately and comically tormented by 'the gods'. He is not even allowed to die tragically. Lear is 'bound upon a wheel of fire' and only death will end the victim's agony:

> Vex not his ghost: O, let him pass! he hates him
> That would upon the rack of this tough world
> Stretch him out longer. (V. iii. 315)

King Lear is supreme in that, in this main theme, it faces the very absence of tragic purpose: wherein it is profoundly different from *Timon of Athens*. Yet, as we close the sheets of this play, there is no horror, nor resentment. The tragic purification of the essentially untragic is yet complete.

Now in this essay it will, perhaps, appear that I have unduly emphasized one single element of the play, magnifying it, and leaving the whole distorted. It has been my purpose to emphasize. I have not exaggerated. The pathos has not been minimized: it is redoubled. Nor does the use of the words 'comic' and 'humour' here imply disrespect to the poet's purpose: rather I have used these words, crudely no doubt, to cut out for analysis the very heart of the play—the thing that man dares scarcely face: the demonic grin of the incongruous and absurd in the most pitiful of human struggles with an iron fate. It is this that wrenches, splits, gashes the mind till it utters the whirling vapourings of lunacy. And, though love and music—twin sisters of salvation—temporarily may heal the racked consciousness of Lear, yet, so deeply planted in the facts of our life is this unknowing ridicule of destiny, that the uttermost tragedy of the incongruous ensues, and there is no hope save in the broken heart and limp body of death. This is of all the most agonizing of tragedies to endure: and if we are to feel more than a fraction of this agony, we must have sense of this quality of grimmest humour. We must beware of sentimentalizing the cosmic mockery of the play.

And is there, perhaps, even a deeper, and less heart-searing, significance in its humour? Smiles and tears are indeed most curiously interwoven here. Gloucester was saved from his violent and tragic suicide that he might recover his wronged son's love, and that his heart might

> 'Twixt two extremes of passion, joy and grief,
> Burst smilingly. (V. iii. 200)

Lear dies with the words

> Do you see this? Look on her, look, her lips,
> Look there, look there! (V. iii. 312)

What smiling destiny is this he sees at the last instant of racked mortality? Why have we that strangely beautiful account of Cordelia's first hearing of her father's pain:

> . . . patience and sorrow strove
> Who should express her goodliest. You have seen
> Sunshine and rain at once: her smiles and tears
> Were like a better way: those happy smilets,
> That play'd on her ripe lip, seem'd not to know
> What guests were in her eyes; which parted thence,
> As pearls from diamonds dropp'd. In brief,

Sorrow would be a rarity most belov'd,
If all could so become it. (IV. iii. 18)

What do we touch in these passages? Sometimes we know that all human pain holds beauty, that no tear falls but it dews some flower we cannot see. Perhaps humour, too, is inwoven in the universal pain, and the enigmatic silence holds not only an unutterable sympathy, but also the ripples of an impossible laughter whose flight is not for the wing of human understanding; and perhaps it is this that casts its darting shadow of the grotesque across the furrowed pages of *King Lear*.

Notes

1. *Troilus and Cressida*, V. ii. 138.
2. This is to be related to *Antony and Cleopatra*, IV. xii. 100, and *Measure for Measure*, III. i 82; also *Hamlet*, IV. iv 62.

THE METAMORPHOSIS
(FRANZ KAFKA)

"Aspects of the Grotesque
in Franz Kafka's *The Metamorphosis*,"
by Robert C. Evans
Auburn University at Montgomery

If any situation can seem inherently "grotesque," the act of waking up one morning and discovering that one has turned into a gigantic insect certainly fits the bill. This, of course, is the central plot device of Franz Kafka's famous story *The Metamorphosis*, in which a young traveling salesman named Gregor Samsa awakes to find that he has been

> . . . transformed in his bed into an enormous bug. He lay on his back, which was hard as armor, and, when he lifted his head a little, he saw his belly—rounded, brown, partitioned by archlike ridges—on top of which the blanket, ready to slip off altogether, was just barely perched. His numerous legs, pitifully thin in comparison to the rest of his girth, flickered helplessly before his eyes. (25)

What could be more grotesque—to oneself as well as to others—than such a transformation? To be changed into a dog, cat, bird, or even a fish, might eventually seem almost appealing, but to be changed, without warning or explanation, into a giant vermin is undeniably grotesque to an extreme degree.

Grotesqueness as a phenomenon and the grotesque as an artistic trait are notoriously difficult concepts to pin down. "The grotesque," Geoffrey Harpham long ago argued, "is the slipperiest of aesthetic categories" (461) and has been defined in numerous ways over many decades and even centuries. "When dealing with the grotesque" (Harpham continues) it seems that "one must deal either with gross generalizations, arbitrariness, or specific statements about specific works" (461). Nevertheless, Harpham himself, following the great German scholar Wolfgang Kayser, associates the grotesque with such elements as suddenness, surprise, and estrangement: "the familiar and commonplace must be suddenly subverted or undermined by the uncanny or alien," and he argues that "Kafka's *The Metamorphosis* gives perhaps the perfect example of instant alienation, brilliantly, suddenly literalizing Dostoevsky's metaphor of man-as-beetle, raising the existential to the grotesque" (462). "For an object to be grotesque," Harpham ultimately contends, "it must arouse three responses. Laughter and astonishment are two; either disgust or horror is the third" (463).

The Metamorphosis is full of obviously astonishing, disgusting, and horrific elements; however, its humor seems less obvious, and certainly Kafka's tale is not humorous in the ways or to the extent that Flannery O'Connor's grotesque stories are often laugh-out-loud funny. Nevertheless, the narrative does offer an often wry and subtly comic perspective on the events it describes, and, as in much grotesque literature, the smiles it provokes are often tinged with guilt. We cannot help being amused by some of Gregor's predicaments—especially his difficulties in getting out of bed—and the reactions of his parents, sister, employers, and others to his transformation are sometimes also sadly funny. In trying to determine the specific ways in which *The Metamorphosis* counts as a grotesque story, then, it may be best to begin by discussing its elements of humor. This is, after all, a story that often seems amusing, even when our impulse to smile or laugh seems somewhat insensitive, tactless, or even tasteless. Perhaps part of the reason the humor of the story counts as grotesque is that when we find ourselves amused by Gregor's situation, we in some ways feel ourselves diminished. We feel less noble, less humane, less worthy of our own respect when we laugh or smile at something that should arouse our pity and sympathy, and so we ourselves (or at least our images of ourselves) are undercut and transformed. We as readers are diminished when we laugh at Gregor.

Even so, it is hard not to smile when (for instance) Gregor tries to go back to sleep but finds that this is now

> totally out of the question, because he was used to sleeping on his right side, and in his present state he couldn't get into that position. No matter how energetically he threw himself onto his right side, each time he rocked back into the supine position. (25)

Kafka implicitly rebukes us for smiling, mentioning that Gregor "must have tried a hundred times" and, as a result, "began to feel a slight, dull pain in his side that he had never felt before" (25). Kafka reminds us, in other words, that Gregor is a desperate, suffering creature and thus in some ways deserving of our pity. At the same time, Kafka makes the episode seem both disgusting and somewhat funny when he also describes how Gregor, during these efforts, closes "his eyes to avoid seeing his squirming legs" (25). Kafka, in other words, achieves a grotesque effect precisely by making Gregor seem pitiable, ugly, laughable, and sympathetic all at once.

Humor of a different sort is on display when Gregor (now increasingly reconciled to his status as a bug) contemplates whether he should call for help from his family, who are on the other side of his locked bedroom door. "Despite all his tribulations," the narrator reports, Gregor "was unable to suppress a smile at the thought" (33). Gregor imagines with amusement how his family will react when they discover his transformation. In some very obvious ways, Gregor's metamorphosis has made him their definite inferior, but in other ways it has given him an odd position of power—the power to shock, disgust, and repel. Gregor, as an intelligent being, cannot help being amused, at least to some extent, by what has happened to him; he still retains the critical distance that allows him to see potential for comedy in his bizarre situation. It is this critical intelligence, ironically, that still makes him seem so fully human despite his external transformation. He has not fully become an insect so long as he can retain his sense of humor.

This same sense of humor and irony is also evident somewhat later, when Gregor, still locked inside his room, with his family and even his boss noisily demanding entrance, feels "eager to learn what the others, who were now so desirous of his presence, would say when they saw him" (41). There is almost a hint here of Gregor taking pleasure in their shock and of enjoying their surprised reactions, but the humor is magnified when he sensibly reasons that if the others "got frightened, then Gregor would have no further responsibility and could be calm. But if they accepted everything calmly, then he, too, would really have no cause to be upset, and, if he hurried, he could really be at the station at eight o'clock" for his previously planned business trip (41). It is hard to know what is funnier here: the idea of an insect thinking so rationally; the idea that the others might in fact be able to stay calm when greeted by a giant beetle; or the idea that that same beetle might actually skitter down to the station and board a train for work. Here and throughout the story, Kafka achieves effects that are both comic and grotesque through his deadpan style of narration. Episodes such as this would be far less amusing if Kafka himself ever cracked an obvious smile; instead, he simply describes Gregor's thoughts as if they make perfect sense.

Interestingly enough, the grotesque humor of Kafka's story is often directed as much at others as at Gregor himself. Thus, when the door finally is opened and his parents and his boss confront Gregor, the insect is "perfectly conscious of being the only one who had remained calm" (45). He even has what seems (to him) a perfectly rational plan to propose to his employer: "I'll get dressed right away, pack the sample case and catch the train. Is it all right, is it all right with you if I make the trip?" (45). When the supervisor begins to retreat in disgust, Gregor attempts to maintain his calm demeanor: "Where are you off to, sir? To the office? Yes? Will you make an honest report of everything? . . . I'm in a jam, but I'll work my way out of it! . . . Speak up for me in the firm!" (47). This is obviously one of the most comic (but also pathetic) episodes in the story. It is impossible not to feel sympathy for Gregor here, but the idea that he can still make the trip, and the idea that an "honest report" will actually help him with the company, and especially the idea that he can "work [his] way out" of his current "jam" are all ridiculous. Any of us would probably respond as Gregor desperately does if we found ourselves in a similar situation, but his responses are incongruously comic nonetheless.

In episodes such as this, then, Kafka's story does display the humor that Harpham and so many other analysts consider crucial to grotesque writing. Two other brief moments, however, should also be mentioned. At one point, Gregor's movements are described thus: "Slowly, still feeling his way clumsily with his antennae, which he was just now beginning to appreciate, he heaved himself over to the door to see what had happened there" (53). That almost-parenthetical phrase ("which he was just now beginning to appreciate") is wonderfully comic, causing us to smile because of the evidence it provides of Gregor's sensible adaptability and his wonderful capacity to look on the bright side of life, even in the most dire of circumstances. Finally, another episode in the story that is often considered comic involves the reaction of the crusty old maid whom Gregor's family hires to help them deal with their new predicament. She seems one of the few people (indeed, perhaps the only person) who is neither afraid of nor disgusted by him. In fact, at "the beginning she even called him over with words she probably thought were friendly, such as 'Come over here, old dung beetle' or 'Just look at the old dung beetle!'" The narrator notes that "Gregor never responded to such calls" (93), and it is hard to know what is funnier: an old woman who treats a giant insect almost like a family pet, or a giant insect with a profound sense of injured personal dignity.

Humor, then, is one element of Harpham's definition of the grotesque that is definitely (if not insistently) present in Kafka's tale, but humor alone would not make the story grotesque. The humor has to be (and is) incongruous, ironic, absurd, or bizarre, and it also has to be combined with "either disgust or horror" (Harpham 463). As it happens, *The Metamorphosis* is brimming with both of these latter qualities, and it is perhaps their presence that makes the story most obviously grotesque. Kafka goes out of his way to literalize the metaphor of a human-turned-insect; he spares us few details of the disgusting aspects of Gregor's transformation. Just when we are getting used to the idea of Gregor as a vermin, with little legs and a bloated body, Kafka will add some new and even more gross detail to the narrative. His intention, it seems, is to keep us shocked, to never let us forget the disgustingly physical aspects of Gregor's repulsive body, even while keeping us sympathetic to his mental and emotional plight. Thus, very early in the story we are treated to a description of Gregor's "itchy place, which was all covered with little white spots" (27); then, later, we are informed that "the balls of his little feet contained some sticky substance," that he has "no real teeth," and that, when he tries to turn a key with his jaws, "a brown fluid issued from his mouth, ran down over the key and dripped onto the floor" (43). Later still, we learn that Gregor's favorite foods now include "old, half-rotten vegetables" as well as bones from his family's supper, "coated with a white gravy that had solidified" (59). And, in an episode that combines humor with gross specificity, the narrator reports that "for amusement" Gregor "acquired the habit of crawling in all directions across the walls and ceiling" and that he "especially enjoyed hanging up on the ceiling," even if doing so sometimes results in an occasional fall (71). Unfortunately, however, "when crawling he left behind traces of his sticky substance here and there" (71). It would be all too easy to add further examples to this list of disgusting details, but there is little point in doing so. The gross facts of Gregor's existence are far more obviously emphasized than the humor of his predicament, but it is partly this combination of grossness and humor that helps make the story grotesque.

Kafka, then, emphasizes the repulsive physical details of Gregor's transformation, but another feature that also helps make the story grotesque is his stress on Gregor's gradual physical degradation. Gregor begins badly, but his situation eventually becomes worse and worse. He becomes even more obviously an insect (and even less obviously a human) by the end of the story than he was at the beginning, and it is this steady degradation that helps add to the grotesqueness of the tale. Although the title of the story alludes to a single metamorphosis, the change is in fact a gradual, on-going process of subtle metamorphoses. The disgusting nature of Gregor's feet, mouth, and eating habits have already been mentioned, but Kafka also emphasizes his growing resemblance to an insect by stressing the degradation of his speech (41), his increasing control over his "little legs" (49), and the unsanitary nature of his living conditions: "Long trails of dirt lined the walls, here and there lay heaps of dust and filth" (91). Gregor also seems physically degraded, not only when he is injured by a splinter (when a dropped bottle shatters on the floor [79]), but especially when his enraged father pelts him with (of all things) an apple, normally a symbol of nourishment and health. The apple actually penetrates his back and becomes embedded there (83), so that Gregor now moves "like an old invalid" and needs "long, long minutes to cross his room" (85). By the end of the story, he is physically, mentally, and emotionally exhausted, and so his death comes as no surprise: "his head involuntarily sank down altogether, and his last breath issued faintly from his nostrils" (109). This is Gregor's final metamorphosis, and it ends a process of many earlier transformations that have led him to seem, both to his family and to Kafka's readers, less and less a human and more and more a vermin. If the initial, sudden metamorphosis from man to insect was startling, the gradual but relentless diminishment of Gregor's physical humanity results in something that is finally even more obviously grotesque.

More grotesque still, in some ways, than the physical degradation Gregor undergoes is his steady spiritual or emotional decline. For much of the first part of the story, Gregor remains admirably human in his thoughts and feelings, despite the profound change in his body. By the second half of the story, however, he has become a more aggressive, more selfish, more threatening creature. His transformation, in other words, has become both physical and spiritual. Thus, in one of the most shocking statements in a generally shocking story, we are told that Gregor "would sooner jump onto" the face of his beloved sister, Grete, than relinquish a framed picture he treasures (79). This, of course, is the same sister who has lovingly cared for him throughout the story. Later, he comes to feel "rage over how badly he was looked after; and even though he couldn't imagine anything he might have had an appetite for, he laid plans for getting into the pantry so he could take what was still his by rights, even if he wasn't hungry" (91). A bit later still, when the rest of the family is in hysterics, Gregor is said to have "hissed loudly with rage because it didn't occur to anyone to close the door and spare him that sight and that commotion" (91). By the end of the story, then, Gregor has come to seem less ideally human, not only physically, but also in his emotional and mental responses. Once more, the full, grotesque effects of his metamorphosis are not completely felt until the conclusion of the tale.

It is not only Gregor, however, who is transformed during the course of the story, nor is it only Gregor who exhibits grotesque behavior. By the end of the narrative, a number of other characters have come to seem grotesque in ways all their own. This is especially true of Gregor's father, whose immediate reaction to his son's transformation is far less sympathetic than the reactions of Gregor's mother and sister. Thus, the father is said to have tried to drive Gregor back into his room by brandishing a folded newspaper and a walking stick:

"Implacably the father urged him back, uttering hisses like a savage"
(51). The word "hisses" is, of course, the key term, for it suggests that
Gregor's father sounds even more like an insect than Gregor does, and
Kafka is careful to emphasize the point: "If only his father had stopped
that unbearable hissing! It made Gregor lose his head altogether. He
was almost completely turned around when, constantly on alert for
that hissing, he made a mistake and turned himself back again a little"
(53). Later, of course, it is the father who seems ready to kick Gregor
and who does pelt him with apples (83). Even the otherwise sympathetic Grete eventually seems degraded by the demands of caring
for her brother: as the story draws to its conclusion, she calls him
an "animal," blames him for the family's sufferings, and accuses him
(highly implausibly) of wanting "to take over the whole apartment
and make us sleep in the street" (105). It is Grete who ultimately locks
Gregor inside his room (107), but it is the elderly maid who adds the
last touch of grotesque inhumanity when, having discovered Gregor's
dead body, she proudly announces to the family, "Come take a look,
it's croaked; it's lying there, a total goner" (109). Later she tells them:
"you don't have to worry your heads about how to clear out that trash
[i.e., Gregor's corpse] next door. It's all taken care of" (113). Arbitrary
fate turned Gregor into an insect, but it takes the inhumanity of other
people to turn him into a wounded, abused, despised piece of "trash."
By the conclusion of the story, we are left wondering what is more
grotesque: Gregor the insect or the people who treat him with such
indifference and contempt.

There are, then, many different respects in which the plot, characters, imagery, and symbolism of *The Metamorphosis* might legitimately
be called "grotesque." By the end of the story, the dignity of practically every character has been undercut. The story has emphasized
disgusting physical details, bizarre events, repulsive conduct, and
strange juxtapositions of the comic and the horrific, the inhuman
and the absurd. What, however, is the point of all this? What are
some possible larger meanings of this story? Or is the story, as one
prominent analyst has suggested, simply a reflection of Kafka's own
idiosyncratic psychology and of his own personal family situation, and
thus lacking in any general or universal significance? (Gray 62-63).
How is the tale possibly relevant to the lives of Kafka's readers? Such
questions can be—and have been—answered in numerous ways. *The
Metamorphosis*, after all, is one of the most-interpreted stories ever

written. Among the ways in which this "grotesque" story achieves its powerful effects is through its appeal to very widespread and very common, almost archetypal, human fears.

None of us ever needs to worry about waking to discover ourselves transformed into giant insects. Nearly all of us, however, need to worry, at some level, about the possibility of sudden, disastrous, and apparently random change—the sort of change that can come, for instance, from a serious accident or some other abrupt loss. Related to this fear is a common human dread of betrayal by one's own body, including loss of control of one's bodily functions or even of one's mind. Both of these kinds of loss are related, in turn, to the fear of losing personal dignity and freedom, and thus to social isolation or ostracism, and thus to fear of abandonment, even (or especially) by one's family. *The Metamorphosis*, in fact, can be seen as reflecting many other common and deep-seated human anxieties, but by now the basic point is clear: this is not simply the bizarre and improbable story of one man who wakes up as an insect; it is the story of any human being who fears finding himself in circumstances that are grotesque in themselves and that threaten to drag that person himself down into the depths of grotesque thoughts, feelings, and behavior.

WORKS CITED OR CONSULTED

Bloom, Harold, ed. *Franz Kafka's* The Metamorphosis: *Bloom's Guides.* New York; Chelsea House, 2007.

Clark, John R. *The Modern Satiric Grotesque and Its Traditions.* Lexington: U of Kentucky P, 1991.

Gray, Ronald. "The Metamorphosis." *Franz Kafka's* The Metamorphosis: *Modern Critical Interpretations.* Ed. Harold Bloom. New York: Chelsea House, 1988: 61-69.

Harpham, Geoffrey. "The Grotesque: First Principles." *The Journal of Aesthetics and Art Criticism* 34.4 (1976): 461-68.

Kafka, Franz. "The Metamorphosis." *Best Short Stories = Die Schönsten Erzählungen: A Dual-Language Book.* Minneola, NY: Dover, 1997. 24-115.

Spilka, Mark. *Dickens and Kafka: A Mutual Interpretation.* Bloomington: Indiana UP, 1963.

MISS LONELYHEARTS
(NATHANAEL WEST)

"Carnival Virtues: Sex, Sacrilege, and the Grotesque in Nathanael West's *Miss Lonelyhearts*,"
by Blake G. Hobby and Zachary DeBoer, The University of North Carolina at Asheville

---

Miss Lonelyhearts sits at his desk in the newspaper office, smoking a cigarette and brooding over a pile of agonizing letters. The desperate, the deformed, and the abused beg Miss Lonelyhearts to help them; they seek Miss Lonelyhearts' wisdom and love. On his desk, taunting Miss Lonelyhearts, lies a blasphemous prayer scribbled by his boss, Shrike, on a piece of cardboard. Addressed to Miss Lonelyhearts, the prayer mocks the advice columnist as a messiah for the pitiful and broken. But in this novel's ironical mode, the prayer captures Miss Lonelyheart's tormented obsession with belief and suffering. For if, on the one hand, God is with us, Lonelyhearts cannot understand why suffering exists. If, on the other hand, God is not with us, then Lonelyhearts is equally puzzled, consumed by a kind of compassionate agnosticism. Lonelyhearts feels responsible for others, yet is never sure how to make things better. In this sense, Lonelyhearts is a kind of perverse Christ-figure whose ultimate death is both serious, affecting real people, yet also horrifyingly comic, for it also grieves the delusional, who found solace in a columnist they misread. Lonelyhearts has a wounded need to fix the world. Thus, West's novel captures a

145

grotesque world: one inhabited by fellow sufferers impervious to their own ironic fate.

Grotesque literature takes its roots in what Mikhail Bakhtin identifies as folk humor and carnival ambivalence, both of which he traces back to the Roman Saturnalia. The Saturnalia was a celebration marked by revelry and freedom, a festival in which all Roman citizens became unified and equalized through participation in ritual irreverence to cultural norms. The tradition of festival continued on to the medieval period, during which celebrants directed the festival's irreverence towards the era's two omnipresent institutions: the Christian Church and feudalism. Representing structure, hierarchy, and oppressive cultural norms, these institutions became targets of carnival parody—that is, a mockery of sacred practices and texts, and a reversal of stately ceremonies.

In a feudalistic Church-State, individuals were classified and stratified. Hierarchical rankings were crucial to these institutions, which both established and mandated them in medieval daily life. How could people tolerate such rigid social, political, and religious order? By ushering in the periodic inversion of this order through the participation in carnival. Carnival, according to Bakhtin, was the manifestation of the people's necessary (albeit temporary) need to depart from the realm of institutional control. Bakhtin writes:

> Carnival festivities and the comic spectacle and ritual connected with them . . . offered a completely different, nonofficial, extraecclesiastical and extrapolitical aspect of the world, of man, and of human relations; they built a second world and a second life outside officialdom, a world in which all people participated more or less, in which they lived during a given time of the year. (196–197)

This "second world" provided relief from the oppression of institutionalized hierarchy by rejecting and defying the very institutions that proliferated cultural standards. These standards included spiritual regulations and codes of social propriety, rules of conduct that the Church and State imposed on medieval European citizens. Standardized seriousness became a requirement for "official" medieval life—a seriousness often asserted through feasts sanctioned by the Church or the State (199). This seriousness is precisely what folk humor intends to disrupt.

Folk humor informs grotesque literature in a variety of ways. For one, it seeks to bring all individuals to a common level, to collapse hierarchy and eliminate distinctions between social rank and class. Carnival brings people together, and through laughter, disorder, and unusual behavior, it degrades all of its participants until they all exist on an equal plane. Grotesque literature, too, seeks to illicit a type of laughter that equalizes its readers—a laughter that celebrates the bizarre, and perhaps disturbing, elements of life. The grotesque operates in a second world, an alternative realm separate from the realm of institutionalized order and social protocol prevalent in typical daily life. In this second world, what once was off-limits becomes fair game: the inappropriate becomes acceptable; the taboo becomes norm. Formal conversation and the multitude of rules that govern it give way to a new form of communication: one in which profanities and abusive language become not only acceptable, but also meaningful (204).

Bakhtin identifies degradation as "the essential principle of grotesque realm . . . the lowering of all that is high, spiritual, ideal, abstract; [the] transfer to the material level, to the sphere of earth and body in their indissoluble unity" (205). This principle, however, is not synonymous with destruction, which implies finality and death. Instead, degradation leads to eventual elevation: as Bakhtin contends, "to degrade is to bury, to sow, and to kill simultaneously, in order to bring forth something new and better" (206). This is one of the ways in which Bakhtin distinguishes folk humor from modern satire: whereas satire criticizes and ridicules something separate from the satirist (that is, something of which the satirist is not, or believes he is not, guilty), folk humor does not distance itself from the source of its laughter. Folk humor links the laughers with their laughter and discourages opposition among people: satire is inherently opposi-tional. Satire indicts, yet does not offer a solution to the problems it aims to expose. Folk humor does not merely accuse, nor merely condemn: it degrades so that it can renew. According to Bakhtin, "to degrade an object does not imply merely hurling it into the void of nonexistence, into absolute destruction, but to hurl it down into the reproductive lower stratum, the zone in which conception and a new birth take place" (206). Carnival's departure from institutionalized order does not intend to obliterate the Church and the State, but it does intend to refresh the humanity of people smothered by inhumane limitations.

Key to the nature of folk humor is the concept of ambivalence—that is, the coexistence of conflicting attitudes or feelings. Bakhtin suggests that much of the modern scholarship regarding folk humor errs by interpreting one of two ways. In the words of the critic, "The present-day analysis of laughter explains it either as purely negative satire . . . or else as gay, fanciful, recreational drollery deprived of philosophic content. [The notion] that folk humor is ambivalent is usually ignored" (201). Grotesque literature, too, is ambivalent—especially in its use of degradation as an agent of rebirth. The grotesque in literature is not one-dimensional: it has a variety of aspects, some perhaps contradictory, which contribute to its purposes. These purposes, to name a few, include defying institutionally standardized notions of what is appropriate and what is not in social and artistic discourse; re-humanizing communication among all people; and embracing the bizarre, disturbing, irrational, and yet entirely natural aspects of the world.

Out of fundamental necessity, societies since the time of Ancient Rome have used carnival and folk humor to cope with the oppressive confusion, monotony, and travesty of day-to-day life. Miss Lonelyhearts is well acquainted with these three forces. He encounters them every day at his job as he reads letters sent to him by downtrodden members of society. Saturated with groans of misery, despondency, and turmoil, the letters plunge the columnist himself into a sea of agony. These epistolary pleas for salvation from despair force Miss Lonelyhearts to come face to face with the most grotesque aspects of the human condition. A sixteen-year-old girl born without a nose writes in for advice. She describes the turmoil that comes from her anomaly:

> I sit and look at myself all day and cry. I have a big hole in the middle of my face that scares people even myself so I cant [sic] blame the boys for not wanting to take me out. My mother loves me, but she cries terrible when she looks at me. (2)

Ultimately, the girl wants to know from Miss Lonelyhearts whether or not she should commit suicide. A fifteen-year-old boy writes in:

his thirteen-year-old sister, deaf and dumb, has been raped. The boy worries that his sister will become pregnant, and he fears that telling his mother will earn his sister a vicious beating since the girl has received abusive punishment for even as little a mistake as tearing her dress (3). A mother writes in: her psychotic husband has a history of physically and psychologically abusing her, has made threats against her life, has been in and out of jail, and has recently disappeared without leaving any provision of financial support for his children. Meanwhile, to support her children, she has rented a room in her house to a boarder—but the man often comes home drunk and makes unwelcome sexual advances on her. She wants Miss Lonelyhearts' advice about what to do (40-43). These are the people who turn to Miss Lonelyhearts for help: the unwanted, the violated, the humiliated, the undone. At first, the columnist found the letters humorous; then they began to trouble and disgust him. Disturbed and heartbroken by the supplicants' plight and earnestness, Miss Lonelyhearts begins to take the requests seriously. He no longer laughs at them. He wants to help them, to comfort them, to save them, and he has come to believe that the only way to do so involves adopting a life of religious devotion.

With pious persistence, Miss Lonelyhearts struggles to look to Christ for renewal and salvation. His attempts at spiritual vitality, however, often result in underwhelming flops. Miss Lonelyhearts has dislodged a figure of the crucified Christ from its cross and nailed it to his bedroom wall, in hopes that it will serve as a beacon to guide him towards humility and devotion. Instead, it hangs lifeless, decorative rather than powerful (8). From childhood onward, Miss Lonelyhearts senses a mysterious, fascinating force when he utters the name of Christ—but he judges that this feeling more closely approaches hysteria than transcendence (8), and in the end Christ's name becomes meaningless and empty to him (39). Miss Lonelyhearts finds his main antagonist in Shrike, the embodiment of the vulgarity, faithlessness, and mockery that Miss Lonelyhearts fights to resist. Shrike embraces the grotesque elements of existence, and in *Miss Lonelyhearts* he functions as grotesquery's spokesman. A perpetual thorn in Miss Lonelyhearts side, Shrike is often blasphemic, hurling disparaging words, and he savors his role. When he isn't profaning Christ (irreverently referring to him as "the Miss Lonelyhearts of Miss Lonelyhearts" on multiple occasions), Shrike either ridicules Miss Lonelyhearts for approaching the column with sincerity and compassion or drunkenly rambles about the most effective ways to escape life's miseries. Often Shrike suggests that Christ is, in fact, the only hope for spiritual solace, but he always does so tongue-in-cheek. These mock-religious speeches parody and patronize Christ, reducing him to a punch line. Early in the narrative, readers learn that "Christ was Shrike's particular joke" (3) and that this ongoing joke "made a sane view of this Christ business impossible" (8) for Miss Lonelyhearts. As much as Miss Lonelyhearts strives to believe in Christ as redeemer, Shrike derides the columnist as a nincompoop religious fanatic.

While Miss Lonelyhearts seeks to exist in the realm of the sacred and spiritual, Shrike operates in the carnival realm. Shrike, parodist of all things religious, embodies the spirit of carnival and folk humor that Bakhtin discusses in his essay on the same topic. Carnival and folk humor, the progenitors of grotesque literature, create an alternative realm to the world governed by the institutions of Church and State. In carnival, irreligion usurps religion, disorder usurps order, and the vulgar usurps the holy; sacred ceremonies are turned upside-down, and stately processions are inverted; people from all social levels cast off their ranks and unite in festive revelry. Folk humor not only shirks the regulatory solemnity of the Church, it also actively mocks it. So, too, does Shrike: he lives according to carnival virtue, as Miss Lonelyhearts attempts to live according to conventional, sacred virtue. As a result, the two men become bitter opponents. Carnival rejects piety and replaces it with fleshly, ribald laughter, and whereas the sacred realm requires seriousness, quiet, and purity, the carnival realm values folk humor, clamor, and obscenity. These two realms stand in direct opposition to one another—the carnival and the sacred cannot occupy the same time and space, and no one can simultaneously inhabit both realms. Reason would have it that a person who operates in one realm opposes the other, and so it is with Shrike and Miss Lonelyhearts.

Shrike's mockery of Christ, ridicule of Miss Lonelyhearts' piety, and inclination for obscenity represent the essence that drives folk humor and carnival. In the novel's second chapter, "Miss Lonelyhearts and the Dead Pan," Shrike insists that Miss Lonelyhearts turn to the pursuit of physical pleasure in order to achieve satisfaction. "You're morbid, my friend, morbid. Forget the crucifixion, remember the Renaissance" (5), Shrike tells Miss Lonelyhearts in the oft-frequented

Delehanty's speakeasy. The editor expresses his admiration for the irreverence and misbehavior of the Renaissance period (especially in the context of sexuality), and he carries this admiration into his affair with the shapely Miss Farkis, whom Shrike praises for her "great intelligence"—a phrase he uses as a code for Miss Farkis' giant bust (6). When Miss Lonelyhearts refuses to share in Shrike's enthusiasm for female anatomy, Shrike seizes the opportunity to tease him about his effort at chastity. "Oh, so you don't care for women, eh? J.C. is your only sweetheart, eh? Jesus Christ, the King of Kings, the Miss Lonelyhearts of Miss Lonelyhearts . . . ." (6), says Shrike in his patent sarcastic deadpan. Later in the scene, Shrike offers a facetious defense of his own spirituality, calling himself a "great saint," before musing on "a bird called the soul":

> The Catholic hunts this bird with bread and wine, the Hebrew
> with a golden ruler, the Protestant on leaden feet with leaden
> words, the Buddhist with gestures, the Negro with blood. I spit
> on them all. Phooh! And I call upon you to spit. (7–8)

In this monologue Shrike not only decries religion for its oppression of humanity, but also makes a concerted movement away from the sacred towards the carnal, fondling Miss Farkis through the duration of his speech. Shrike is a model carnival participant: he despises religion, parodying it mercilessly; he adores sex and lauds the human body; he is loud, irreverent, and crude. He abides by the virtues that folk humor and carnival (and by extension, the grotesque) uphold.

In his waking life, Miss Lonelyhearts behaves with average morality, but in his sleeping life he experiences recurring dreams and visions rich with the vulgarity of carnival and folk humor. After the first scene with Shrike in Delehanty's, Miss Lonelyhearts returns home, agitated and exasperated. That night he dreams of a carnivalesque procession, consisting of himself and two college buddies, in which they drunkenly lead a lamb to its slaughter:

> They paraded the lamb through the market. Miss Lonelyhearts
> went first, carrying the knife, the others followed, Steve with the
> jug [of applejack] and Jud with the animal. As they marched,
> they sang an obscene version of "Mary Had a Little Lamb."
> . . . Miss Lonelyhearts was elected priest, with Steve and Jud

as his attendants. While they held the lamb, Miss Lonelyhearts crouched over it and began to chant.

"Christ, Christ, Jesus Christ. Christ, Christ, Jesus Christ."
(9–10)

This sacrilegious ceremony is the essence of folk humor and carnival. Miss Lonelyhearts and his friends disgrace the Church by declaring themselves clergyman, they corrupt the innocence of a children's song, and they profane the name of Christ with Miss Lonelyhearts' blasphemous incantation—actions fit for any carnival, in the sense described by Bakhtin. For someone like Miss Lonelyhearts, who on one level strives for piety and belief in Christ, this behavior should be unacceptable, even if the actions occur in a dream world rather than in reality. The presence of this latent grotesquery in his mind is enough to disconcert Miss Lonelyhearts, to whom order becomes an ever-growing obsession (10). Confined to his room on account of a debilitating physical illness (perhaps a manifestation of his spiritual woes), Miss Lonelyhearts contemplates the perpetual war that order and chaos wage against one another:

> He sat in the window thinking. Man has a tropism for order. Keys in one pocket, change in another. Mandolins are tuned G D A E. The physical world has a tropism for disorder, entropy . . . Keys yearn to mix with change. Mandolins strive to get out of tune. Every order has within it the germ of destruction. All order is doomed, yet the battle is worthwhile.
> (30–31)

Miss Lonelyhearts then experiences a grotesque vision in which he first constructs a phallus out of old watches and rubber boots, and later uses pawnshop junk and flotsam and jetsam from the sea to form a massive cross (31).

As this war wages on, Miss Lonelyhearts behaves badly. Contrary to his intermittent desire for pious purity, he engages in acts of violence and sex. With a drinking buddy, he finds and old man sitting in a park toilet, whom Miss Lonelyhearts verbally and physically assaults (16-18). He participates in a bizarre affair with Shrike's wife—an affair of which Shrike has full awareness and to which he gives ambivalent permission. In one scene, Miss Lonelyhearts has a sexual encounter with Mrs. Shrike outside the door of the Shrikes' apartment, stripping her naked in the hallway before releasing her. Moments later, a half-nude Shrike himself arrives at the floor in an elevator (24). Later in the novel, Miss Lonelyhearts begins another scandalous dalliance, this time with Mrs. Doyle, a married woman sexually frustrated by her crippled husband. Mrs. Doyle is a grotesque figure, with "legs like Indian clubs, breasts like balloons and a brow like a pigeon" (27). Nevertheless, Miss Lonelyhearts, in keeping with carnival virtues, sinks into Mrs. Doyle's sea of flesh. He continues his battle to become Christ-like, however, and by the end of the novel transcends the obscene influence of carnival and folk humor—only to die at the hands of Mr. Doyle, who murders Miss Lonelyhearts in an act of misguided revenge. Thus the novel ends the same way it begins: with a flourish of grotesque, undeserved, and unnecessary suffering.

What, then, do we as readers take from this grotesque, absurd tale? *Miss Lonelyhearts* shows the world as confusing and confused, and it shows the people who inhabit it as they cling in desperation to whatever they believe might keep them afloat while tumultuous waters toss them to and fro. This is the world as *Miss Lonelyhearts* captures it: a grotesque place rife with ambivalent forces. Forces both obscene and pious, sexual and chaste; a place in which opposing realms of order and disorder, sanctity and blasphemy, collide.

Works Cited

Morris, Pam, ed. *The Bakhtin Reader: Selected Writings of Bakhtin, Medvedev, Voloshinov.* London: Edward Arnold, 1994.

West, Nathanael. *Miss Lonelyhearts & The Day of the Locust.* New York: New Directions, 1962.

THE MYSTERIOUS STRANGER (MARK TWAIN)

"Grotesque Bodies in Twain's The Mysterious Stranger"
by Matthew J. Bolton, Loyola School

It could be said (with certain reservations, of course) that a person of the Middle Ages lived, as it were, two lives: one that was the official life, monolithically serious and gloomy ... the other was the life of the carnival square, free and unrestricted, full of ambivalent laughter, blasphemy, the profanation of everything sacred ...

—Mikhail Bakhtin, *Problems of Dostoevsky's Poetics* (129–30)

Russian formalist critic Mikhail Bakhtin's writings on medieval culture and literature provide a powerful lens through which to read works that might otherwise be dismissed as fragmentary, disjointed, or even incoherent. Whether writing about medieval authors, such as Rabelais, or nineteenth-century novelists, such as Dostoevsky, Bakhtin gravitated toward those instances in a narrative where "the official life" is disrupted or subverted by the intrusion of the grotesque. He saw such grotesqueries as being at once destructive and generative, arguing,

> The essence of the grotesque is precisely to present a contradictory and double-faced fullness of life. Negation and destruction (death of the old) are included as an essential phase,

inseparable from affirmation, from the birth of something new
and better. (*Rabelais and his World* 62)

Bakhtin's focus on the messy collisions between the official life and
the life of the carnival represents a powerful counterpoint to the Aristotelian model of formal and thematic wholeness, in which a dramatic
situation revolves around the "three unities" of time, character, and
action. Aristotle's model illuminates the classical tragedies from which
it was derived—and any number of subsequent works of literature and
art—but can sometimes cloud the issue when misapplied to a work
that is inherently comic and fragmentary. A work may fail to meet
Aristotle's criteria of formal unity precisely because it expresses the
"double-faced fullness of life:" its form is as grotesque and contradictory as life itself.

One such double-faced work is Mark Twain's novella *The Mysterious Stranger*, cobbled together by his literary executor from three
unfinished manuscripts and first published a decade after the author's
death. *The Mysterious Stranger* has often been dismissed on the
grounds of its dubious authenticity and its incompleteness. Yet to take
issue with the novella for lacking formal unity is to read it through
the wrong lens.

Twain's greatest novel, *The Adventures of Huckleberry Finn*, might
be read as conforming to the Aristotelian dramatic model, with the
journey upriver serving as the story's unifying element. *The Mysterious
Stranger* will not brook comparison with *Huckleberry Finn*, for it operates on a very different set of principles. Instead of coalescing around a
single episode, such as the journey upriver, Twain's final story unfolds
according to a gothic or grotesque series of scenes. Such an organizing
principle is particularly appropriate to a story set in the Middle Ages.
After all, many of the great medieval works of literature, including *The
Canterbury Tales*, are unfinished and discursive. That the manuscript
of *The Mysterious Stranger* is the product of a heavy-handed process of
editing further locates it in a medieval tradition, for the very notions of
authorial and textual authority were less stable before the Renaissance
than they would become in the modern era. Perhaps the best way to
appreciate this darkly-comic work is therefore to adopt a Bakhtinian
approach, seeing its grotesque elements not only as breaking down
social, ethical, and literary structures, but as establishing new structures—fragmented, discursive, and divergent as they may be—in

their place. Nowhere is this grotesque principle more apparent than in the novel's representation of the human body, and in particular, in the series of mutilations, hangings, burnings, drownings, and other violent deaths that litter the story's plot. The suffering of the body in the name of spiritual salvation and Christian orthodoxy becomes Twain's mode of satirizing man's preoccupation with abstraction and religious faith.

Many of the novel's dramatic conflicts arise from the profoundly different attitudes toward the human body that the narrator and the angel Satan hold. When Satan first appears to the narrator and his friends (assuring them, incidentally, that he is the archfiend's nephew rather than the devil himself), he delights the boys by creating out of thin air a miniature castle, peopled by tiny but fully-realized people. The boys quickly lose themselves in watching these citizens bustle about the business of erecting the castle. Yet when two workmen set to quarreling, Satan responds in a manner that horrifies the boys:

> In buzzing little bumblebee voices they were cursing and swearing at each other; now came blows and blood; then they locked themselves together in a life-and-death struggle. Satan reached out his hand and crushed the life out of them with his fingers, threw them away, wiped the red from his fingers on his handkerchief, and went on talking where he had left off. (730)

When the weeping of the other townspeople begins to annoy Satan, he does something even more horrifying: "he took the heavy board seat out of our swing and brought it down and mashed all those people into the earth just as if had been flies, and went on talking just the same" (731). Then he wracks the little city with miniature thunderstorms, bolts of lightning, and, finally, an earthquake that swallows it down into a chasm in the earth.

These acts are disturbing enough, but the gap between Satan's actions and words are even more so. For throughout the destruction of the miniature city, the angel has not stopped expounding on his own incapacity to do evil. Not having eaten of the Tree of the Knowledge of Good and Evil, as did Adam and Eve, this younger Satan and his fellow angels lack "the moral sense" with which men and women are burdened. He concludes: "We others are still ignorant of sin; we are not able to commit it; we are without blemish; we shall abide in that estate always. We—" and it is precisely at this point that he murders the little workmen. There is a strange and inverted logic to Satan's understanding of the nature of evil. He assumes, as have the church fathers and most theologians, that man lived in a state of grace before he ate of the tree. The angels who did not rebel against God continue to share in that state of grace. But Satan's capricious destruction of the miniature city suggests just the opposite: not knowing the difference between good and evil is a form of ignorance rather than grace. Throughout *The Mysterious Stranger*, the angel causes great pain to others without ever seeming to acknowledge that he has done so.

Satan's destruction of the miniature city foreshadows the disregard with which he views the suffering and death of full-sized humans. He offers two explanations for why the destruction of the human body is of no consequence to him. First, he sees mankind as entirely *other*. As mortal beings, men are by nature perishable and expendable in a way Satan is not. At several points he draws analogies with the animal kingdom: if a human is like a small red spider, he explains, than an angel is like an elephant (772). Angels and mortals simply cannot be thought of as existing on the same plane. Satan's attitude toward the tiny but sentient people he creates at the start of the novella—people no bigger than the red spiders of his analogy—is of a piece with his attitude toward the narrator, his friends, and their fellow townspeople. Furthermore, people, like ants, are an abundant resource: there will always be more of them, and the death of one here or there, or of a whole city, is of little consequence. "They were of no value," he consoles the boys after destroying the castle and its inhabitants, "we can make plenty more" (733).

Satan's other reason for disregarding human suffering and death is grounded in a *reductio ad absurdum* distortion of Christian doctrine. Being himself a spirit rather than a body, Satan does not care how greatly or how unjustly a person suffers in life if upon death his or her soul can enter Heaven. To a certain extent, Satan and the narrator see eye to eye on this issue, for the narrator and his friends are very concerned with whether any given person is bound for salvation or damnation. Their first response when Satan destroys the inhabitants of the miniature castle, for example, is to lament, "They are gone to Hell!" (733). Yet whereas the boys can only speculate as to whether someone has been saved or damned, Satan actually knows each person's fate as a surety. When the boys express their horror that a woman will be burned at the stake, Satan chastises them:

> What you are thinking is strictly human-like—that is to say, foolish. The woman is advantaged. Die when she might, she would go to heaven. By this prompt death she gets twenty-nine years more of heaven than she is entitled to, and escapes twenty-nine years of misery here.

According to Satan's logic, to be a soul in heaven is better than to be a body on earth, and bodily death is therefore a fair price to pay for spiritual salvation. Not having a body himself, Satan cannot be moved by seeing the bodies of others in agony.

Satan's inability to sympathize with human suffering becomes apparent when he and the narrator witness an accused heretic being tortured into confessing his sins. Responding to the narrator's fleeting thought that he would like to see the inside of the town's jail, where his favorite priest has been locked away, Satan instantly transports the two of them there. The narrator finds himself in a smoky torture chamber, where he and Satan witness an inquisition:

> A young man lay bound, and Satan said he was suspected of being a heretic, and the executioners were about to inquire into it. They asked the man to confess to the charge, and he said he could not, for it was not true. Then they drove splinter after splinter under his nails, and he shrieked with the pain. Satan was not disturbed, but I could not endure it, and had to be whisked out of there. (752)

It is a disturbing scene that the narrator quite understandably refers to as "brutal." Satan objects, arguing, "no brute ever does a cruel thing—that is the monopoly of those with the Moral Sense" (752). Satan lacks the moral sense, as attested to by his various acts of destruction and his blind disregard for human suffering. Yet in man, the moral sense seems to license even more destructive modes of violence: The torturers believe that they have a moral imperative to cause the young man pain. His suspected spiritual or intellectual deviation from church orthodoxy obligates them to take moral action. They cannot get direct access to the man's mind and soul, but his bound body is at their disposal.

The torturers therefore share in Satan's privileging of spirit over body. They rationalize the pain they cause the youth by presuming that his spiritual salvation is more important than his physical suffering. By their own lights, they are not so much torturers as ministers, attending to the state of the man's soul by working through his body. Satan whisks the narrator away before he can witness the conclusion of this torture session, but we can assume what the outcome will be: the young man will eventually confess to whatever crimes his torturers accuse him of having committed. A man who is being tortured eventually stops thinking in terms of truth and falsehood or right and wrong. His body, and the pain it is suffering, becomes his whole world. When the inquisitors first ask the man to confess to heresy, "he said he could not, for it was not true." But truth is an abstraction in a way one's fingernails are not, and the accused will soon abandon his fidelity to abstract principles if by so doing he can bring an end to the pain he is suffering.

A more protracted scene of torture and interrogation shows just this process at work. The narrator tells of how eleven girls in a nearby school were accused of bearing "the Devil's marks," which they at first protested were merely flea bites. Yet after being locked away in dark and solitary confinement for ten days, one confessed to her crimes. She admitted to all manner of wild and unholy things: riding broomsticks and dancing with the Devil and other evil acts. The narrator recalls:

> That is what she said—not in narrative form, for she was not able to remember any of the details without having them called to her mind one after the other; but the commission did that, for they knew just what questions to ask, they being all written down for the use of witch commissioners two centuries before. (758)

The narrator seems here to accept the commissioners' premise that by torturing a person's body one may get at the truths that he or she holds in mind. By attacking the physical body, one may attain to the mind and soul. Yet when he attends the burning at the stake of the eleven girls, the narrator sees one he remembers playing with as a child, and his abstract acceptance of the commission's tactics falters. He

recalls: "It was too dreadful and I went away." Bakhtin argues that the
grotesque "leads man out of the confines of the apparent (false) unity,
of the indisputable and stable" (*Rabelais* 48). For the narrator, seeing
the grotesque image of his childhood friend bound to a stake leads
him away from his former acceptance of the commission's "indisputable" ruling. His turning away from the crowd is not merely a physical
act, but a moral one.

While religious hypocrisy is the primary target of Twain's satire
in *The Mysterious Stranger*, both Satan and the narrator expand the
scope of their argument to include economic and social structures that
sacrifice the human body to abstract belief systems. After visiting the
torture chamber, for example, Satan brings the narrator to a French
industrial village. They tour living and working conditions that are
no less dismal than the dungeon they have just left and see factory
workers who are "worn and half starved, and weak and drowsy" (753).
Satan details the workers' plight and then draws a connection between
how they are treated and how the imprisoned heretic was tortured:
"You see how they treat a misdoer there in the jail; now you see how
they treat the innocent and the worthy. Is your race logical?" (753).
Whereas the heretic and the accused witches are tortured and killed
for having committed offenses against the church's teachings, the
men and women of the industrial town have been sacrificed to an
economic principle. The owners of the factory, Satan argues, "are rich,
and very holy," yet somehow their very holiness justifies the conditions in which they keep their workers. Their faith in the abstract
system of capitalism and in the promise of salvation blinds them to
the bodily suffering of their workers. In thinking of Heaven, they fail
to see that their factory town is a hell on earth.

An even more grotesque coupling of economic concerns with the
material body comes later in the novella, when a little girl's corpse is
seized as collateral:

> At the graveyard the body of little Lisa was seized for debt by
> a carpenter to whom the mother owed fifty groschen for work
> done the year before. She had never been able to pay this, and
> was not able now. The carpenter took the corpse home and kept
> it four days in his cellar, the mother weeping and imploring
> about his house all the time; then he buried it in his brother's
> cattle-yard, without religious ceremonies.

As in the case of the factory workers, religion and economics become entangled in the treatment of the body. The carpenter not only keeps Lisa's body as collateral on her mother's debt to him, but keeps the body from the religious rites and Christian burial that would help to assure that her soul is bound for heaven. Burying the corpse in a cattle-yard is more than an indignity; it is an act that endangers the state of Lisa's soul itself. As in the scenes of inquisition, torture, and witch burning, the body, be it living or dead, is a means of accessing the spirit.

All societies have a set of rituals and taboos associated with the treatment of the dead body, and it would be hard to find a place and time where the carpenter's actions—seizing a corpse in order to secure repayment of a loan—would be socially acceptable. Homer's *Iliad*, for example, ends with the story of Achilles' grotesque mistreatment of Hector's corpse. Only when Hector's aged father, King Priam, comes to beg for the right to bury his son, does Achilles see the injustice of what he has done. In the *Iliad*, the mistreatment of a dead body is an act of epic proportions, and Homer treats the episode with great dignity. The mistreatment of Lisa's corpse, on the other hand, is represented in very different terms. Relaying the facts in an abrupt, telescopic, and matter-of-fact manner, Twain's narrator denies the event the tragic proportions that Homer gives to the death of Hector. Instead, the narration itself is as grotesque as are the carpenter's actions. Injury and death comes suddenly and without sentiment, as functions of comedy rather than of tragedy or epic.

Having been told by Satan that their friend Nikolaus will drown while attempting to save a young girl who has fallen into a river, the narrator and his friend, Seppi, try valiantly to keep their friend from leaving the house on the day of his imminent death. Nikolaus's mother presses cake and other treats on them, then, seeing their pallor and misinterpreting it as heartburn, plies them with medicine and cordials. Unbeknownst to any of the three, Nikolaus has slipped out of the house during his mother's ministrations:

> Then she watched the effect, and it did not satisfy her; so she
> made us wait longer, and kept upbraiding herself for giving us
> the unwholesome cake. Presently the thing happened which
> we were dreading. There was a sound of tramping and scraping

outside, and a crowd came solemnly in, with heads uncovered,
and laid the two drowned bodies on the bed. (786)

One minute Nikolaus is alive and well in his bedroom; the next
minute his dead body is being carried in by a sudden crowd. The
episode is cartoonish and anti-climactic; the actual drowning receives
no mention at all, and instead the text dwells on the cake and the
cordials. The effect is to leach from Seppi's death any sense of pathos
or emotional weight. The narrator may be profoundly affected by his
friend's death, but his narrative itself fails to move the reader.

The grotesque elements of *The Mysterious Stranger* are therefore
located not only in the suffering bodies of the men and women
that people the story, but in the body of the text itself. The narrator,
with his anti-climactic and cartoonish representations of suffering,
is partly responsible for these formal grotesqueries, but Satan is far
more so. Inquisitors and witch hunters need to torture the body to
get at the mind and soul, but Satan, being spirit rather than body,
has direct access to the narrator's thoughts. This produces a series of
odd and disconcerting moments in which Satan responds to the text
of the narrative itself rather than to the narrator's words. The effect
is to warp the traditional distinction between narrative and dialogue,
between what is conveyed to the reader and what is conveyed among
the characters.

When Satan compares human beings to "bricks or manure," for
example, the narrator holds his tongue: "I could see he meant no
offense, but in my thoughts I set it down as not very good manners."
Yet the narrator's thoughts are as readily accessible to Satan as
his words would be, and the angel responds as if the narrator has
spoken: "'Manners!' he said. 'Why, it is merely the truth, and the
truth is good manners; manners are a fiction'" (732). Again and
again, Satan intrudes on the thoughts and idle musings of the
narrator with a direct access that the inquisitors could only dream
of having. Satan therefore shoulders aside both the narrator and
the reader, for he can "read" the first-person narrative of Twain's
story as readily as either of them. Satan bends the text out of shape,
blurring the boundaries between narration and dialogue, between
narrator and reader, and between the text and the world that the
text describes.

Satan's closing words represent a final grotesquerie. Whereas once he was content to challenge the narrator's moral vision of the world and the human body, Satan now challenges the very reality of the narrator's world and body. Satan tells the youth:

> You are not you—you have no body, no blood, no bones, you are but a thought. I myself have no existence; I am but a dream—your dream, creature of your imagination. In a moment you will have realized this, then you will banish me from your visions and I shall dissolve into the nothingness out of which you made me . . . (813)

The novella has structured itself around grotesque representations of the human body in pain. Those who would police the thoughts or beliefs of their neighbor must do so through the crude instrument of the body, torturing or imprisoning it to access the secrets of the mind. Now Satan inverts this relationship between body and mind. It is the body itself that is an abstraction, for the narrator's true existence is as a "thought." The novella ends with this sudden descent into solipsism, in which the narrator finds himself suddenly and profoundly alone. Satan spells out the larger implications of such solipsism:

> It is true, that which I have revealed to you; there is no God, no universe, no human race, no earthly life, no heaven, no hell. It is all a dream—a grotesque and foolish dream. Nothing exists but you. And you are but a thought—a vagrant thought, a useless thought, a homeless thought, wandering forlorn among the empty eternities! (814)

The patient suffering of those who thought themselves bound for Heaven is revealed to be fruitless, as Satan collapses the distinctions between body and soul, life and afterlife, the self and the other. All is but a "grotesque and foolish dream."

Should Twain's final work therefore be read as profoundly nihilistic? If we see Satan as speaking for Twain himself, then the author seems to be rejecting the very foundations of humanity and morality. One would do well, however, to remember that *The Mysterious Stranger*—despite the tortured, burned, and hanged bodies with which it is littered—is a comedy rather than a tragedy. Nowhere does

Satan speak more clearly for Twain than when he speaks of the comic. Counseling the rather humorless narrator, Satan tries to get the youth to see how incongruous, strange, and hilarious man's behavior really is. It is here, perhaps, that Satan gives voice to the underlying principle of *The Mysterious Stranger*: "Your race, in its poverty, has unquestionably one really effective weapon—laughter."

WORKS CITED

Bakhtin, Mikhail. *Rabelais and his World*. Bloomington: Indiana University Press, 1984.

———. *Problems of Dostoevsky's Poetics*. Minneapolis: University of Minnesota Press, 1984.

Twain, Mark. *The Complete Short Stories*. New York: Bantam Classic, 1981.

———. *The Mysterious Stranger Manuscripts*. Edited and with an introduction by William M. Gibson. Berkeley: University of California Press, 1969.

"THE OVERCOAT"
(NIKOLAI GOGOL)

"Reading Gogol's Grotesque 'Overcoat'"
by James N. Roney, Juniata College

As Boris Eikhenbaum illustrated in his 1919 essay, "How Gogol's 'Overcoat' Is Made," Nikolai Gogol's "Overcoat" uses *skaz*, a narrative technique that draws upon oral speech, first-person narration, and speech commonly used by the lower class, the lesser educated, and those living in regional, often rural areas with their own dialect. Because the narrator's speech and attitudes differ from those of educated readers, readers construct not only the events and characters but also the teller and his motivations, asking: Who is this narrator? Why has Gogol chosen to speak in this voice to tell us this story? By casting the story in such language while targeting the story to an educated audience, Gogol creates a bizarre effect. The narrator's distorted language, filled with the many irregularities of colloquial speech and the sort of puns and language games we associate with folklore or urban gossip, evokes both empathy and disgust from its readers, a characteristic response to the grotesque.

Vissarion Belinsky praised Gogol for building sympathy for the poor by describing their situation. Gogol's story seems to provoke such sympathy when the clerks, while mocking the main character, are suddenly taken aback by his response to their interrupting his work:

> Only if the fun got quite out of hand . . . and he was prevented from continuing his work, would he protest: "Leave me alone, why do you torment me?" And there was something

> strange about his words, and about the tone in which they were spoken. His voice contained something which inclined the listener to pity, which caused one young man of recent appointment, who followed the others' example in poking fun at him, suddenly to stop dead in his tracks, and thenceforth to see everything around him in a quite different light. Some unnatural force drew him away from his new friends, whom he had previously seen to be decent, cultivated people. . . . in these words he could hear quite a different message: "I am thy brother." (117)

Yet the key to understanding the significance of this passage lies in its tone. A meaningful aura emanating from some otherworldly presence, the young man's own consciousness, or Akaky's soul (of whose existence neither he nor we are very aware) permeates the government office and Akaky's normally inarticulate speech. The young man responds with only a comically exaggerated gesture: "At these moments the poor young man would cover his face with his hands" (117). The narrator's tone parodies the literature of effusive empathy:

> Many a time during his life did he shudder at the sight of man's cruelty to man, at the violent and brutish nature concealed behind a refined, educated and civilized veneer and, heaven help us! to be found even in those whom society has recognized as noble and honest. (117)

Consider another passage of explicit sympathy for Akaky:

> St. Petersburg continued its life without Akaky Akakievich just as if he had never existed. No trace remained of this creature defended by no one, dear to no one, of interest to no one, who failed even to attract the attention of the naturalist who will leap at the chance of putting a common housefly on a pin and studying it under a microscope; a creature who had endured with humility the jeers of his fellow clerks and had gone to his grave without any great achievement to his name, yet whose wretched life, for one brief moment so shortly before its end, had nevertheless been brightened by a radiant visitation in the form of a new overcoat, but who had then been crushed by

an intolerable blow of misfortune, as crushing as those which
befall the potentates and sovereigns of this world. (140)

This brotherly creature's grotesque behavior provokes our laughter,
even as his humanity elicits our sympathy. The exultant narrator uses
overly exalted rhetoric for the description of simple things; Gogol's
style requires his readers to be responsive to the grotesque, the combination of incompatible elements in a single whole with no dominant
organizing principle. A monster is a monster; a person is a person.
Neither of these is grotesque. Grotesquerie lies in a single being
with inseparable monstrous and human parts. Gogol's story is such
a being.

Gogol's narrator belongs to the lower level of the educated classes.
He is obviously literate but lacks the perspective and linguistic control
of the literary elite. He is a storyteller, a lover of puns and anecdotes
who relishes a joke about a "haemorrhoidal" (115) complexion as
much as an effusive call to love our neighbors. He claims faulty
knowledge, he is too frightened of authority to tell us where events
happened but not afraid to mock others. He represents a public that
repeats rumor at face value, loves strong effects, and is neither aware
of nor interested in its own contradictions. Sometimes absurdities
yield intentional jokes, as in the confusion over the *Bashmachkins* (or
Shoes) wearing "boots, only having them resoled three times a year"
(115). Sometimes they cause self-mockery: "who, as the reader will
know, are the butt of the jokes and mockery of many a writer, given to
the commendable habit of hitting out at those who cannot hit back"
(115). The narrator uses language not for its referential value, but for
its effect on the audience, giving us a little too much of everything:
too many explanations, too much expressed sympathy, and too many
anecdotes after Akaky's death.

The narrator offers a lengthy justification for Akaky's mother
picking his "somewhat strange and contrived" (115) name: "We have
made this digression in order that the reader might see for himself
that this was a matter of sheer necessity and it would have been
quite impossible to give him any other name" (116). His explanation
is absurd; we are suspicious not of the mother, but of the narrator
and Gogol. The educated reader is either frustrated or amused by a
narrator who believes, as a member of an oral culture, that the length
of a narrative can serve as proof of its truth. When Akaky visits Petro-

vich, the narrator ostentatiously yields to literary fashion "as it is now customary in stories to give a full account of the character of each of the dramatis personae . . . we shall have a close look at Petrovich too" (121). However, we get only anecdotes about Petrovich's drinking and how guardsmen "twitch their moustaches and utter a strange noise" (121) when they pass his wife. This satire of literary realism's emphasis on how environment and background shape character raises the question: Is the narrator mocking an expectation he has no intention of meeting, inadvertently mocking himself by claiming to meet a standard he does not understand, or both?

The narrator provides a humorous portrayal of a lowly clerk. The educated reader develops an image of him as someone who either does not understand the meaning of words or who is consciously baiting us. This distances the reader from narrator and story. Closer to Akaky in social status, the narrator sometimes humanizes him, conveying the uncanny presence of a higher sympathy. At other moments, his lack of perspective dehumanizes Akaky, making him the target of our laughter. This shifting distance between reader, author, narrator, and character makes the text mobile.

The narrator's hyperbole and inconsistencies make us doubt him. However, Gogol, whose fame as a provincial writer of folk grotesques made him doubt his own status in the literary elite, shares much in common with his narrator, causing us to find intentional irony or serious metaphysical writing rather than simple clumsiness in problematic passages. The square on which Akaky has his overcoat stolen appears as a kind of romantic void opening up in the middle of the city. Anyone who enters it can lose the external trappings that sustain identity by concealing the inner alienation of urban life. This is not just a funny tale about a silly clerk and a clumsy narrator but a sophisticated commentary on Petersburg life. The mobile relationship between character, narrator, and author culminates neither in humor, nor in moral empathy. The grotesque discourse of Gogol's *skaz*-narrator places everything on an equal level, frustrating attempts to distinguish between an author who has the beliefs of an educated writer and the humorous quirks of a narrator for whom all stories are valid if they produce strong effects. Critics err in praising Gogol for his humorous verbal play, spiritual insight, social criticism or sympathy for the poor, while attributing contradictory elements either to his own or his narrator's shortcomings. Gogol himself may have died because he could not reconcile the *skaz* at the heart of his talent with the moral demands he and his society placed on the author.

The story's narrator derives comic effects from the external description of characters' states of mind: "perhaps he was not thinking this at all—after all, you cannot see into the mind of another person and discover what he is thinking" (131). Even characters at their most comic suddenly become objects for sympathy in ecstatic moments of redemption or damnation. Since the characters lack a stable inner self or the narrator lacks the ability to depict it, Petersburg appears as a place in which human identity is precarious; barely existing and subject to various social and cosmological influences. Inner selves or instances of moral empathy appear only as acts of grace either deeply spiritual, if believed, or comical, if unbelievable. The narrator's humor complicates our reaction: "This adventure had the most profound effect on him. He even stopped saying so often to his inferiors: 'How dare you?—Do you realize who you are speaking to?' and if he did say it, it was not without first listening to what the other had to say" (144). Should we judge or empathize with the characters? Should we judge ourselves for alternating sympathy with laughter?

Akaky Akakievich's life has three stages: his early life as a perfect clerk, his new identity emerging around the overcoat, and his vengeful spirit after death. Akaky "was of the genus eternal Titular Councillor" (115). He grimaces at his birth as if he knows his fate; everyone imagines "that he must have been born into the world in exactly that state, complete with uniform and bald pate" (116). Immersed in the surface existence of copying, he lives only for his work: "there were certain letters that he particularly favoured and if he encountered them he would be quite transported; he would chuckle and wink and make sounds" (118). Barely aware of where he is, "he only saw all about him the even lines scripted in this neat hand, and only if a horse . . . should thrust its nose over his shoulder . . . might he realize that he was in the middle of the street and not in the middle of a sentence" (119). He spends whatever extra time he has at home copying some document which catches his interest by "the unusual identity or importance of its addressee" (119). He never notices what he eats and is unable to handle the stress of changing a few verbs in a document the one time he is offered an opportunity for advancement. "Such was the peaceful life led by a man who, with a salary of four hundred rubles, could be content with his lot, and such would it have continued" were it not for the natural aging of his overcoat and the "implacable enemy" (120) of the Petersburg climate. Akaky wraps himself in the routines and objects of his clerkish life; the narrator derives humorous effects from depicting his life. Together they create a hollow, puppet character.

The overcoat interrupts the superficial eternity of Akaky's life, giving him a past and a future, and forcing him to encounter new places, objects and characters. He almost makes a mistake in his copying. The overcoat becomes a future object, a potential spouse, a source of spiritual nourishment, and a life goal. "With this new regime his whole existence became somehow more fulfilled, as if he had got married, as if there were some other person with him" (127). Previously he lived in an eternal present defined by his job; now he imagines other existences and changes his behavior, no longer copying at home: "he chuckled whenever he thought of the appalling state of his old smock" (130). The early, will-less Akaky spoke

> with the use of prepositions, adverbs, and all sorts of particles which have absolutely no meaning at all. If the situation was particularly awkward he would even not complete his phrases . . . as he would be under the impression that he had said all he intended to say. (122-3)

Now he thinks in coherent paragraphs, maintains a "line of reasoning" (125) when deciding what to do after visiting Petrovich, and asserts his will by challenging the officials after his coat is stolen. Tragic irony hovers over these passages. He is not really capable of either socializing with the clerks or acting on his new erotic desires (staring at a bare leg in an ad; scampering after a woman on the street). The externals of office life have been traded for the externals of a consumer existence in which Akaky's overcoat and its owner lose their novelty value, becoming unnoticed and forgotten: "[H]e slipped out of the room surreptitiously, and hunted for his coat, which, to his distress, he observed lying on the floor" (132).

Akaky survived as a clerk by remaining unnoticed within a system valuing him only as an object for the plans and words of others, whether officials, fellow clerks, or authors. His desire for the coat causes interactions that cost him his life: "Such is the effect a good dressing-down can have!" (139). The dying Akaky is once again unable to communicate with others; lost in visions, he unleashes frightening curses in his delirium. The narrator, who has a popular sense of justice and loves oral tales of supernatural intervention, tells us Akaky returns after death to reclaim his coat. Did Akaky's assertion of self result in loss of self? Is his life after death only a new mask for his lack of a soul?

The clerks and officials live on different levels of a government hierarchy in which individuals define themselves by their ability to imitate or control others: "For such is the pass to which Holy Russia has come; imitation is the order of the day and each man spends his time aping and imitating his superiors" (136). The clerks buy the trappings of higher-class existence; officials force others to wait, practicing threatening expressions in front of the mirror. The clerks live in a swirling present governed by current rumor: "Somehow or other everyone in the department had learned that Akaky Akakievich has a new coat and that the old smock was no more. They all dashed out into the lobby to admire their colleague's latest acquisition" (130). They have good moral impulses but quickly forget Akaky and his coat and are subject to the whims of authority, "the sum [collected for Akaky] was only trifling because the department staff had already been made to pay out a lot of money in contributions, first towards a portrait of the director and then towards some new book, which their section head had recommended, being a friend of the author's" (135). Assuming the official rules are not as important as unofficial connections, they send Akaky to an inspector and the *important personage*, inadvertently causing his death from a stern rebuke. Their world is not so much evil as soulless and amoral; human responses are muted by propriety and good stories.

The overcoat also changes the tailor and the *important personage*. Petrovich lives outside polite society up a back staircase, "which, to be perfectly truthful, was thoroughly steeped in dishwater and slops, and everywhere gave off that acrid smell which so stings the eyes and which, as the reader will know, is an inescapable adjunct of all back staircases in St. Petersburg" (121). Petrovich enjoys frightening poor clerks: "He was very fond of strong effects, liked to say things which would shock, and then slyly watch the expression which these words brought to the face of his stunned listener" (124). Petrovich, given demonic aspects by Akaky's fear (Chizhevsky 319-320), becomes "conscious of the great chasm that divides tailors who merely stitch in linings and do repairs from those who create new garments" (Gogol 129). Petrovich, whose repairs "did no credit to the art of the tailor and were baggy and unsightly" (121), produces a fine garment from inexpensive materials by going over every seam with his teeth, following Akaky to see how the coat looks. He is a drunken, henpecked tailor who enjoys whatever power he exercises over others but is surprisingly capable of dedication and creativity when the coat enters his life. The *important personage*'s promotion prevents him from interacting with people of lower rank for fear of appearing undignified. He "preserves his silence," acquiring "the reputation of a crashing bore" (137). He delivers a crushing rebuke to Akaky merely to impress his visiting friend and is delighted "that his word alone was sufficient to scare the living daylights out of another person" and "that his friend was in a most uneasy state and was even beginning to show visible signs of alarm" (139). This rebuke kills Akaky but also troubles the *important personage*, who "experienced something in the nature of regret" since "compassion was not an entirely alien emotion to him; his heart was stirred by many kindly impulses, although his rank usually prevented him from revealing them" (142).

Gogol's humor mocks the behavior of characters who have no inner self and behave badly until those moments when something triggers a good impulse or pain, which is rarely properly expressed: the *important personage*'s sympathy causes him to seek consolation with his mistress for his suffering over Akaky's fate; the clerks forget Akaky or help him with insufficient funds and bad advice; the narrator describes sincere actions with such hyperbolic rhetoric that we start to laugh at our own sympathy. Petersburg extends into an eternal modern city in which the soul is absent and human interaction is threatened with amoral dissolution. Only when the narrator's "perfectly authentic" story takes a "fantastic twist" (142) can Akaky's ghost and his army of real thieves save souls. These comments and actions enhance the story's moral grotesquery because they are barely manifest in the here and now of everyday life.

Near the story's end, the *important personage*

> wrapped himself luxuriously in his warm overcoat, and lapsed into that state so cherished by the average Russian, when he no longer has to think for himself, for the thoughts come crowding

into his head of their own will, each more pleasing than the
last, and require no exhausting pursuit. (143)

The violent theft of his coat breaks this receptive state, shocking him
into a more moral life. An "average Russian," Gogol's *skaz*-narrator
delights in recounting everything he hears, deriving full aesthetic
and comic pleasure from his story's contradictory elements. A naïve
raconteur, he refuses to engage in the "exhausting pursuit" of consistent moral judgment or logical consistency. Readers wanting to derive
a consistent message from a comic story told by a narrator who alter-
nates between amorality and moral effusiveness are tempted to judge
the narrator and themselves for being too quick to enjoy life's absurdities before assuaging their guilt by leaping to a level of meaning where
all can be explained and judged.

For Harold Bloom, such desire threatens the existence of the
western canon, replacing the essentially solitary perceptions of
aesthetic competition with moral or political considerations. Gogol's
story embraces and mocks political and moral readings. The narrator
himself is both amoral and ostentatiously moral, espousing multiple
moralities. The authorial voice mocks both him and its own desire to
feel superior to him. Every respectable, consistent reading is caught
up in the story's grotesque laughter. The story can be read as a verbal
game whose narrator glories in puns and shocking events, playing
with language and our expectations. However, the comic passages
of moral empathy and fear of higher judgment also mock such
aesthetic amorality. Are we, as in Gogol's plays, actually laughing
at ourselves? Our reading cruelly duplicates the actions of those
characters that use others only as objects of a speech displaying
its own power. Only the rare work of art brings us to experience
the momentary insight and existential unrest found in a story like
Gogol's, which finds humor in our lives as finite beings, both laughable and worthy of empathy.

WORKS CITED

Bakhtin, Mikhail. *Rabelais and His World.* Trans. Helene Iswolsky.
    Bloomington: Indiana UP, 1984.
Bloom, Harold. "An Elegy for the Canon." Introduction. *The Western Canon.*
    The Books and School of the Ages. New York: Harcourt Brace, 1994: 15–41.

Chizhevsky, Dmitry. "About Gogol's 'Overcoat'." *Gogol from the Twentieth Century. Eleven Essays.* Ed. and Trans. Robert Maguire. Princeton: Princeton UP, 1974: 293–322.

Eichenbaum, Boris. "How Gogol's 'Overcoat' Is Made." *Gogol from the Twentieth Century. Eleven Essays.* Ed. and Trans. Robert Maguire. Princeton: Princeton UP, 1974: 269-294.

Gogol, Nikolai. "The Overcoat." *Plays and Petersburg Tales.* Trans. Christopher English. Oxford: Oxford University Press, 1995: 115–145.

Maguire, Robert. "The Legacy of Criticism." Introduction. *Gogol from the Twentieth Century. Eleven Essays.* Ed. and Trans. Robert Maguire. Princeton: Princeton UP, 1974: 3–54.

Terras, Victor. *Belinsky and Russian Literary Criticism. The Heritage of Organic Aesthetics.* Madison: U of Wisconsin P, 1974.

"REVELATION"
(FLANNERY O'CONNOR)

"The Grotesque Protagonist"
by Gilbert H. Muller,
in *Nightmares and Visions: Flannery O'Connor and the Catholic Grotesque* (1972)

INTRODUCTION

Gilbert Muller hails Flannery O'Connor's short story "Revelation" as a "triumph of the comic grotesque," one whose protagonist, Ruby Turpin, "turns the story into a punitive fable on arrogance, hypocrisy, and pride." Discussing O'Connor's place in the Southern grotesque tradition and her use of grotesque characterizations, Muller claims "the grotesque was [her] ideal vehicle for objectifying [the] fears, obsessions, and compulsions" she perceived in Southern culture. The presence of the grotesque, for Muller, "suggests that the visible world is incomprehensible and unregenerate [i.e. unredeemed]." This fearful and revelatory vision leaves readers, and O'Connor's Ruby Turpin, "floundering in a sea of contradictions and incongruities," yearning for spiritual redemption.

Muller, Gilbert H. "The Grotesque Protagonist." *Nightmares and Visions: Flannery O'Connor and the Catholic Grotesque.* Athens, GA: University of Georgia Press, 1972: 19–50.

The moral vision of writers like West, Sophocles, and Faulkner was obviously congenial to Flannery O'Connor, because she found her natural idiom in stories where the characters—Miss Lonelyhearts, Oedipus, the Bundrens—confront the limits of mystery. As Miss O'Connor once remarked in delineating her own work, "the look of this fiction is going to be wild ... it is almost of necessity going to be violent and comic, because of the discrepancies that it seeks to combine." [1] And the writer who cultivates this type of vision, based on characters "who are forced out to meet evil and grace and who act on a trust beyond themselves," [2] will inevitably be interested in the grotesque.

Miss O'Connor began writing about grotesques because she could, as she readily admitted in a letter to James Farnham, recognize them. "Essentially the reason why my characters are grotesque," she explained, "is because it is the nature of my talent to make them so. To some extent the writer can choose his subject; but he can never choose what he is able to make live. It is characters like the Misfit and the Bible salesman that I can make live." [3] Flannery O'Connor was preeminently successful in character depiction because she realized that the grotesque was the ideal vehicle for objectifying fears, obsessions, and compulsions. Within her southern landscape (only two of her stories are set outside the South, and they involve southern characters), it is the common everyday confrontations, such as a family trip or a visit to the doctor's office, that are filled with horror, and it is the sudden irrationality of the familiar world that induces distortions in character. Thus the grotesque suggests that the visible world is incomprehensible and unregenerate, and that the individual is floundering in a sea of contradictions and incongruities.

The typical grotesque character in Miss O'Connor's fiction is an individual who projects certain extreme mental states which, while psychologically valid, are not investigations in the tradition of psychological realism. To be certain, the reality of the unconscious life—incorporating dream, fantasy, and hallucination—is expressed, but grotesque characterization is not interested in the subtleties of emotion and feeling, but rather in their larger outlines. This method actually tends toward the symbolic, where distillation of character into a basic set of preoccupations serves to crystallize attitudes toward the ethical circumstances being erected. Here a basic point to emphasize is that grotesque characterization does not necessarily make the characters in a story remote or improbable, since the sacrifice in psychological realism is more counterbalanced by the impact of the grotesque. [...]

Although there is no counterpart in her fiction to Faulkner's Yoknapatawpha, to Eudora Welty's Natchez Trace, or to the dark and bloody ground of Robert Penn Warren, O'Connor's writing does bear an intrinsic relationship to the historicity of her region. As she observed in her essay "The Catholic Novelist in the Protestant South":

> The two circumstances that have given character to my own writing have been those of being Southern and being Catholic. This is considered by many to be an unlikely combination, but I have found it to be a most likely one. I think that the South provides the Catholic novelist with some benefits that he usually lacks, and lacks to a conspicuous degree. The Catholic novel can't be categorized by subject matter, but only by what it assumes about human and divine reality. It cannot see man as determined; it cannot see him as totally depraved. It will see him as incomplete in himself, as prone to evil, but as redeemable when his own efforts are assisted by grace. And it will see this grace as working through nature, but as entirely transcending it, so that a door is always open to possibility and the unexpected in the human soul.[4]

The operation of grace through nature is one of the author's major fictional and religious concerns, and this explains why she valued her region and its culture so highly—precisely because it revealed certain manifestations of the spirit grounded in the concrete world. This spiritual dimension of reality led Miss O'Connor to remark in "The Regional Writer": "To call yourself a Georgia writer is certainly to declare a limitation, but one which, like all limitations, is a gateway to reality. It is a great blessing, perhaps the greatest blessing a writer can have, to find at home what others have to go elsewhere seeking."[5] The South provided Miss O'Connor with two main attributes of her fiction—a sense of manners and a sense of religious mystery. Manners are a part of the concrete world which every serious novelist must acknowledge. "You get manners," she observed in "Writing Short Stories," "from the texture of existence that surrounds you. The great advantage of being a Southern writer is that we don't have to go anywhere to look for manners; bad or good, we've got them in abundance. We in the South live in a society that is rich in contradiction, rich in irony, rich in contrast, and particularly rich in speech."[6] This sense of historical ambiguity, rooted in the concrete, extends outward until it embraces the realm of mystery, and the coincidence of these two qualities, as Robert Heilman has observed in one of the most penetrating essays on the nature of southern literature, is what makes the fiction of this region so distinctive. Heilman terms the sense of mystery a "sense of totality," yet it is easy to discern that he and Miss O'Connor are discussing the same phenomenon:

> Inclined to question whether suffering is totally eliminatable or unequivocally evil, the Southerners are most aware that, as Tate has put it, man is incurably religious, and that the critical problem is not one of skeptically analyzing the religious impulse of thinking as if religion did not exist for a mature individual and culture, but of distinguishing the real thing and the surrogates. . . . For them, totality is more than the sum of the sensory and the rational. The invention of gods is a mark, not of a passion for unreality, but of a high sense of reality; is not a regrettable flight from science, but perhaps a closer approach to the problem of being.[7]

The burden which a sense of reality and of mystery imposes upon a writer is one of honesty toward one's region, rather than of slavish devotion to it. As Miss O'Connor mentioned in "The Fiction Writer and His Country," truthful depiction of these two qualities requires "a delicate adjustment of the outer and inner worlds, in such a way that, without changing their nature, they can be seen through each other. To know oneself is to know one's region. It is also to know the world, and it is also, paradoxically, a form of exile from that world."[8] To be an exile from the world implies a detachment from it, and this in turn permits a degree of objectivity in rendering it. This feeling of exile places O'Connor at the center of what Lewis Simpson, in an elegant and carefully wrought investigation of the southern writer, terms the Great Literary Secession.[9] Miss O'Connor is able to appreciate the cultural and historical richness of her region because of this detachment, which does not negate her willingness to utilize the South's firm guidelines: "... these guides have to exist in a concrete form, known and held sacred by the whole community. They have to exist in the form of stories which affect our image and our judgement of ourselves."[10] By being in partial exile from her region, Flannery O'Connor never succumbs to what C. Van Woodward has called those illusions of innocence and virtue which afflict all aspects of the southern mind—and the broader American character as well.

[...]

In her facetious moments Miss O'Connor was fond of asserting that to be a Georgia author was "a rather specious dignity, on the same order as, for the pig, being a Talmadge ham."[11] Yet seen within the larger context analyzed above, it is obvious that for her the term "regional writer" was certainly a valuable restriction. Indeed her origins were an asset, because Flannery O'Connor realized that the interplay of social and religious forces in the South worked to produce both characters and situations that were inherently grotesque. Thus, when asked why she wrote about grotesque characters, she replied:

> Because we can still recognize one. In the South, where most people still believe in original sin, our sense of evil is still just strong enough to make us skeptical about most modern solutions, no matter how long we embrace them. We are still held by a sense of mystery, however much against our will. The prophet-freaks of Southern literature are not images of the man in the street. They are images of man forced out to meet the extremes of his own nature. The writer owes a great debt to everything he sees around him, and in Georgia he is particularly blessed in having about him a collection of goods and evils which are intensely stimulating to the imagination.[12]

Realizing that the South was "Christ-haunted and that ghosts cast strange shadows, very fierce shadows, particularly in our literature,"[13] Miss O'Connor made the vast majority of her characters attest to a religious presence by either fanatically embracing or denying it, by remaining dangerously apathetic about it, or by replacing it with a more contemporary explanation of human destiny. The communal displacement which is so evident in her "farm" stories, for example, serves as an index of the spiritual displacement of the characters. With a regional background rooted in a sense of evil and of original sin, incredible grotesques emerge, since the history of the area tends to foster extreme behavior.

Delineation of the cultural grotesque as a main character type establishes Flannery O'Connor as a very special kind of regionalist, as one who both utilizes the South's special resources and who is decidedly at odds with it, for what she once described as the division of Christendom is rooted largely in the failure of community. Her cultural grotesques do not cultivate the land but instead pursue moral and spiritual decay. They debase their own traditions, and consequently Miss O'Connor found little civic virtue in her rural folk. She assailed the myth of agrarian perfection promulgated from Jefferson to Allen Tate. This led her to conclude that the Catholic novelist in the Protestant South "will feel a good deal more kinship with backwoods prophets and shouting fundamentalists than he will with those politer elements for whom the supernatural is an embarrassment and for whom religion has become a department of sociology or culture or personality development."[14] Realizing that the Agrarians could no longer speak for her generation, she evolved a new attitude based on physical and spiritual isolation within the community. Her fiction reveals that the norms of southern life have lost their sacredness and have become disastrously secular in orientation. The reality of this situation in turn forced her to concentrate upon the atypicality of southern life, because the new southern identity must derive not "from the mean average or the typical, but from the hidden and often the most extreme."[15]

For Flannery O'Connor communal life in the South *should* have a spiritual basis, yet its very absence forced her not only to attack this dissociation but also to locate the divine in the extreme. "I am always having it pointed out to me," she wrote, "that life in Georgia is not at all the way I picture it, that escaped criminals do not roam the roads exterminating families, nor Bible salesmen prowl about looking for girls with wooden legs."[16] The point is that people like the Misfit and the Bible salesman, or the insane Singleton of the uncollected story "The Partridge Festival" (1961), who kills even more people than the Misfit, are necessary in order to force a recognition of man's radical dependence on God upon the average man. The true cultural grotesques are the invariably well-mannered members of the community who ignore the spiritual foundations of their culture. Miss O'Connor sees the South as struggling to preserve this spiritual identity, not only against the Raybers and the Sheppards, but also against those numerous members of the community who substitute sanctimoniousness for true Christian virtue. This insight into human nature applies especially well to her earth mothers—to Mrs. May in "Greenleaf," to Mrs. McIntyre in "The Displaced Person," to Mrs. Cope in "A Circle in the Fire," and to Mrs. Turpin in "Revelation." These women traipse their fields, pastures, and woods with a single-minded sense of righteous proprietorship that prevents them from recognizing a fundamentally spiritual estrangement from their surroundings, an estrangement rooted in their inability to act charitably toward their neighbors. Unaware of their alienation, these ordinary individuals are extremely vulnerable to extraordinary events which test their harshness and rigidity of spirit.

One of the most remarkable of these cultural grotesques is Ruby Turpin, the protagonist of Flannery O'Connor's short story, "Revelation." Unlike many writers whose energies atrophy in middle age, Miss O'Connor had talents that were constantly improving, and a story as nearly flawless as "Revelation" (which won a posthumous first prize in the O'Henry competitions) is a poignant testament to a talent thwarted by death. First published in the *Sewanee Review* in 1964, it is a fable of God's providence operating in a doctor's office and in a pig pen. A triumph of the comic grotesque, the story opens in a doctor's waiting room, where an extraordinary collection of patients who form a miniature society—a ship of fools—awaits examination. Assembled in this almost claustrophobic office are representative diseases of the body, the mind, and the spirit: the crippled bodies of the aged, the maimed intelligences of the poor and the neuroses of the intellectually gifted, and the defective souls of the self-righteous. Their illnesses represent the maladies of society, and the traits of this society are progressively revealed to a point where the absurdity implicit in the characters' behavior must explode.

Ruby Turpin, who self-indulgently speculates about the blessings bestowed on her by the Lord, unconsciously turns the story into a punitive fable on arrogance, hypocrisy, and pride. She gradually emerges as a high-toned Christian lady whose sense of social and moral superiority and whose extreme self-absorption and pride border on narcissism. Negative aspects of her character are progressively revealed and thrown into grotesque perspective, and each brushstroke fills in a canvas that is unrelieved by any redeeming qualities. Mindless of her faults, she establishes herself as a type of white culture heroine, aligned with a pitiful minority against the encroachments of Negroes, poor-white trash, and the baser elements of humanity. Because of her obsessions and her spiritual deformities she is inherently grotesque; her thoughts and her actions reveal her as a negative moral agent, unaware of her own absurdity because she is so attached to an inauthentic existence.

It is relevant that Miss O'Connor plots this story at a pace that is discernibly slower than most of her short fiction and that Ruby's unbearable self-righteousness is gradually reinforced to the point of the reader's exasperation. The lack of any physical action, counterpointed by Ruby's constant speculation on the mysteries of creation and by the mechanical conversation of the patients, creates a repressed narrative pace wherein the slightest disruption in movement could have the unusual effect of releasing tensions which lie just beneath the surface of the story. Thus the dramatic escalation which occurs abruptly after Ruby thanks the Lord for having created in her such a fine creature is so unanticipated that the shocking impact creates one of the revelations to which the title of the story alludes. As the Wellesley girl strikes Ruby Turpin in the eye with a hurled book and pounces on her in a frenzy, the astonishing disclosure of the girl's imprecation is not only authoritative in moral terms, but approximates, as perfectly as the literary medium can, the actual force of revelation.

The execration which the girl hurls at Ruby Turpin is both shocking and convincing, for it calls Ruby's self-contained egocentric existence into question. Ruby tries to rebel against this revelation, which in theological terms is a manifestation of God's providence, and which in emotional terms is cathartic. Because of this revelation she becomes an inhabitant of a world which suddenly appears estranged to her. Her initial revelation—that she is, in the girl's words, a wart-hog from hell—is at first incomprehensible and then outrageous, and the remainder of the story traces the process whereby she painfully learns obedience, which is a prerequisite of true faith and of salvation.

Ruby's failure to present a suitable defense of herself shifts from outrage to hatred and bitterness toward God, and the image of this woman marching out to the pig parlour to wage battle with the Lord is a brilliant and hilarious picture of the false believer journeying to meet her apocalypse. Still actively engaged in an attempt to reconstruct the world in her own image, she subsumes any conception of God to her own blueprint, an act that constitutes absolute heresy. This is her central crisis—and the crisis of all of Flannery O'Connor's cultural grotesques: as the landscape transforms itself from the brightness of late afternoon to a deepening and mysterious blue, the reality of this crisis begins to catch up with her.

Ruby Turpin is one of the author's countless grotesques who are largely the creations of themselves. Their own misconception of self and of social laws places them in opposition to a higher justice which assures the ultimate triumph of their opposites—the humble and the meek. Assuredly the lame shall enter first, while the superior citizen, conducting his life for his own sake, shall suffer a humiliation even more acute than total damnation.

Conscious elaboration of the cultural grotesque was merely a part of Flannery O'Connor's incisive depiction of degeneracy at all social levels. All her characters are susceptible to defects in nature and spirit, and these deficiencies are what estrange them from the community and from God. Whether it is Haze Motes trying nihilistically to overturn his culture, or Ruby Turpin attempting to preserve it, Miss O'Connor ridicules pride and hypocrisy wherever she finds it. She unmasks her grotesques by exposing their perversity, affectation, and vanity, and she frequently reduces them to impotence through satire. For O'Connor it is the grotesque which underlies all forms of failure. Revealing the dilemmas in the quest for human identity, she shows how the lack of an integrated society—which for the author would be a Christian society—prevents the possibility of an integrated personality. All her grotesques eventually come to the realization of the fact that they are aspiring toward illusory points in a secular world. This defect in vision, epitomized by Haze Motes, whose very name suggests his confused condition, creates an abnormality which is not easily cured.

The grotesques of Flannery O'Connor are individuals who cannot erase the horrors of their obsessions. Few images of peace and beauty populate their world, few are the interludes of order. Implicit in their behavior are all the conventions of the grotesque—the nightmare world, the perversion, the satanic humor. These people wear their deficiencies of spirit as scars—as emblems of a world without order, meaning, or sense of continuity. In an attempt to transcend their painful condition, to rise above that which is alienated and estranged, Miss O'Connor's protagonists invariably descend into the demonic.

Obsessed with their own sins, with weakness, evil, and suffering, they turn inward upon themselves and act out their agonies in extraordinary ways. Because O'Connor's grotesques are—to paraphrase T. S. Eliot in his essay on Baudelaire—men enough to be saved or damned, their actions in this world become reflections of the interior life of the soul. It is one of the triumphs of Flannery O'Connor's art—and a mark of her vital faith—that she is willing to write about all types of malefactors who, utterly out of harmony with the world and with Creation, risk exile and damnation for their disbelief.

NOTES

1. "Some Aspects of the Grotesque in Southern Literature," in *Mystery and Manners*, ed. Sally and Robert Fitzgerald (New York: Farrar, Straus & Giroux, 1969), p. 43. This essay was published originally in *Cluster Review* (March 1965). Miss O'Connor was one of the few writers of the grotesque who commented on the tradition and genre which she was using in her fiction.
2. Ibid., p. 42.
3. "Flannery O'Connor—A Tribute," p. 23.
4. *Mystery and Manners*, pp. 196-197. This essay appeared initially in the Georgetown magazine, *Viewpoint* (Spring 1966).
5. Ibid., p. 54. "The Regional Writer" was first published in *Esprit*, 7 (Winter 1963).
6. Ibid., p. 103.
7. "The Southern Temper," in *Southern Renaissance*, ed. Louis D. Rubin, Jr., and Robert D. Jacobs (Baltimore: Johns Hopkins Press, 1953), p. 11. Many of the most astute critics of southern literature have acknowledged this holiness of the secular. See in this anthology the essays by Richard Weaver and Andrew Lytle, and in the editors' *South: Modern Southern Literature in its Cultural Setting* (Garden City: Doubleday, 1961) the essay by Louise Cowan, who writes:

> . . . as a community adapts itself to a way of life, a conciliation of the divine and the human orders may be effected within it. In such a society, economic, moral, and aesthetic patterns, transformed by a kind of grace,

lose their exclusively secular character and begin to assume a sacredness within the community; and loyalty between members of the community rests on this essentially metaphysical basis. Men do not bow to each other but to the divine as it manifests itself in the communal life (pp. 98–99).

8. "The Fiction Writer and His Country," in *The Living Novel: A Symposium*, ed. Granville Hicks (New York: Collier, 1957), p. 163.

9. "The Southern Writer and the Great Literary Secession," *Georgia Review*, 24 (Winter 1970), 393-412. As with Heilman and others, Simpson connects the posture of the literary exile with manifestations of the divine. "The vision of the Agrarians," he writes, "always had . . . a strong religious and metaphysical quality. This indeed is the quality of the whole modern effort toward a renewal of letters, which ultimately is an expression of an increasing alienation of modern man from the mystery of the Word" (p. 411).

10. *Mystery and Manners*, p. 202.

11. Ibid., p. 52.

12. Margaret Meaders, "Flannery O'Connor: Literary Witch," *Colorado Quarterly*, 10 (Spring 1962), 384.

13. *Recent Southern Fiction: A Panel Discussion*, Bulletin of Wesleyan College, 41 (January 1961), p. 11.

14. *Mystery and Manners*, p. 207.

15. Ibid., p. 58.

16. Ibid., p. 38.

Six Characters in Search of an Author
(Luigi Pirandello)

"Luigi Pirandello's *Six Characters in Search of an Author* and the Grotesque"
by J. R. Holt, Centenary College

In general, the word "grotesque" refers to the appearance of incongruity, distortion, abnormality, or just plain ugliness. Normally we seek to avoid beholding such appearances because they elicit discomfort and pain (as opposed to the pleasure we feel upon beholding what is beautiful). Since all art invites us to behold it, thus to experience aesthetic pleasure, an art that is *deliberately* ugly or grotesque seems to be a contradiction. The grotesque aesthetic is a "beautiful ugliness" because it breaks down our conventional notions of beauty, harmony, order, and meaning, forcing us to find sense beyond our familiar categories of beauty and knowing. In the process, we come to realize that those familiar categories themselves are artificial, and as such can distort the truth behind appearances. Grotesque art, then, employs distortion to correct distortion.

The distortion addressed in *Six Characters in Search of an Author* is articulated by Pirandello in the play's "Preface." The problem he was trying to get at in this play, he said, is "the inherent tragic conflict between life (which is always moving and changing) and form (which fixes it, immutable)." That is, any work of art seeks to express vital matters of meaning and value through finite, fixed forms. A play script, once written, is fixed, immutable. Yet its subject matter—generally, human existence—is constantly changing from moment to moment; and more, these changes do not cancel previous changes but rather add to them, thus making for endless complexity. The reductive simplifications of art, then, clash with the indefinite complexities of human living. Pirandello sees this conflict as tragic because *any* order—which we humans truly need—is *artificial*, or "made by human artifice." The trick is to not see this artificial order as a natural order, but that is very difficult for us to do. (The notion, by the way, that all order is artificial rather than natural is one of the hallmarks of the post-modern perspective.)

Six Characters, then, uses distortion to correct distortion. One distortion is our illusion that a work of art is transparent: that we can see through the art to the reality it represents. An actor represents a character, which represents a person; but, unless that person is based on a historical human being (e.g., King Henry V, but not Prince Hamlet), the represented person is imaginary. But even if the person has a historical basis, his or her representation is as artificial as if it were purely imaginary. So the main characters in this play—the Father, the Step-Daughter, and the Son—insist that actors cannot play their roles because their roles are somehow real. As opposed to actual persons existing in time and space, they have been imagined into a state of being by an author. They are as real as an idea or a design. But, like an unfinished symphony, their design is unresolved. Like souls in Limbo, they crave resolution so that they may rest, complete and whole.

In his "Preface to *Six Characters in Search of an Author*," which he wrote four years after the premiere of the play to address the puzzlement of its audiences, Pirandello tells of how these six characters were formed in his "fantasy" in response to a "spiritual need" for meaning within him. He then goes on to explain how the story he began to construct for them failed to meet that need: "Now, however much I sought, I did not succeed in uncovering the meaning in the six characters. And I concluded therefore that it was no use making them live." When these characters nonetheless lingered in his imagination—begging, as it were, for resolution—he hit upon the idea of this play, in which "they had each to appear in that stage of creation which they had attained in the author's fantasy at the moment when he wished to drive them away."

The six characters are members of a family: Father, Mother, and their 22-year-old Son, along with a step-family consisting of a young woman (Step-Daughter), the 14-year-old Boy, and the 4-year-old girl

(Child), who are children of Mother and her second husband, who
has recently died, which explains why the step-family wears black
clothing. Apparently, the point at which Pirandello "wished to drive
them away" is the drowning of Child in a fountain and the subsequent
suicide of Boy. We know that these terrible events have not been
improvised or added on in their enactment for two reasons: (1) no one
has assumed the task of "author" to resolve the family's story; and (2)
the suicide is anticipated (foreshadowed, foreknown, fated, scripted)
at the beginning of Act II, when Step-Daughter, seeing a gun in Boy's
pocket, tells him, "If I'd been in your place, instead of killing myself,
I'd have shot one of those two, or both of them: father and son."

It is fair to speculate on why Pirandello chose to abandon the
project at this particular point. In his "Preface", Pirandello provides an
important clue to this question when he describes his passive, authorial role in the creative process:

> I can only say that, without having made any effort to seek them
> out, I found before me, alive—you could touch them and even
> hear them breathe—the six characters now on the stage. And
> they stayed there in my presence, each with his secret torment
> and all bound together by the one common origin and mutual
> entanglement of their affairs, while I had them enter the world
> of art, constructing from their persons, their passions, and their
> adventures a novel, a drama, or at least a story.

The inspiration of his fantasy was the image of a family, a family
where each member suffers a particular torment, though they all share
a common origin. What Pirandello had to add was a story or plot that
would link a set of related events in a rough cause-effect sequence
so as to make their suffering meaningful. When Child drowns in a
fountain and Boy commits suicide, Pirandello appears to have given
up his search for the meaning he wants to achieve. It is not clear
whether Child fell into the fountain or was deliberately pushed into
it by Boy; nor is it clear why Boy has a gun or how he got one. It
is clear, however, that Boy, who seems mentally disturbed, perhaps
autistic, either failed to save Child, or did not try to save her at all. The
implication is that his state of mind is affected by the whole family
dynamic, which is one of moral sickness. A further implication is that
the root cause of this sickness is the decision on the part of Father to

leave Mother when he finds out that she has fallen in love with one of the clerks who works for him. He thinks that she needs a simpler, more humble partner than he, and he insists (Out of concern for her happiness? Or his own happiness, in recognition that he had made a mistake in marrying someone intellectually beneath him?) that she take up with the clerk. When she remarries, he takes custody of their son and, in what certainly seems to be a moral mistake, sends him off to be raised by an unrelated family "so that he could grow up healthy and strong in the country." This action is the germ, at least, of the root cause: an unhappy marriage that results in Mother seeking love with another man, Father's proud dismissal of Mother, and, despite his protestations, the Father's rather selfish abandonment of Son.

Now, given the passive role that Pirandello assigns himself in the creation of these characters, we must claim the obvious—that the situation of Father and Mother emerged from Pirandello's unconscious mind, and that it symbolically represents one of his deep moral concerns. Pirandello's own wife began showing signs of mental illness after his wealthy parents suddenly became bankrupt in 1903. Her illness progressed to such a point that she exhibited inappropriate sexual feelings for their daughter as well as paranoid delusions that led to violent behavior. In 1919, after sixteen years of taking care of his wife and fearing for the safety of their daughter, Pirandello had his unstable spouse placed in an asylum, where she remained for the rest of her life. It is also a fact that Pirandello adored his mother and had severe conflicts with his father, in part over his anger at his father's alleged extramarital affairs. This brief background is suggestive of Pirandello's own secret torments and sufferings related to familial entanglements, and why in such matters he would seek spiritual meaning in the sufferings of an imaginary family that, indirectly and symbolically, represented his own.

Mother and her second husband move away to another town, but Father goes to keep watch over them from time to time and observes the children growing up, especially Step-Daughter (for whom, it is insinuated, he has a sexual interest). After about twenty years, Mother's second husband dies, and she returns to the city where Father lives without telling him. To help support Mother and her siblings, Step-Daughter gets work at the shop of "Madame Pace," ostensibly as a clerk for fashionable women's wear, but in fact as a prostitute. One evening Father comes to Madame Pace's "shop" to visit with a prostitute, and he is about to undress Step-Daughter when he suddenly recognizes her. In their shame and degradation, Mother and Step-Daughter agree to be taken care of by repentant Father and to live with him. The eventual arrival of the son from the original marriage completes this reunited family, which at this point can be called truly grotesque; full of resentment, bitterness, guilt, shame, and vengefulness. Out of this situation come the tragic deaths of the two young innocents, who, in their wordless pathos, are pure victims of their situation.

Indeed, how could one bring this story to a satisfying conclusion? It is all self-laceration and pathos, with suffering at every turn. Pirandello was not up to the task. He could not find any meaningful way out. And yet, of course, he did in a sense complete the story by framing it with another story, a story about the difficulty an author sometimes has in completing a story.

Although Pirandello says in his "Preface" that the conflict between life and art (or "form") is "tragic," he nonetheless describes this play as "A Comedy in the Making" and refers to the "vain attempt" of the six characters to improvise their "drama" on a theater stage as a "comedy." This ambiguity of genre reveals another aspect of the grotesque aesthetic: the implied breakdown of order. According to Harmon and Holman, "the Grotesque is the merging of the comic and the tragic, resulting from the loss of faith in the moral universe essential to tragedy and in a rational social order essential to comedy." Thus, at the end of the play, when Boy commits suicide with a gun, some of the "actors" cry out that he's dead, while others insist that "it's only make-believe, it's only pretence!" to which Father responds, "Pretence? Reality, sir, reality!" The last word on this metaphysical quandary, however, belongs to the Director: "Pretence? Reality? To hell with it all! Never in my life has such a thing happened to me. I've lost a whole day over these people, a whole day!" The last word, then, is a comic perspective. The shameful, terrible story of the imaginary family of six suffering souls, in the Director's view, amounts to an utterly vain pursuit of meaning, a waste of time. The Director's attitude would seem to reflect in a comic way that of the imaginary "author" who had imagined them into being and implies why, in despair, he has left their story unfinished. Of course, the imaginary author is only one step removed from Luigi Pirandello, the actual author.

This playful solution to a problem well known to all artists—how to bring a creative project to closure—points to another aspect of the grotesque aesthetic: reflexivity. Not only is *Six Characters* a play about theater, with the rather old device of the play within the play, but it also exhibits an extreme of reflexive self-consciousness that is characteristic of much modern and post-modern art. The play the "actors" are about to rehearse, "Mixing It Up," is in fact one of Pirandello's own early plays, and the Director, who is staging it without enthusiasm, refers to "Pirandello's works, where nobody understands anything, and where the author plays the fool with us all" In directing the Leading Man he refers to one of Pirandello's typical ideas: "You stand for reason, your wife is instinct. It's a mixing up of the parts, according to which you who act your own part become the puppet of yourself. Do you understand?" The Leading Man responds, "I'm hanged if I do," and the Director confesses, "Neither do I. But let's get on with it. It's sure to be a glorious failure anyway." This dialogue echoes Pirandello in his "Preface", where he explains that "the Father, the Step-Daughter, and also the Son are realized as mind; the Mother as nature." Pirandello, then, as the author behind the "author," includes in this play explicit and ironically unflattering references to himself and his work. Indeed, he is echoing typical criticisms of his manner of writing, as if to acknowledge both their validity and their irrelevance at the same time. The themes are presented in straightforward fashion, but the mockery of these themes, especially since it is self-mockery, forces us into a critical examination of the action while it is happening. Pirandello's technique here makes us self-conscious, aware that we are aware. We are constantly reminded that we are watching a play rather than action going on behind an invisible fourth wall.

The actual story that binds the virtual fates of the six characters together into an ineluctable unity, though compelling, is really quite secondary to the main theme of the play, which may be expressed as the perspective made available by a "distortion of unnatural combinations" (see "grotesque," *Oxford Standard Dictionary*). This perspective by incongruity helps us to overcome what Burke calls our "trained incapacities" of thinking in limited categories, so that we can begin to get at the truth of things. Mikhail Bakhtin argues that this grotesque aesthetic has the effect of "subverting the dominant order" which, when it becomes "hegemonic," is itself a distortion of true order. This idea of order can be social and political, but it also pertains to the aesthetic, moral, and metaphysical orders as well; and it is with these latter orders that Pirandello is most concerned.

The human need for order beyond the order of Nature, which governs all that is except certain aspects of the human realm, is rooted in human freedom. Humans, unlike the rest of animate and inanimate beings, can choose their actions with an awareness that these choices affect their happiness or misery. Freedom entails responsibility for one's own happiness and, more or less, the happiness of others. Wisdom consists of the ability to see the connections between choices and consequences, and especially to anticipate those connections. Pirandello, in *Six Characters*, reminds us of these simple truths by showing how conscious and unconscious motives can easily become entangled, how one choice leads to another, how attempts to correct bad choices can make matters worse instead of better, and how our perceptions of reality can be distorted by the various ways we frame that reality. A close examination of this play should bring us to respect the complexity of human existence, and to be more generous in our judgments of others and ourselves.

When we go to see a play, we do so with certain expectations. Upon entering a theater we expect to see rows of seats facing an empty stage, concealed by a curtain before it. We expect other people—mostly strangers—to join us in this theater, to sit in the seats facing the stage, and to await the beginning of the play. We expect that at a certain appointed moment the house lights will dim and the curtain will rise, thereby revealing a set suggesting a scene illuminated by stage lights. We then expect people called actors pretending to be characters to move about the stage, to talk to each other, and use gestures to express how they feel. We become aware of the situation of these characters; we anticipate a conflict that motivates the characters to behave in such ways as to engage this conflict and to try to resolve it. When that conflict is finally resolved, we feel a certain satisfaction and a sense of completeness as the curtain descends, the house lights brighten, and we join the rest of the audience in getting out of our seats to leave the theater. We have beheld a performance, a dramatic work of art, and, let us hope, we have been spiritually enriched by the experience.

How then do we react when these expectations are deliberately subverted, turned inside-out? For that is just what happens in a performance of Luigi Pirandello's *Six Characters in Search of an Author*. We see, upon entering the theater, that the curtain is already raised, and the semi-darkened stage has small tables and several chairs scattered about, as during rehearsals. We fear we have come too early, or to the wrong theater. But, with the play's odd title in mind, we sit and wait for something to happen. Our expectations are jarred a bit, but we are curious about what is to come. And indeed, a number of people in casual street clothes begin coming into the theater, heading straight for the stage, and we guess they are actors gathering for a rehearsal. Then a man enters, followed by another person who, when the man sits next to a table in a prominent spot, gives him what appears to be the man's mail, which he sorts through. He calls out, "I can't see. Let's have a little light, please!" and in a moment the stage brightens. When the man then claps his hands and calls out, "Come along! Come along! Second act of 'Mixing It Up,'" we guess that the man is a director, and we are about to witness a rehearsal of a play called "Mixing It Up." Even though we have come to view a play called "Six Characters in Search of an Author," however, we do not leave thinking we have made a mistake; for the actors and the director, who must surely be aware of our presence as an audience, behave as if we were not present. And so we guess, correctly, that this rehearsal is part of the play we came to see.

Six Characters, then, is a play about play-acting, a theater piece about theater art. As such, it is what has been called meta-theater, which is a type of meta-art, or art that draws attention to its status as art. What is the point of this?

All theater, and especially theater that uses the stylistic method of realism, is based on an illusion: that the play's performance is not a performance but rather something real. We view the action as if it were natural rather than artificial. That is why we come to care about what happens in the performance, even though we know that it is just a performance.

This artificiality of art, this illusion that as we view it we take it to be real, is part of what *Six Characters* is about. When the expected six characters arrive during the rehearsal looking for an author to complete their story—a story supposedly abandoned unfinished by the author who had imagined them into being—we enter a zone of metaphysical ambiguity. Reality and illusion become difficult to distinguish. We know we are witnessing a performance—that seems true and real enough—but because of its reflexive theater-about-theater quality, we become unsure of our grasp of reality itself. The conception of the play is like a magician's trick, only here the magician is showing us how his trick is done, and we still are puzzled.

WORKS CITED

Bakhtin, Mikhail. *Rabelais and His World.* Helene Iswolsky, trans. Cambridge, MA: M.I.T. Press, 1968.

Bentley, Eric, ed. *Naked Masks: Five Plays by Luigi Pirandello.* New York: E. P. Dutton, 1952. [This edition includes the "Preface to *Six Characters in Search of an Author.*"]

Burke, Kenneth. *Permanence and Change: An Anatomy of Purpose.* 2nd rev. ed. New York: Bobbs-Merrill, 1965.

Harmon, William and Hugh Holman. *A Handbook to Literature.* 10th ed. Upper Saddle River, NJ: Pearson Prentice Hall, 2006.

WINESBURG, OHIO
(SHERWOOD ANDERSON)

"The Book of the Grotesque"
by Irving Howe, in *Sherwood Anderson* (1951)

INTRODUCTION

In this chapter from his study of Sherwood Anderson's fiction, Irving Howe calls *Winesburg, Ohio* "a fable of American estrangement, its theme the loss of love." Depicting a forlorn community populated by characters "stripped of their animate wholeness and twisted into frozen postures of defense," Howe explores grotesquery in Anderson's portrayal of rural American life. In his analysis of the novel, Howe discusses Anderson's explanation of the grotesque existence his characters endure, an existence where "the deformed exert dominion, [where] the seeming health of our state derives from a deep malignancy."

In rather shy lyrical outbursts [*Winesburg, Ohio*] conveys a vision of American life as a depressed landscape cluttered with dead stumps, twisted oddities, grotesque and pitiful wrecks; a landscape in which ghosts fumble erratically and romance is reduced to mere fugitive

---

Howe, Irving. "The Book of the Grotesque." *Sherwood Anderson*. New York: William Sloane, 1951. 91–109.

brushings at night; a landscape eerie with the cracked echoes of village queers rambling in their lonely eccentricity. Again and again *Winesburg* suggests that beneath the exteriors of our life the deformed exert dominion, that the seeming health of our state derives from a deep malignancy. And *Winesburg* echoes with American loneliness, that loneliness which could once evoke Nigger Jim's chant of praise to the Mississippi pastoral but which has here become fearful and sour.

Winesburg is a book largely set in twilight and darkness, its backgrounds heavily shaded with gloomy blacks and marshy grays—as is proper for a world of withered men who, sheltered by night, reach out for that sentient life they dimly recall as the racial inheritance that has been squandered away. Like most fiction, *Winesburg* is a variation on the theme of reality and appearance, in which the deformations caused by day (public life) are intensified at night and, in their very extremity, become an entry to reality. From Anderson's instinctively right placement of the book's central actions at twilight and night comes some of its frequently noticed aura of "lostness"—as if the most sustaining and fruitful human activities can no longer be performed in public communion but must be grasped in secret.

The two dozen central figures in *Winesburg* are hardly characters in the usual novelistic sense. They are not shown in depth or breadth, complexity or ambiguity; they are allowed no variations of action or opinion; they do not, with the exception of George Willard, the book's "hero," grow or decline. For Anderson is not trying to represent through sensuous images the immediate surface of human experience; he is rather drawing the abstract and deliberately distorted paradigm of an extreme situation, and for that purpose fully rounded characterizations could only be a complicating blemish.

The figures of *Winesburg* usually personify to fantastic excess a condition of psychic deformity which is the consequence of some crucial failure in their lives, some aborted effort to extend their personalities or proffer their love. Misogyny, inarticulateness, frigidity, God-infatuation, homosexuality, drunkenness—these are symptoms of their recoil from the regularities of human intercourse and sometimes of their substitute gratifications in inanimate objects, as with the unloved Alice Hindman who "because it was her own, could not bear to have anyone touch the furniture of her room." In their compulsive traits these figures find a kind of dulling peace, but as a consequence they are subject to rigid monomanias and are deprived of one of the great blessings of human health: the capacity for a variety of experience. That is why, in a sense, "nothing happens" in *Winesburg*. For most of its figures it is too late for anything to happen, they can only muse over the traumas which have so harshly limited their spontaneity. Stripped of their animate wholeness and twisted into frozen postures of defense, they are indeed what Anderson has called them: grotesques.

The world of *Winesburg*, populated largely by these back-street grotesques, soon begins to seem like a buried ruin of a once vigorous society, an atrophied remnant of the egalitarian moment of 19th-century America. Though many of the book's sketches are placed in the out-of-doors, its atmosphere is as stifling as a tomb. And the reiteration of the term "grotesque" is felicitous in a way Anderson could hardly have been aware of; for it was first used by Renaissance artists to describe arabesques painted in the underground ruins, *grotte*, of Nero's "Golden House."

The conception of the grotesque, as actually developed in the stories, is not merely that it is an unwilled affliction but also that it is a mark of a once sentient striving. In his introductory fantasy, "The Book of the Grotesque," Anderson writes: "It was the truths that made the people grotesques . . . the moment one of the people took one of the truths to himself, called it his truth, and tried to live his life by it, he became a grotesque and the truth he embraced a falsehood." There is a sense, as will be seen later, in which these sentences are at variance with the book's meaning, but they do suggest the significant notion that the grotesques are those who *have* sought "the truths" that disfigure them. By contrast the banal creatures who dominate the town's official life, such as Will Henderson, publisher of the paper for which George Willard works, are not even grotesques: they are simply clods. The grotesques are those whose humanity has been outraged and who, to survive in Winesburg, have had to suppress their wish to love. Wash Williams becomes a misogynist because his mother-in-law, hoping to reconcile him to his faithless wife, thrusts her into his presence naked; Wing Biddlebaum becomes a recluse because his wish to blend learning with affection is fatally misunderstood. Grotesqueness, then, is not merely the shield of deformity; it is also a remnant of misshapen feeling, what Dr. Reefy in "Paper Pills" calls "the sweetness of the twisted apples."

Winesburg may thus be read as a fable of American estrangement, its theme the loss of love. The book's major characters are alienated from the basic sources of emotional sustenance—from the nature in which they live but to which they can no longer have an active relationship; from the fertility of the farms that flank them but no longer fulfill their need for creativity; from the community which, at least by the claim of the American mythos, once bound men together in fraternity but is now merely an institution external to their lives; from the work which once evoked and fulfilled their sense of craft but is now a mere burden; and, most catastrophic of all, from each other, the very extremity of their need for love having itself become a barrier to its realization.

The grotesques rot because they are unused, their energies deprived of outlet, and their instincts curdled in isolation. As Waldo Frank has noticed in his fine study of *Winesburg*, the first three stories in the book suggest this view in a complete theme-statement. The story, "Hands," through several symbolic referents, depicts the loss of creativity in the use of the human body. The second story, "Paper Pills," directly pictures the progressive ineffectuality of human thought, pocketed in paper pellets that no one reads. And the third story, "Mother," relates these two themes to a larger variant: the inability of Elizabeth Willard, *Winesburg's* mother-figure, to communicate her love to her son. "The form of the mother, frustrate, lonely, at last desperate," Frank writes, "pervades the variations that make the rest of the book: a continuity of variation swelling, swirling into the corners and crannies of the village life; and at last closing in the mother's death, in the loss forever of the $800 which Elizabeth Willard had kept for twenty years to give her son his start away from Winesburg, and in the son's wistful departure." In the rupture of family love and the consequent loss of George Willard's heritage, the theme-statement of the book is completed.

The book's central strand of action, discernible in about half the stories, is the effort of the grotesques to establish intimate relations with George Willard, the young reporter. At night, when they need not fear the mockery of public detection, they hesitantly approach him, almost in supplication, to tell him of their afflictions and perhaps find health in his voice. Instinctively, they sense his moral freshness, finding hope in the fact that he has not yet been calloused by knowledge and time. To some of the grotesques, such as Dr. Reefy and Dr. Parcival, George Willard is the lost son returned, the Daedalus whose apparent innocence and capacity for feeling will redeem Winesburg. To others among the grotesques, such as Tom Foster and Elmer

Cowley, he is a reporter-messenger, a small-town Hermes, bringing news of a dispensation which will allow them to re-enter the world of men. But perhaps most fundamentally and subsuming these two visions, he seems to the grotesques a young priest who will renew the forgotten communal rites by which they may again be bound together. To Louise Trunnion he will bring a love that is more than a filching of flesh; to Dr. Parcival the promise to "write the book that I may never get written" in which he will tell all men that "everyone in the world is Christ and they are all crucified"; to the Reverend Curtis Hartman the willingness to understand a vision of God as revealed in the flesh of a naked woman; to Wash Williams the peace that will ease his sense of violation; and to Enoch Robinson the "youthful sadness, young man's sadness, the sadness of a growing boy in a village at the year's end [which can open] the lips of the old man."

As they approach George Willard, the grotesques seek not merely the individual release of a sudden expressive outburst, but also a relation with each other that may restore them to collective harmony. They are distraught communicants in search of a ceremony, a social value, a manner of living, a lost ritual that may, by some means, re-establish a flow and exchange of emotion. Their estrangement is so extreme that they cannot turn to each other though it is each other they really need and secretly want; they turn instead to George Willard who will soon be out of the orbit of their life. The miracle that the Reverend Curtis Hartman sees and the message over which Kate Swift broods could bind one to the other, yet they both turn to George Willard who, receptive though he may wish to be, cannot understand them.

In only one story, "Death," do the grotesques seem to meet. Elizabeth Willard and Dr. Reefy embrace in a moment of confession, but their approach to love is interrupted by a stray noise. Elizabeth leaves: "The thing that had come to life in her as she talked to her one friend died suddenly." A few months later, at her deathbed, Dr. Reefy meets George Willard and puts out "his hand as though to greet the young man and then awkwardly [draws] it back again." Bloom does not find his Daedalus; the hoped-for epiphany comes at the verge of death and, as in all the stories, is aborted; the ritual of communal love remains unrealized.

The burden which the grotesques would impose on George Willard is beyond his strength. He is not yet himself a grotesque mainly because he has not yet experienced very deeply, but for the role to which they would assign him he is too absorbed in his own ambition and restlessness. The grotesques see in his difference from them the possibility of saving themselves, but actually it is the barrier to an ultimate companionship. George Willard's adolescent receptivity to the grotesques can only give him the momentary emotional illumination described in that lovely story, "Sophistication." On the eve of his departure from Winesburg, George Willard reaches the point "when he for the first time takes the backward view of life. . . . With a little gasp he sees himself as merely a leaf blown by the wind through the streets of his village. He knows that in spite of all the stout talk of his fellows he must live and die in uncertainty, a thing blown by the winds, a thing destined like corn to wilt in the sun. . . . Already he hears death calling. With all his heart he wants to come close to some other human, touch someone with all his hands. . . ." For George this illumination is enough, but it is not for the grotesques. They are a moment in his education, he a confirmation of their doom. "I have missed something. I have missed something Kate Swift was trying to tell me," he says to himself one night as he falls asleep. He has missed the meaning of Kate Swift's life: it is not his fault: her salvation, like the salvation of the other grotesques, is beyond his capacities.

In the story "Queer" these meanings receive their most generalized expression, for its grotesque, Elmer Cowley, has no specific deformity: he is the grotesque as such. "He was, he felt, one condemned to go through life without friends and he hated the thought." Wishing to talk to George Willard, he loses courage and instead rants to a half-wit: "I had to tell some one and you were the only one I could tell. I hunted out another queer one, you see. I ran away, that's what I did." When Elmer Cowley does call George Willard out of the newspaper office, he again becomes tongue-tied in his presence. Despairing over "his failure to declare his determination not to be queer," Elmer Cowley decides to leave Winesburg, but in a last effort at communication he asks George Willard to meet him at the midnight local. Again he cannot speak. "Elmer Cowley danced with fury beside the groaning train in the darkness on the station platform. . . . Like one struggling for release from hands that held him he struck, hitting George Willard blow after blow on the breast, the neck, the mouth." Unable to give Elmer Cowley the love that might dissolve his queerness, George Willard suffers the fate of the rejected priest.

From the story "Queer," it is possible to abstract the choreography of *Winesburg*. Its typical action is a series of dance maneuvers by figures whose sole distinctive characteristic is an extreme deformity of movement or posture. Each of these grotesques dances, with angular indirection and muted pathos, toward a central figure who seems to them young, fresh, and radiant. For a moment they seem to draw close to him and thereby to abandon their stoops and limps, but this moment quickly dissolves in the play of the dance and perhaps it never even existed: the central figure cannot be reached. Slowly and painfully, the grotesques withdraw while the young man leaves the stage entirely. None of the grotesques is seen full-face for more than a moment, and none of them is individually important to the scheme of the dance. For this is a dance primarily of spatial relationships rather than solo virtuosity; the distances established between the dancers, rather than their personalities, form the essence of the dance. And in the end, its meaning is revealed in the fact that all but the one untouched youth return to precisely their original places and postures.

When Anderson first sent his *Winesburg* stories to the *Masses*, *Seven Arts*, and the *Little Review*, he intended each of them to be a self-contained unit, as in fact they may still be regarded. But there was clearly a unifying conception behind all the stories: they were set in the same locale, many of the characters appeared in several stories, and there was a remarkable consistency of mood that carried over from story to story. Consequently, when Anderson prepared them for book publication in 1919, he had only to make a few minor changes, mostly insertions of place and character names as connectives, in order to have a unified book.

Particularly if approached along the lines that have been suggested here, *Winesburg* seems remarkably of a piece. The only stories that do not fit into its pattern are the four-part narrative of Jesse Bentley, a failure in any case, and possibly "The Untold Lie," a beautiful story measuring the distance between middle-age and youth. Of the others only "Tandy" is so bad that its omission would help the book. On the other hand, few of the stories read as well in isolation as in the book's context. Except for "Hands," "The Strength of God," "Paper Pills," and "The Untold Lie," they individually lack the dramatic power which the book has as a whole.

Winesburg is an excellently formed piece of fiction, each of its stories following a parabola of movement which abstractly graphs the book's meaning. From a state of feeling rather than a dramatic conflict there develops in one of the grotesques a rising lyrical excitement, usually stimulated to intensity by the presence of George Willard. At the moment before reaching a climax, this excitement is frustrated by a fatal inability at communication and then it rapidly dissolves into its original diffuse base. This structural pattern is sometimes varied by an ironic turn, as in "Nobody Knows" and "A Man of Ideas," but in only one story, "Sophistication," is the emotional ascent allowed to move forward without interruption.

But the unity of the book depends on more than the congruous design of its parts. The first three stories of *Winesburg* develop its major theme, which, after several variations, reaches its most abstract version in "Queer." The stories following "Queer" seem somewhat of a thematic afterthought, though they are necessary for a full disposal of the characters. The one conspicuous disharmony in the book is that the introductory "The Book of the Grotesque" suggests that the grotesques are victims of their wilful fanaticism, while in the stories themselves grotesqueness is the result of an essentially valid resistance to forces external to its victims.

Through a few simple but extremely effective symbols, the stories are both related to the book's larger meaning and defined in their uniqueness. For the former of these purposes, the most important symbol is that of the room, frequently used to suggest isolation and confinement. Kate Swift is alone in her bedroom, Dr. Reefy in his office, the Reverend Curtis Hartman in his church tower, Enoch Robinson in his fantasy-crowded room. Enoch Robinson's story "is in fact the story of a room almost more than it is the story of a man." The tactful use of this symbol lends *Winesburg* a claustrophobic aura appropriate to its theme.

Most of the stories are further defined by symbols related to their particular meanings. The story of the misogynist Wash Williams begins by rapidly thrusting before the reader an image of "a huge, grotesque kind of monkey, a creature with ugly sagging, hairless skin," which dominates its subsequent action. And more valid than any abstract statement of theme is the symbolic power of that moment in "The Strength of God" when the Reverend Curtis Hartman, in order to peek into Kate Swift's bedroom, breaks his church window at precisely the place where the figure of a boy stands "motionless and looking with rapt eyes into the face of Christ."

Though *Winesburg* is written in the bland accents of the American story teller, it has an economy impossible to oral narration because Anderson varies the beat of its accents by occasionally whipping them into quite formal rhetorical patterns. In the book's best stretches there is a tension between its underlying loose oral cadences and the stiffened superimposed beat of a prose almost Biblical in its regularity. Anderson's prose is neither "natural" nor primitive; it is rather a hushed bardic chant, low-toned and elegiacally awkward, deeply related to native speech rhythms yet very much the result of literary cultivation.

But the final effectiveness of this prose is in its prevalent tone of tender inclusiveness. Between writer and materials there is an admirable equity of relationship. None of the characters is violated, none of the stories, even the failures, leaves the reader with the bitter sense of having been tricked by cleverness or cheapness or toughness. The ultimate unity of the book is a unity of feeling, a sureness of warmth, and a readiness to accept Winesburg's lost grotesques with the embrace of humility. Many American writers have taken as their theme the loss of love in the modern world, but few, if any at all, have so thoroughly realized it in the accents of love.

Acknowledgments

Firth, C. H. *The Political Significance of* Gulliver's Travels *from The Proceedings of the British Academy Vol. IX*. Norwood, PA: Norwood Editions, 1977 (read 10 December 1919).

Heine, Heinrich. "Heine on Cervantes and the *Don Quixote*." *Temple Bar*, Vol. XLVIII (October 1876), 235-49.

Howe, Irving. "The Book of the Grotesque." *Sherwood Anderson*. New York: William Sloane, 1951. 91-109. Copyright 1951. Reproduced by permission of Nina Howe, literary executor of Irving Howe.

Kayser, Wolfgang. "The Grotesque in the Age of Romanticism: *Tales of the Grotesque and Arabesque*." *The Grotesque in Art and Literature*. Trans. Ulrich Weisstein. New York: Columbia UP, 1981. 76-81. Reproduced by permission.

Knight, G. Wilson "*King Lear* and the Comedy of the Grotesque." *Twentieth Century Interpretations of King Lear: A Collection of Critical Essays*. Ed. Janet Adelman. Englewood Cliffs, NJ: Prentice Hall, 1978. p. 34-49. First published as a chapter of *The Wheel of Fire*. London: Methuen & Co., 1949. p.160-76. Reproduced by permission.

Melchinger, Siegfried. "The Bacchae." *Euripides*. Trans. Samuel R. Rosenbaum. New York: Frederick Ungar, 1973. 177-89.

Muller, Gilbert H. "The Grotesque Protagonist." *Nightmares and Visions: Flannery O'Connor and the Catholic Grotesque*. Athens, GA: University of Georgia Press, 1972. 19-50. Copyright 1972 by University of Georgia Press. Reproduced by permission.

Ruskin, John. "Grotesque Renaissance." *The Stones of Venice, Volume the Third: The Fall*. New York: John Wiley & Sons, 1880. 112-65.

Schevill, James. "Notes on the Grotesque: Anderson, Brecht, and Williams." *Twentieth Century Literature*, Vol. 23, No. 2 (May 1977): 229-38. Copyright 1977 by Twentieth Century Literature. Reproduced by permission.

Voltaire. "Optimism." *Voltaire's Philosophical Dictionary, Vol. IV.* Trans.
    William F. Fleming. New York: Lamb Publishing (1903, 1910).
    80–89.

Index

211